PRIVATIZATION AND COMPETITION IN TELECOMMUNICATIONS

International Developments

Edited by Daniel J. Ryan

D0209756

Privatizing Government: An Interdisciplinary Series
Simon Hakim, Gary Bowman, and Paul Seidenstat, Series Advisers

Westport, Connecticut
London

Library of Congress Cataloging-in-Publication Data

Privatization and competition in telecommunications : international
  developments / edited by Daniel J. Ryan.
     p.   cm. — (Privatizing government, ISSN 1087–5603)
  Includes bibliographical references and index.
  ISBN 0–275–95813–2 (alk. paper)
  1. Telecommunication policy. 2. Telecommunication—Deregulation.
3. Privatization. 4. Competition, International. I. Ryan, Daniel
J. II. Series.
HE7645.P753   1997
384'.041—DC20   96–36358

British Library Cataloguing in Publication Data is available.

Library of Congress Catalog Card Number: 96–36358
ISBN: 0–275–95813–2
ISSN: 1087–5603

First published in 1997

Praeger Publishers, 88 Post Road West, Westport, CT 06881
An imprint of Greenwood Publishing Group, Inc.

Printed in the United States of America

The paper used in this book complies with the
Permanent Paper Standard issued by the National
Information Standards Organization (Z39.48–1984).

10 9 8 7 6 5 4 3 2 1

PRIVATIZATION AND COMPETITION IN TELECOMMUNICATIONS

CONTENTS

TABLES AND FIGURES

TABLES

FIGURES

ABBREVIATIONS

Where appropriate, countries or organizations are mentioned in parentheses and chapters are given in brackets; important technology terms are defined.

ADC   Access Deficit Contribution [7]

APEC   Asia–Pacific Economic Cooperation

ASEAN   Association of SouthEast Asian Nations

ATM   Asynchronous Transfer Mode: Advanced data transmission technique wherein users can dynamically select the amount of bandwidth and transmission speed required.

BOT   Build–Operate–Transfer

BTO   Build–Transfer–Operate

CAT   Communications Authority of Thailand [1]

CBT   Companhia Brasileira de Telefone [12]

CCITT   International Telegraph and Telephone Consultative Committee (ITU)

CDMA   Code Division Multiple Access: A technique to increase throughput by subdividing the transmission spectrum into various code sequences.

CEE   Central and Eastern Europe [9]

CEPT   Conference of European Post and Telecommunications Administrations

CITIC   China International Trust and Investment Corporation [5]

CMEA   Council for Mutual Economic Assistance

COCOM   Coordinating Committee for Multilateral Export Controls

CP   Charoen Pokphand (Thailand) [6]

CPA   Centrais de Programacoa Armazenada (Brazil) [12]

CPqD   Brazilian Telecommunications Research Center [12]

CTC   Chunghwa Telecommunications Company (Taiwan) [1]

CTO	Czech Telecommunications Office [8]
DAMA	Demand Assigned Multiple Access: A technique to increase throughput by allocating transmission capacity on an as-needed basis.
DECT	Digital European Cordless Telecommunications
DELs	Direct Exchange Lines
DGT	Directorate-General of Telecommunications (Taiwan) [1]
DSC-LBR	Digital Satellite Channel - Low Bit Rate [4]
DTI	Department of Trade and Industry (United Kingdom) [7]
EBRD	European Bank for Reconstruction and Development
EC	European Community
ECJ	European Court of Justice
EDI	Electronic Data Interchange: high-speed computer-to-computer transmission of data in machine-readable format; can also refer to a combination of data, voice, and text transmission.
EEC	European Economic Community
EIB	European Investment Bank [9]
ERMES	European Radio Message System
EU	European Union
FTC	Fair Trade Commission (Japan) [2]
FTP	First Telecommunications Project (Czech Republic) [8]
GATS	General Agreement in Services
GATT	General Agreement on Tariffs and Trade
GDP	Gross Domestic Product
GII	Global Information Infrastructure
GSM	Global System for Mobile Communications (Groupe Special Mobile)
HKT	Hong Kong Telecom Ltd. [1]
HKTC	Hong Kong Telephone Company
HKTI	Hong Kong Telecom International [1]
HUF	Hungarian Forint (currency) [9]
IDR	Intermediate Data Rate [4]
IFC	International Finance Corporation (World Bank)
IPFs	Investment Privatization Funds (Czech Republic) [8]
IPO	Initial Public Offering
ISDN	Integrated Services Digital Network: digital system that can manage voice and data transmission simultaneously; can convert from analog to digital and vice versa; potentially a standard for global connectivity.

IT   Information Technologies [10]

ITU   International Telecommunications Union (United Nations) [1]

Kcs   Koruny (Czech currency) [8]

KMT   Korea Mobile Telecom Corp. [3]

KT   Korea Telecom Co. [3]

LDC   Less Developed Country

LEO   Low Earth Orbiting satellite

MAV   Hungarian Railway Company [9]

MCL   Mercury Communications Ltd. (United Kingdom) [7]

MFN   Most Favored Nation

Mincom   Ministry of Communications (Brazil) [12]

MITI   Ministry of International Trade and Industry (Japan) [2]

MMC   Monopolies and Mergers Commission (United Kingdom) [7]

MMDS   Microwave Multipoint Distribution Systems

MNC   Multinational Corporation

MOF   Ministry of Finance

MPT   Ministry of Posts and Telecommunications

MTTW   Ministry for Transport, Telecommunications, and Water Management (Hungary) [9]

NAFTA   North American Free Trade Agreement

NCC   New Common Carrier [2]

NECA   National Exchange Carriers Association

NICs   Newly Industrializing Countries

NPF   National Property Fund (Czech Republic) [8]

NTT   Nippon Telegraph and Telephone (Japan)

NZ$ New Zealand dollars

NYSE   New York Stock Exchange

OECD   Organization for Economic Cooperation and Development

OECF   Overseas Economic Cooperation Fund

ONP   Open Network Provision (EU) [10]

OTC   Overseas Telecomunications Corporation (Australia) [1]

PBX   Private Branch Exchange: A telephone line switching device located on the user's premises; routes all inbound and outbound calls.

PCN   Personal Communication Networks

PCS   Personal Communication Service

PHS   Personal Handyphone System (Japan)

PLA   People's Liberation Army (China) [5]

PLC   Public Limited Company (United Kingdom) [7]

PLDT   Philippines Long Distance Telephone Company [1]

POSCO   Pohang Iron and Steel Co. (Korea) [3]

PPI   Producer Price Index

PSPDN   Packet-Switched (Public Data Network): PS is a transmission technology that reduces messages and data into individually routed packets and reassembles them before they reach their final destination.

PSTN   Public Switched Telecommunications Network

PTAs   Provincial Telecommunications Authority (China) [1]

PTD   Posts and Telegraph Department

PTO   Public Telecommunications Operator/Organization

PTT   Post, Telegraph, and Telephone Administration

RBOCs   Regional Bell Operating Companies ("Baby Bells")

R&D   Research and Development

REA   Rural Electrification Administration (United States) [13]

RPI   Retail Price Index (United Kingdom) [7]

SCPC   Single Channel Per Carrier (analog) [4]

SCT   Secretary of Communication and Transportation (Mexico) [11]

SDH   Synchronous Digital Hierarchy: A high-speed transmission standard.

SEC   Securities and Exchange Commission (United States)

SONET   Synchronous Optical Network: Protocols for operating fiber-optic transmission facilities at very high multimegabit speeds.

SHC   State Holding Company (Hungary) [9]

SOTE   State-Owned Telecommunications Enterprise

SPA   State Property Agency (Hungary) [9]

SPHC   State Privatization and Holding Company (Hungary) [9]

STRM   Telephone Workers' Union (Mexico) [11]

TA   TelecomAsia (Thailand) [6]

TAs   Telecommunications Administrations

TDMA   Time Division Multiple Access: A technique to increase throughput by assigning channels to users in discrete blocks of time.

TF   Telecommunications Fund (Hungary) [9]

TOT   Telephone Organization of Thailand [1, 6]

TT&T   Thai Telephone and Telecommunication [6]

USD   United States dollar

UTV   Universal Cable Television Network (Thailand) [6]

VANs   Value-Added Networks: Enhanced services such as electronic funds transfers, message storage and processing, and credit card verification.

VAT   Value-Added Tax

VSAT   Very Small Aperture Terminal: Very small satellite earth stations, typically situated on user premises.

WATTC   World Administrative Telegraph and Telephone Conference (ITU)

WTO   World Trade Organization

INTRODUCTION

Throughout the world, governments are reducing their involvement in tele-communications. Some telephone companies are being fully or partially privatized; others are being allowed a freer hand in managing themselves; and in nearly all cases more competition is being allowed. In fact, it seems that competition cannot be prevented: Private firms frequently arrange their own telecommunications network (e.g., with microwave or satellite technology) to bypass an overpriced monopoly provider; and with the rapid growth of cellu-lar telephony, even private citizens have an alternative to the state-owned company. Often it is these changes that have forced the hand of government to either repress the innovations or to try to accomodate them. The latter choice usually prevails; exactly how different countries respond to the new environment is the subject of this volume.

The chapters in this book examine countries outside of North America. There are six chapters on Asia: one overview and five dealing with specific countries. There are four chapters on Europe: one on BT in the United King-dom and three on CEE countries. Two chapters deal with Latin America, and the last concerns developing countries. In all chapters, we see the interaction of encroaching competition, new technology, and a desire for the greater effi-ciency that traditional state firms cannot provide; but events tend to evolve differently in each case.

In Chapter 1, John Ure and Araya Vivorakij present an overview of the many changes taking place in Asian telecommunications. They begin with the im-portant point that "privatization" must be defined carefully, especially in regard to Asian countries, where control and ownership may not be as clearly demar-cated as in Western countries. Proceeding from this point, they outline the vari-ous reforms occurring throughout the greater Asian continent and islands.

Significant change has occurred in recent years; nearly all countries have allowed at least some liberalization, while a few have allowed complete privatization (including stock market listings) and competition. Ure and Vivorakij present the different variations of privatization; for example, a state-operated telecommunications enterprise might be sold directly to the public, to other private-sector firms, or to another state-owned entity.

Motives for the privatization of telecommunications are also discussed: the potential productivity gains, financial benefits to the government, and promotion of economic development in general (a point taken up by Heather E. Hudson in Chapter 13). Although these all encourage some sort of privatization, the actual form it takes depends on other factors: ideology regarding the role of the state; the extent of nationalism; and the strength of various affected groups (labor unions, consumer and business interests).

Finally, they discuss the closely related topics of competition, welfare and pricing, and employment. Privatization by itself actually leads to higher prices, whereas competition leads to lower prices; the former tends to be the choice when the interests of the owners (often the state) dominate, the latter if the consumers' interests predominate. Regarding employment, layoffs have been limited to the more advanced countries, reflecting the labor intensity of the different stages of telecommunications development.

The Japanese telecommunications industry, and NTT in particular, is the subject of Chapter 2. Daniel J. Ryan provides a brief historical review, then describes the gradual erosion of NTT's monopoly position over the past ten years. Although there was virtually no opposition to the privatization of NTT in 1985, the subsequent years have been contentious. Since NTT operates in both the (still monopolized) local service and in long-distance service, there is constant debate as to whether NTT is allowing competing long-distance firms fair access to the local system. For this reason, a special council to the MPT has argued that NTT should be broken up (as was AT&T); thus far, the management of NTT and its institutional investors have successfully resisted. No decision on this issue is expected in the near future; and in light of the intense competition generated by new technology (especially mobile telephony), the concern over interconnection may become irrelevant.

Jeong-ja Lee presents her analysis of Korean telecommunications in Chapter 3. As in many countries, the former monopoly provider (KT) has been separated from the government and has had its subsidiaries spun off into separate firms. One of the firms, Dacom, is gradually being allowed to enter into KT's markets (international in 1991, long-distance in 1996); the other competes in mobile telephony. Lee describes the ongoing privatization process for these three firms (new share issues, limits on share ownership, etc.). She also describes the price advantage allowed by the government for new, small entrants, and the licensing process; both are designed to encourage competition. It seems clear that the Korean government's goals of privatization and competition are being met.

Bruce Rowe covers a specific topic in Chapter 4: digital satellite telephony in Indonesia. Since Indonesia is composed of thirteen thousand islands, its future telecommunications development can be achieved most cost-effectively via satellite communication rather than by wire. He documents the efficiency gains from using modern digital technology; for example, replacing 150 analog modems with one digital modem. This is a good example of "leap-frogging," wherein a developing country can jump from a low level of technology to the newest, most advanced technology.

The relationship between foreign trade, foreign capital, and the Chinese telecommunications industry is the subject of Chapter 5. Meheroo Jussawalla describes how the fast-growing (41.6% per year) telephone sector in China has been purchasing large amounts of foreign equipment (e.g., US$100 million per year from AT&T alone) and is attracting foreign investment. Since the telecommunications sector is greatly in need of funds, and since the provincial governments now have a freer hand in negotiating joint ventures with foreign firms, it is not surprising that investment in China has risen rapidly. Many cases are highlighted, demonstrating that few multinationals intend to miss the opportunity to sell to or invest in China. She also points out that some domestic competition has been allowed (from new firms Liantong and Ji Tong), providing further evidence that the government will not take actions that restrict the market's growth.

Chapter 6 presents the experience of NYNEX (one of the RBOCs spun off in the AT&T divestiture) in Thailand. After a review of the great disparity in teledensity around the world and its strong correlation with economic development, Maureen D. Piché, Ben Park, and Roger Carlson provide an in-depth view of Thailand's telecommunications infrastructure. Despite fast overall growth (10% per year) in the late 1980s and early 1990s, Thailand's telecommunications network was not advancing quickly; this raised concerns that communication bottlenecks might retard growth in the future. Since there are other infrastucture developments in Thailand that also require funds (a situation shared by other Asian countries), it was determined that foreign investment should be tapped to accelerate development. This was done with a BOT scheme, wherein NYNEX (through its partner, TelecomAsia) would assist in the construction of two million telephone lines, then receive a share of the revenues for twenty-five years.

The authors describe the many benefits for Thailand, such as state-of-the-art technology, private funding, and market liberalization. As one would expect, allowing a long-term concession ensures that foreign partners will provide the best technology, since they will reap the benefits of greater volume and lower costs in the future. In addition, a BOT has a political advantage over traditional foreign investment: Since ultimate ownership reverts to Thailand, there is less nationalistic opposition. For these reasons, one would expect similar schemes to be used in other countries, and as the authors point out, that is exactly what is happening in many developing Asian nations.

Another international telecommunications firm, BT, is represented in Chapter 7. Marcus Brooks describes the privatization of BT, including the restrictions placed on it by the government (limits on share ownership, the appointment of directors), the establishment of the regulatory body Oftel, and BT's service obligations.

A major part of the chapter concerns the competitive environment. As in other countries, access by competitors to the network is regulated to ensure fair treatment (BT has 95% of the direct fixed connnections) and to prevent cross-subsidization. Until 1991, the competition was mainly Mercury Communications and some wireless firms; since then, dozens of new firms have entered the industry, including large network providers. BT is also subject to price controls and has been allowed price increases less than the rate of inflation, thus the real price of a phone call is now about half of the 1984 price. Despite this, BT has maintained a high level of profitability, to a large extent because of its heavy investments in modernization.

Chapters 8, 9, and 10 detail the transitions of three former Communist countries in CEE. First is the privatization of SPT Telecom, the Czech Republic's telephone company. Maria Michalis and Lina Takla begin with a description of the Czech telecommunications industry: Under Communist rule it was underfunded (and forced to subsidize postal operations), thus resulting in dated technology, poor quality, and shortages. With the move toward a market economy, SPT Telecommunications was gradually privatized; even foreign telecom firms were allowed to bid for one quarter of the firm, which was eventually bought by a Swiss–Dutch consortium for US$1.45 billion. The main goal of the government is to upgrade and expand the network, a task private investors are willing to do since SPT Telecom will maintain a near monopoly until the year 2000. The regulatory environment (other than that exercised through the state's shareholding) consists of adjusting tariffs and eventually allowing new entrants, but there is still considerable uncertainty as to how fast and to what extent these changes will take place.

Chapter 9 is Anna Canning's study of telecommunications in Hungary. With only 10 main lines per 100 inhabitants (one-fourth of the EU average) in 1990, Hungary's transformation to a market economy came none to soon; "leap-frogging" to the newest technology is now possible, but the expense will be great. Some funds were raised from domestic bond issues and by increasing service charges (few funds were lent by foreign countries, as Hungary already had a large external debt), and some direct investment by multinational firms (Siemens, Ericsson, US West) took place in related industries (e.g., equipment). But it is the privatization of Matáv, the state telephone company, that this chapter concentrates on. The German–U.S. consortium MagyarCom bought 30 percent for US$875 million in late 1993; this was done with certain preconditions in place (e.g., that Matáv would be required to build a certain number of lines every year). In addition, the local market was split into regions and privatized, with Matáv automatically receiving the most developed ones; the selling of the remaining regions has been slow due to disagreement over the fair value of existing capital and to political corruption. But the uncertainty regarding the future political and regulatory environment has not diminished the rapid changes in the industry. Mobile communications is growing quickly, and overall competition is expected to heat up when Matáv's monopoly status expires in a few years.

In Chapter 10, Piotr Jasiński focuses on the EU's telecommunications policies and how they can promote competition and modernization in Poland as part of Poland's entry into the EU. He first points out the complicated choice between regulating to maintain competition without overregulating to the detriment of competition, then details how telecommunications policy in the EU has developed in recent years. Liberalization has been encouraged, both through the creation of new laws and the enforcement of existing laws (with interpretation by the ECJ). These have been designed to encourage competition and diminish the monopoly status of PTOs, although voice telephony can still receive special treatment.

These laws may be useful in promoting competiton in Poland and mitigating the de facto monopoly position of Telekomunikacja Polska S.A. (Polish Telecom); this is particularly important, because Poland will be investing heavily in new equipment in coming years. As the Polish government harmonizes its laws with that of the EU Council and Commission directives, it should correct some of its more pressing problems: the monopoly status (legal and de facto) of Telekomunikacja Polska; restrictions on ownership and equipment production; and the conflict of interest of the Minister of Communication as both the regulator of telecommunications and the owner of Telekomunikacja Polska.

In Chapter 11, Lilia Pérez Chavolla and Rohan Samarajiva discuss telecommunications in Mexico, one of two Latin American countries covered in this volume. Telmex, the state-owned phone company, was inefficient and suffering from inadequate investment and was thus slated for privatization under President Salinas. In 1990, the concession title guaranteed Telmex's monopoly status in local service until 2026, but the long-distance market would be open to competition in 1996; as in other countries, the government required that Telmex allow other firms to interconnect with its local service. To attract foreign investment, taxes were reduced and prices were altered (long-distance rates decreased, local rates increased) to yield higher profits. As a result, the privatization earned nearly US$2 billion from a French–U.S. consortium.

The Telmex privatization also served as a signal that the goverment was serious about reducing its role in the economy; by 1995, the government owned no shares in Telmex. The privatization also had the desired effect of making Telmex more efficient in managing its assets and undertaking profitable investments. But the recent peso devaluation and recession in Mexico has slowed the deregulation process and has made the government more timid with regard to allowing increased competition.

Joseph Straubhaar and Christine Horak analyze the development of Brazilian telecommunications in Chapter 12. Specifically, they examine the influence of government policies over the last thirty years. The presence of different interest groups (the military, MNCs, government ministers) with differing goals (consolidating power, encouraging industrialization, promoting a national cultural identity) helps explain why the actual events in the telecommunications sector often differed from the planners' rhetoric. For example, national planning documents in the 1970s frequently advocated a greater role for private capital and a reduced role for multinational corporations; however, alliances between MNCs and domestic firms and the fact that Brazilian firms did not have access to the latest technology meant that foreign firms maintained their positions.

Priorities also changed over time. There was a policy shift in the 1980s as social considerations (e.g., extending the telephone network to low-income regions) claimed higher priority. This was partly due to the election of a democratic government but was also a reaction to the poor quality of telephone service; the latter was due to insufficient investment in the 1970s, which in turn resulted from politically motivated pricing policies. More recently, after Cardoso's election in 1994, some modest liberalization took place because of pressure from private interests and business groups. In general, it seems that government policies always became compromised by the reality of the telecommunications sector.

Chapter 13 presents Heather G. Hudson's study of telecommunications in developing countries. She first documents the low teledensity in poorer countries, especially in rural areas. But this is not entirely due to the countries' low incomes; television sets are fairly common even in the poorest countries. So to meet the potential market in telephony, new technologies need to be adopted that can reach large numbers of people at low cost (wireless, VSATs, voice messaging). Policy changes (less dependence on monopoly providers) and incentives to provide service in outlying areas (selling franchises) should be implemented. Other government policies that can improve and expand the industry are incentives for good performance (e.g., price caps, which allow firms to keep as profits some of their efficiency gains). And if subsidies are required in rural areas, they must be provided within a competitive environment; that is, one firm should not be expected to cross-subsidize a high-cost area, as this will simply make it uncompetitive in other markets. Prescriptions such as these are gaining widespread acceptance throughout the world, and should yield significant direct benefits (greater availability of communications) and indirect benefits (faster economic growth).

PRIVATIZATION OF TELECOMS IN ASIA

1

John Ure and Araya Vivorakij

Privatization, viewed as a panacea for the most pressing problems besetting the modernization and development of telecommunications, has become, in recent years, a widely accepted part of orthodox thinking (Wellenius, Stern, Nulty, and Stern 1989, illustrate the point). "How should privatization be defined?" asks the IFC (1995). "A generous stance would admit any transfer of ownership or control from public to private sector. A more exacting definition would require that the transfer be enough to give the private operators substantive independent power."[1] Hence, privatization usually means the transfer of state-owned assets to private-sector ownership, management, and control typified by the sale of part or all of the shares of an SOTE. We shall argue that the "more exacting definition" is appropriate for the experience of Western economies from which it originates (as we will show), while it is too narrow, too precise, and insufficiently "generous" to capture the less clearly defined lines of demarcation between public and private capital in the context of Asian telecommunications. We shall argue that this is because the delineation between state (political society) and civil society is less well developed in Asia, certainly less well articulated in law, and unevenly developed even within single, large Asian countries.

Rather, we shall use privatization as a broader concept to refer to the process through which private capital is brought into the PSTN likely to lead to an extension of private-sector management and control over part or all of the PSTN, including privatization in the form of private network bypass of the PSTN. This broader, looser conceptualization of privatization overlaps with the concept of liberalization (e.g., the issuing of competing PSTN licenses, which allows private operators to win public network traffic) although it is possible to have one without the other.

Asian economies each had their own reasons for choosing to reform their state and industrial policies. Some, like Burma (Myanmar) and North Korea, have made no significant changes, remaining locked in policies of autarky. Others, such as Singapore, Hong Kong, and the tiny Portuguese colony of Macau, base their entire island-economies upon being open ports and international hubs for communications and trade. Their telecommunications reforms reflect this openness. Between these two ends of the spectrum stand societies which differ widely in their state ideologies, social and ethnic make-up, cultures and religions, and levels of development. But what they share is a relative lack of independent institutions of civil society. This stands in contrast to most highly developed Western societies and cultures, and it undermines the notion that privatization implies a clearly defined line between the state and the private sector as it does in the West.

A study of how and why civil society is relatively underdeveloped in Asia falls well beyond the scope of this chapter, and it is not our contention that Asian societies share common political structures—which they clearly do not—or that the factors governing the relations between state and society and the features characteristic of those relations are similar across Asia. Quite the contrary, all these vary enormously. Rather we contend that, in their very different ways, the lines of distinction between the role of the state and the productive, commercial, and cultural life in Asian societies tend to be (1) less formalized than those in the West, and therefore (2) the exercise of state prerogatives, the administration of laws, and the allocation of resources often can appear arbitrary. Policy-making and the exercise of policy administration, such as the decision to issue licenses to new telecommunications operators, the choice of how many licenses, and the choice of who they should be awarded to, are frequently opaque, lacking in transparency even to the point where it remains unclear which government agency is responsible for what, and where and when and how a particular decision was made, or indeed if a decision was made at all. Nor is it entirely unusual for commercial agreements reached by the outgoing minister of one government to be rescinded by the incoming minister of another, or for those agreements to be overturned after a legal challenge. This adds political risk to telecommunications investment, which may already carry substantial commercial risk.

The role of family, military, political, or religious ties is usually very strong in Asian societies, a condition accentuated by the relative lack of independent civil institutions through which social matters can be debated. This heightens the potential role of the state as the arbiter of social issues, where private interests directly lobby those who hold power not as an action complementary to their public bids but as an action which substitutes for public declarations of interest. In the case where the state itself becomes a terrain of conflict and struggle between competing social and ideological groups, policymaking experiences a paralysis. In his study of telecommunications in Latin America and Asia, Petrazzini (1995) argues that reforms were more likely to succeed in cases where the relative autonomy of the state was high, where the reforms were relatively insulated from political pressure, and where power within the state apparatus was highly concentrated than in cases where political power was more evenly contested and administrative power diffused. He contrasts the success of the privatization of Telekom Malaysia with the failure of Thailand's privatization effort despite years of debate within the Thai state.

Under these circumstances it makes far better sense to discuss the issue of privatization as a series of policy approaches that encourage private-sector capital but which leave the lines of demarcation between public- and private-sector management and control of networks and services unclearly, or pragmatically, defined. Examples range from the efforts in Thailand to keep ownership of joint-venture assets within the hands of the SOTE, to controls that the Singapore government exerts over nominally private companies (although companies in which the government may indirectly own shares) to self-censor if, for example, they are handling information coming into Singapore, including over the Internet, or to promote particular technologies, such as videotex or adopt certain technologies, such as EDI.

Asian economies are developing economies, their societies undergoing radical transformation, and overseeing them are Asian governments very much in the process of state-building. Privatization, under these circumstances, is a policy-instrument which can serve many different purposes and different interests—and therefore takes a variety of different forms. Hence we adopt an approach which (1) acknowledges common factors at work (as we will show) but which sees privatization less as an act of transfer and more as a partial process of restructuring the relationship between state and private capital;[2] and (2) emphasizes the need to explore that variety of forms to explain differences between Asian economies and the reform process. In the limited scope of this chapter, we confine ourselves to the task of providing an overview of privatization developments in Asia's telecommunications and of conceptualizing a model which can provide a means by which to conduct country studies in greater depth.

PRIVATIZATION IN ASIA

In many countries in Asia, privatizing the SOTE is seen as one of the important steps in telecommunications sector reform. Privatization is also the mainstream of the reform in other sectors and regions of the world. The number of privatizations in all sectors of developing countries has significantly increased about eightfold, from less than 100 in 1988 to almost 800 in 1993.

Privatization of infrastructure—including telecommunications, energy, water, and transportation—accounted for the largest share of total sales volume of privatization in the developing countries, which peaked at US$29 billion in 1992 and fell slightly to US$24.4 billion in 1993 (IFC 1995). Asia had only a minimal share of this total sales volume as compared with other regions such as Latin America and the Caribbean. This is because reform and privatization of telecommunications in Asia has been slower and of more limited scope (see Smith and Gregory 1994). But as Table 1.1 indicates, few Asian countries have not embarked on telecommunications reforms.

Prior to 1988, when the shares of HKT were sold on the Hong Kong, New York, and Pacific stock exchanges, the only traded Asian telecommunications stocks in East and South-East Asia were those of the PLDT.[3] By mid-1994, as Table 1.2 shows, the number of listed Asian telecommunications companies had risen to twenty-seven, with the Japan Telecom Company, PT Indosat (Indonesia), being added later in the year and PT Telkom (Indonesia), Philtel (Philippines), and TACS, the Thai cellular operating company of Ucom, which has listed on the Singaporean exchange, being added during 1995.

This leap in numbers represents not only "privatization" in the narrow sense of the selling of parts of SOTEs, but also, using a "generous stance" definition, "privatization" in the sense of opening the market to the entry of private operators. Only one-third of the listed companies in Table 1.2 represent SOTEs, while many nonlisted private operators have also gained licenses to operate in Asian markets in recent years.

In the most straightforward case, privatization is the sell-off of shares of the SOTE to private investors, and this is usually one of two types. First is shareholder privatization through an IPO leading to a stock exchange listing, an approach adopted by Telekom Malaysia in 1991 and Singapore Telecom in 1993 when they listed around 18 percent and 10 percent of their shares, respectively. Similarly, in 1994 PT Indosat (Indonesia) and in 1995 PT Telkom (Indonesia) launched IPOs of around 25 percent and 20 percent of their shares on the New York, London, and Jakarta stock exchanges to raise US$1 billion and US$1.68 billion of private investment. In all these cases, only a fraction of total shares were on offer. For a thorough discussion of IPO procedures and methods of placing an initial value upon the shares of an SOTE, see the analysis of NTT's IPO in Takano (1992).

Second is operator privatization involving the sale, normally through a sealed-bid auction, of the SOTE to one or more private telecommunications operators, usually international carriers or substantial national operators with deep pockets and a wealth of managerial and technological experience. For example, in 1990 New Zealand Telecom was auctioned to Bell South (U.S.) and Ameritech (U.S.) for NZ$4.25 billion.

Market liberalization is also a form of privatization that opens the market to new entrants backed by private capital, although in principle the new entrant could be another state-owned entity as is the case in China and Vietnam.[4]

Table 1.1
Telecommunications Sector Reform and Privatization in Asia–Pacific

Japan	Privatization of PSTN in the 1980s; domestic market liberalized; three international carriers.
Four Dragons	
Hong Kong	Four private PSTN operators since 1995; four cellular operators and seven licenses; international nonvoice traffic liberalized.
Singapore	Partial privatization 1993; a second cellular license awarded; further liberalization announced.
South Korea	VANS liberalized from 1985; a second international carrier licensed in 1990; cellular competition from 1996; partial privatization of PSTN planned.
Taiwan	Liberalization reform agreed 1996; cellular licenses to be awarded; partial privatization of PSTN planned.
Southeast Asia	
Indonesia	Partial privatizations 1994, 1995; liberalization on a SOTE joint-operating scheme (KOS) basis 1996.
Malaysia	Partial privatization of PSTN 1990; liberalization of VANS.
Philippines	Liberalization of private PSTN 1994 and VANS.
Thailand	BTO schemes 1990; privatization under policy review.
South Asia	
India	Partial privatization of international; liberalization in cellular 1995 and in local PSTN 1996.
Pakistan	Partial privatization 1994.
Bangladesh	Partial liberalization of rural PSTN.
Sri Lanka	Partial privatization 1992.
China and Indochina	
China	State-controlled local competition since 1994.
Vietnam	Business cooperation contracts with foreign companies.
Burma	No reform to date.
Cambodia	State joint-venture concessions to foreign companies.
Laos	State joint-venture concessions to foreign companies.
Pacific Islands	
Fiji	Public offering planned for PSTN. International is 49% JV with Cable & Wireless.
Solomon Islands	Cable & Wireless 51% JV.
Vanuatu	France Cable et Radio 49% JV.
Australia	Liberalization in 1992.
New Zealand	Liberalization in 1990.

Table 1.2
Quoted Telecommunications Service Companies in the Asia–Pacific Region (August 1994)

Company	Country	Year Quoted
Hong Kong Telecom	Hong Kong	1988
Champion Technology	Hong Kong	1992
Star Paging	Hong Kong	1991
ABC Communications	Hong Kong	1991
Philippine Long Distance Telephone	Philippines	NA
Philippine Telegraph and Telephone	Philippines	NA
Globe Telecom	Philippines	NA
Easycall	Philippines	1991
Time Engineering	Malaysia	NA
Technology Resources Industries	Malaysia	NA
Telecom New Zealand	New Zealand	1991
Telekom Malaysia	Malaysia	1991
Singapore Telecom	Singapore	1993
TelecomAsia	Thailand	1993
Shinawatra	Thailand	1991
Advance Info Services	Thailand	1991
United Communications	Thailand	1993
Loxley	Thailand	1993
Thai Telephone and Telegraph	Thailand	1994
Jasmine	Thailand	1994
Samart	Thailand	1994
Shinawatra Satellite	Thailand	1994
Korea Telecom	Korea	1994
Korea Mobile Telecom	Korea	1992
DACOM	Korea	1992
Videsh Sanchar Nigam Limited	India	1992
Mahanagar Telephone Nigam Limited	India	1992

Source: Andrew Harrington (Salomon Brothers), "Companies and Capital in Asia–Pacific Telecommunications," in *Telecommunications in Asia: Policy, Planning and Development,* edited by John Ure (Hong Kong University Press, 1995).
NA: Not available

In 1991, the Australian government, having merged Telecom Australia and OTC (Overseas Telecommunications Corporation) into Telstra, created a duopoly by awarding a second carrier license to Optus Communications, a consortium consisting of Bell South (U.S.), Cable & Wireless (U.K.), and four local partners. As part of the deal, the government sold to Optus Australia's debt-burdened satellite, Aussat, for US$800 million. In both Australia and New Zealand, these steps were seen as the first toward further market liberalization.

A related form of privatization through market entry is the outsourcing of telecommunications business to the private sector. Pressure from two principle sources gives rise to this development. In the case of a privatized company operating in a liberalized market, there exists an imperative of competition to drive costs to a minimum and shareholder value to a maximum. Telecommunications firms in all liberalized markets have sought ways to outsource business considered vital to their operations but inessential to their commercial competitive advantage; for example, the ducting of telephone cables, the building of new exchanges/central offices, building and office security, and certain nonstrategic data management functions.

In the case of a SOTE in a developing economy, the pressure usually arises from a lack of capital and management resources to meet subscriber demand. In 1990 Thailand's two SOTEs, the TOT and the CAT, responsible for domestic and international telecommunications respectively, broke new ground when they began a series of BTO agreements with private-sector companies, such as Charoen Pokphand, Loxley, Samart, Shinawatra, and others. Under the BTO arrangement, the private sector builds the network and transfers ownership to the TOT or CAT—or the PTD in two of the three cases of VSAT—but continues to run the network on a revenue-sharing basis for the period of the franchise. The BTO has been used in Thailand to steer around the problem that the telecommunications laws, which date to the 1950s and 1970s, require services to be state controlled. Fixed-wire and wireless services are now extensively offered on a BTO basis. In Indonesia, PT Telkom adopted a similar approach in 1989 when PBH (Pola Basi Hasil) revenue-sharing agreements were reached with nine private-sector companies to build fixed-wire local loops. In this case, both ownership and operation were transferred to PT Telkom, although line maintenance was subcontracted to the PBH partners.

There is another reason for outsourcing. It is common in developing countries, such as Malaysia and Indonesia, for SOTE's subject to corporatization and privatization to be required to guarantee the employment and pension rights of staff as a means of softening labor union opposition. One strategy used to guarantee employment but shift excess staff off the books of the operating company is to set up subsidiary or auxiliary companies to undertake outsourcing. In Asia, this approach was first adopted by NTT in Japan following corporatization in 1985 and the beginnings of privatization in 1986. Even so, by 1990 NTT had cut back its 1984 workforce of 310,000 by 50,000. (Takano 1992). In the case of Indonesia, today the foreign companies being invited to participate in the Joint Operating Scheme (JOS) in different regions of the country are required to employ PT Telkom staff.

PRIVATIZATION AS A DEVELOPMENT ISSUE IN ASIA

Privatization is now widely promoted as a way to tap into a wider pool of investible funds—though corporatization alone usually ensures access to major capital markets—and as a milestone on the route towards a greater responsiveness to the market and to customer needs. Privatization is seen as a stepping stone toward, if not the actual achievement of, competition in facilities and services. And in the world's poorest economies even the thorniest of problems, such as the goal of a universal basic telephone service, are now seen as being eased rather than exacerbated by privatization (see Smith and Gregory 1994).

These perceptions have been espoused in a stream of papers, publications, and reports from the World Bank and its affiliate, the IFC; in the APEC Telecoms Working Group forums; in the GATT, GATS, and WTO debates; in ITU forums; as well as in an uncountable number of international telecommunications and information technology trade conferences. And increasingly they are being accepted across Asia. Among the many reasons, three are outstanding.

First, a shift in perceptions was triggered by the apparent success of radical policy changes in the early 1980s, which notably included the antitrust divestiture of AT&T in the United States and Prime Minister Thatcher's privatization of Cable & Wireless and BT in Britain. These policy shifts provided both templates for other governments, including Japan,[5] and strong practical and ideological arguments for the process. On the practical side was the sale of state assets, the rundown of state liabilities, and the promotion of local stock markets; on the ideological side was the commitment to markets in opposition to state ownership and control.

Second, the countries of the OECD, led by the United States, were increasingly determined to force open world markets for trade in services, and in consequence brought considerable pressure to bear on the more advanced developing economies, especially in Asia. These pressures came both directly through trade negotiations and political contact and indirectly through the recommendations of multilateral lending and aid agencies and other international bodies, including those listed previously.

Third, although the debt crisis of the early 1980s generally affected Asia less than other parts of the world such as Latin America and Eastern Europe— although there were notable exceptions, such as the Philippines—many Asian governments, in Malaysia for example, did feel the impact of a fiscal crisis as world trade threatened to collapse. Fiscal tightening in South Korea and Taiwan in the late 1980s and early 1990s arose for similar balance-of-trade and payments reasons. These pressures, which derived from the growing integration of the world's production, trade, and financial systems, affected alike the more export-oriented economies found mostly in Southeast and East Asia and the more closed or protected economies concentrated on the Indian sub-continent of Southern Asia and Indochina. Under these circumstances of fiscal uncertainty, privatization became an increasingly attractive option, quite independent of any intrinsic merits or relevance to the industries concerned. In India, for example, the program of privatization announced in 1991 by Prime Minister P. V. Narasimha Rao departed radically from the policies of all post-Independence governments in India.

In Vietnam, where the Communist Party and government remain staunchly statist, the Stalinist constitution of 1980 was replaced with a new one in 1992, the guiding principle of which is *doi moi* or economic renovation through innovation, laying the groundwork for a greater role for private capital, including foreign. Foreign investment has also been encouraged by China, although in the area of telecommunications this remains restricted to equipment manufacture and does not extend to network ownership or operation. In the early 1990s, China's open door policy, initiated by paramount leader Deng Xiaoping after 1978, was given significant impetus by the declaration of a "socialist market economy" involving state enterprise reforms, including partial privatization.

The aims of privatization differ as widely as the variety of forms. At one radical extreme there stands an ideological commitment to minimize the role of the state as a direct agency of production, distribution, exchange, and redistribution. Undoubtedly, the privatization program of the Thatcher government in Britain after 1979 was conducted in this spirit, and it is interesting to note that Prime Minister Thatcher's first privatization was the sale of a SOTE, Cable & Wireless.[6] After Chile, the New Zealand case may come closest to being an example in the Asia-Pacific region. At the other end of the spectrum is the view that telecommunications is a security issue and a national asset that must not fall into foreign hands. But even in this case, there is a pragmatic recognition of the need to tap into a wider pool of capital for the development of the network. China, for example, has encouraged the use of Build–Transfer–Lease arrangements in telecommunications. Local state enterprise, and in at least two cases overseas capital,[7] has been permitted to "invest" in building fixed-wire and wireless networks either by leasing equipment to the PTAs or by building and transferring networks to the PTA and then leasing them back on a local joint-venture operating and revenue-sharing basis.

Behind such pragmatism lies a recognition of the changing role of telecommunications within modern economies. The technological transformation of the industry over the past decade has changed its entire relationship to the productive economy, making it central to economic and industrial development. With the world market encroaching upon every society, the developing countries of Asia know full well how strategic a modern telecommunications network is for their survival in a competitive global economy. The broad principles of these radical changes were already evident to industry specialists by the early 1980s, although policy makers were then more likely aware of the role computers and microprocessors were going to play in the transformation of industry than of the role of telecommunications. From the early 1980s, and in some cases earlier, the NICs of Asia, especially the "four dragon" economies of Hong Kong, Singapore, South Korea, and Taiwan, but also a second tier including China, India, Malaysia, Pakistan, and Thailand, were developing policy initiatives to encourage the adoption and diffusion of the new technologies. For a discussion of telecommunications policy across Asia in this context, see Chapters 2 and 3 in Ure (1995).

With the recognition growing across Asian economies of the need to place telecommunications development on the fast track, there were two courses of action open to governments. The first was to commit more public funds to investment within the industry. The problem with this option was threefold. First is the fiscal crisis which hit many states in the early-mid-1980s, triggered by a recession in global trading and the world debt crisis. This was certainly the factor behind the Malaysian government's 1983 plan for the privatization of telecommunications.[8] Second, governments in developing countries have tended to view the telecommunications sector as a source of scarce foreign exchange, and telecommunications has been a net contributor, not a net recipient, of funds. In Indonesia and Taiwan, for example, as much as 60 percent of annual telecommunications revenue has gone to the treasury during periods of fiscal tightening. Third, a state bureaucracy is not well adjusted to the management of a sector which is subject to fast changing technologies. Technological transformations raise the risk level of investment because it is difficult to predict which technologies will prove successful and which will not. The greater the risk, the greater the need to spread it across multiple operators.

The second course of action was to open the telecommunications sector to private capital through privatization, liberalization, and deregulation.[9] This is now the favored policy direction, although as Petrazzini (1995) and Ure (1995) point out there are numerous interest groups in developing Asian countries, ranging from ministries (e.g., China) and the military (e.g., Thailand) to labor unions (e.g., Bangladesh) and state managers (e.g., Taiwan), who have reasons to oppose or delay such plans. Since each of these steps, privatization, liberalization, and deregulation, involves the greater participation of the private sector in the industry, we shall continue to use the term privatization in its broadest sense to mean the transfer of at least some ownership or control of telecommunications from the state to the private sector through the opening of an enterprise or the industry to private capital.

The societies of South and Southeast Asia are undergoing a historical change similar to the changes Europe experienced from the sixteenth to the twentieth centuries, except at an accelerated pace. Within the span of one century, they are nation–state building, seeing the struggle to life of political and civil societies, experiencing population shifts from rural to urban communities, industrializing–albeit very unevenly–and becoming integrated into a world system of production, trade, and finance. The Singapore government, for example, in recognition of the need to develop the city-state into a regional financial center, saw the privatization of Singapore Telecom as a way to boost the status of Singapore's stock exchange (see Hukill 1994). The process of economic integration is inevitably uneven, and different centuries of development are evident within quite small geographies, as telephone densities illustrate. Throughout South, Southeast, and East Asia, which is home to 50 percent of the world's 5.5 billion population, most people do not live within twenty-four hours walking distance of a telephone. At the same time, the region is home to some of the most advanced telecommunications network facilities in the world, in Japan, Hong Kong, and Singapore; and by the year 2000 many of the metropolitan cities of the region, Beijing, Shanghai, Bangkok, Kuala Lumpur, and Jakarta, will have telephone penetration rates of between 30 and 50 percent. This will be dial tone. At the same time, digital mobile cellular telephony will be widespread, cellular roaming services, including satellite systems, will be common across Asia, and Internet access will have become ubiquitous, while ATM high-speed data-switching and SDH (SONET) high-speed data transmission will be fully operational in the region's most international cities.

This is the context within which Asian countries view telecommunications, a context of development, and it overrides specific ideologies. In the case of telecommunications, development has a double meaning. It means how to bring telecommunications within reasonable access to the people who will benefit from it—the goal of universal service. However, because of radical changes in technology, it now also means how to modernize the economy through information technology. The reason for this second imperative arises not from the technology per se but from the growth of the world market. The growth of Asian economies is dependent upon their integration into the world economy, and those deliberately isolated from it, such as Burma (Myanmar) and North Korea, or unable to enter, simply stagnate. The 1990s is the decade when this convergence of world economic forces and information technology has become a priority development issue (see the *World Telecommunication Development Report*, ITU 1995) and forms the backdrop to telecommunications policy throughout Asia.

MODELING PRIVATIZATION IN ASIA

Understanding the background of a country does not answer the following questions: when and why did a particular government in a particular country decide to reform, including privatize, its telecommunications industry? Having decided to do so, what determined the form of privatization? How successful was the implementation of the reforms, and what factors were decisive in the outcome? A detailed and comprehensive answer to these questions must await further study—at the time of writing an APEC consultancy study is being undertaken into these very questions—but we can give some review of the issues and Asian experiences to date.

We may begin with a consideration of the objectives of privatization. Having argued previously that the aims of telecommunications privatization in Asia are better understood in terms of national development than in terms of ideologies, it is appropriate to model the argument in terms of driving forces and mediating factors which may act as constraints or issues which determine final outcomes. One set of factors would be contingencies, such as a fiscal crisis, a sudden change of government, or the overall course of government policies. We have already cited Malaysia as an example of fiscal crisis. Another set of factors would arise from the private business sector, the major users of telecommunications services who are looking for a better quality of service and competitive pricing, especially the foreign multinationals who can choose their foreign locations and regional communications hubs. This is a demand-side factor. A third set of factors would arise from international pressures, for example from the WTO, APEC, and the United States. A fourth set of factors would be associated with the issue of development—the need to provide an infrastructure for local development and to provide an attractive environment for foreign investment. The latter issue may be regarded as the supply-side of the demand from multinationals referred to previously. We can use the following as shorthand for each of these sets of factors: fiscal crisis, private capital, WTO, and teledensity.

Interacting with each of these are local constraining or driving elements. The government, as represented by the MOF, stands to lose recurrent foreign exchange revenue from privatization, but gain a windfall income from the sale of shares, while reducing its liabilities. It is interesting to note from Table 1.3 that besides the Philippines, only Hong Kong and Japan operate entirely private international carriers.

Table 1.3
International Carriers

Company	International Communications Revenue ($m 1994)	World Rank	State Ownership
KDD (Japan)	2,869	7	0%
Hongkong Telecom	1,944	8	0%
Singapore Telecom (Singapore)	1,185	15	89%
DGT (Taiwan)	936	17	100%
Korea Telecom (South Korea)	604	25	80%
IDC (Japan)	586	27	0%
PLDT (Philippines)	563	28	0%
ITJ (Japan)	532	29	0%
Indosat (Indonesia)	394	33	65%
China Telecom (China)	382	34	100%
Telekom Malaysia (Malaysia)	379	35	75%
VSNL (India)	335	37	85%

Source: *Communications Week International*, November 27, 1995, 17, which lists HKT under Cable & Wireless, ranked number 3.

Labor unions can be another powerful influence on the timing, extent, and form of privatization. In India, Pakistan, Sri Lanka, and Bangladesh unions have effectively blocked privatization either totally or to a large extent, as they have in Thailand. In Malaysia and Indonesia they have lobbied hard for government commitments to protect employment, as they have in Taiwan, where in January 1996 the government was forced to concede to workers' representation on the soon-to-be incorporatized CTC which is currently part of the DGT. Nationalism, which is systematized throughout much of Asia in this period of state-building, is a further constraint. In Indonesia, for example, the government has felt it necessary to step warily toward privatization, less it be accused of selling-out to foreign interests. In China, foreign direct investment in telecommunications remains taboo, despite openness in other areas. Telecommunications continues to be treated as a sacred cow, a national and security asset, rather than as a mass consumption commodity.

Finally, there are local interest groups, lobbyists who have an interest in the industry. These could include local users, including consumer groups who oppose opening the market for fear that tariff rebalancing will disadvantage domestic subscribers, but also local aspiring new entrants who want a share of the pie. They may welcome foreign partnerships or wish to protect the market for themselves. In each case, a study of the local situation, its politics and personal and business networks, needs to be undertaken to reveal its dynamics. Table 1.4 suggests a possible set of forces at work, some showing negative reactions (−) against pressure to open markets and privatize in the broadest sense, others showing positive responses (+) in favor.

Table 1.4 is schematic, but illustrates some of the potential drivers behind policy making and some of the constituent constraints and influences upon policy making. Further research at country level reveals what the ITU (1995) calls three waves of liberalization: the first in the mid-1980s led by Japan, Australia, and New Zealand; the second coming in the later 1980s involving many of the ASEAN countries, such as Malaysia, Indonesia, Thailand, and Singapore, but also Hong Kong, South Korea, and Taiwan; and the third (current) wave in southern Asia and Indochina. But as we indicated above, in each

Table 1.4
Matrix of Negative Reactions and Positive Responses

Drivers	MOF	Labor Unions	Nationalism	Local Lobby
Fiscal crisis	−/+	−	+	+
Private capital	+	−	+/−	+
WTO	+/−	−	−	+/−
Teledensity	−/+	−	−/+	−/+

telecommunications jurisdiction very different local circumstances led to many different forms of private capital entry and state–capital relations.

Krzywicki (1994) offers an interesting perspective on the forms of entry of private capital in Asia's telecommunications markets. He suggests a trade-off between the risk associated with operator-privatization, which is most likely in the least developed countries where a "junk-the-local-operator-and-start-again" approach may be the ideal option, and the inherited skill-set that comes with the stockholder or equity privatizations of SOTEs in the developed economies. He places most of Asia somewhere between the two extremes and argues that operator privatization does not guarantee that the benefits accrue to the privatizing country. The main point is that outside operators may restructure the local network to their own advantage, but, significantly, his example comes not from an LDC but from North America, where AT&T took operational control of Unitel, Canada's second long-distance carrier, and steadily shifted Unitel's research and development out of the country. Equally problematic with the model is that within Asia–Pacific operator-privatization was pioneered in New Zealand—although the networks in the ex-colonial protectorate islands of the Pacific are largely foreign controlled—while in the developing countries of Asia there is considerable caution shown toward foreign network operators.

Perhaps the more interesting trend across Asia is not the entry of foreign carriers—although many American Baby Bells and European and Australian carriers are entering strategic alliances—but the role of Asian telecommunications companies entering the regional market (see Ure 1995, especially Chapter 4 by Andrew Harrington). Thai companies like Charoen Pokphand, Jasmine, Loxley, and Shinawatra, Malaysia companies like Sapura and TRI, Singapore Telecom, HKT, Hong Kong's Hutchison Telecom, Champion Technologies, Star Paging, KT, and others large and small are penetrating each other's markets in local alliances. Japanese companies, like NTT, are also very active, using their traditional alliances with Japanese trading houses such as Itochu, Marubeni, and Sumitomo to open doors in Indonesia and the Philippines. The nation-state–private capital relationship is therefore being overlaid with capital which is distinctly Asian regional.

The advantage that Asian capital has in this context is that the commercial risks associated with a potentially volatile and ill-defined state–private capital relationship—one where licenses issued today may disappear tomorrow, government policies can alter radically over short periods, regulation is opaque, the hidden costs of doing business can be very high, and so on (to say nothing of uncertain market demand) are excessive. International Western companies, with stockholder considerations uppermost and every contract and negotiation put under the close scrutiny of corporate lawyers, are either loath to entangle themselves or find themselves ill-informed and uncertain. Local Asian capital, often controlled by families and perhaps more used to the ways of doing business in the region, can enjoy lower transactions costs and are able to accept higher risk on the basis of extracontractual understandings.

Of course, there are some economies of scale not available to the small private Asian companies, while companies like HKT (Cable & Wireless) and Singapore Telecom are just as international as AT&T or BT. But it is interesting to speculate that as the region grows and technologies break down the distinctions between fixed-wireline and wireless communications, it will be Asian capital that dominates the Asian marketplace and Asian states that aid that process.

WELFARE EFFECTS OF PRIVATIZATION IN ASIA

No comprehensive study of the welfare effects of telecommunications privatization in Asia has yet been undertaken. In the absence of firm evidence, we may refer to more generic studies and to the partial evidence that does exist. The World Bank (1992) covered twelve enterprises in its study of the welfare effects of privatization in Chile, Malaysia, Mexico, and Britain and came out with a positive overall assessment, but admitted problems in separating the effects of privatization from contemporaneous changes in state policies regarding investment, labor regulation, and the organizational restructuring of state-owned enterprises. However, only three telecommunications companies were included in the study, none of them Asian, and in the case of one of them, Telmex of Mexico, it concluded that consumers were actually worse off, at least in terms of prices. Of course, higher residential tariffs may be offset by tariff reductions to the business sector which later show up in lower manufacturing and consumer service prices. Furthermore, the dynamic efficiencies associated with the implementation of new technologies which privatization can encourage cannot be measured in the short timeframe of these policy changes.

Petrazzini and Clark (1996) offer preliminary findings based upon a study of the effects of liberalization in twenty-six developing countries. Because competition is likely to be the primary driver toward dynamic welfare effects; privatization alone does not guarantee competition; and, since, until very recently, competition in Asian countries has been confined to value-added services; the authors choose to use the presence or absence of competitive entry in the cellular telephone market to correlate to changes in cellular teledensity as a test of the impact of competition on accessibility. On this welfare measure, the results are unambiguously positive. But they also confirm that the threat of competitive entry may be as positive in fixed-wireline teledensity as the onset of competition. The speed with which the PLDT introduced its Zero-Backlog program, designed to abolish waiting lists in the Philippines by 1997, following the announced opening of the market is the outstanding example. They also confirm a correlation between privatization and growth in teledensity, which by intuition we can surmise is associated with the encouragement of increased investment in the sector.

Whereas they find a correlation between competition and price reductions, they find no similar correlation in the case of privatization on its own. On the contrary, like the World Bank study, they find price increases. Circumstantial evidence would suggest that this is associated with the interests of private—especially overseas institutional—investors to protect their asset value. The difficulties encountered by PT Telkom's IPO in 1995, for example, suggests that country risk is placing a premium upon income protection. Investors prefer a period of exclusivity to protect their investments, and the approach adopted in Hong Kong during the 1980s and in Singapore in the 1990s has been to grant it. Another factor influencing local tariffs is tariff rebalancing, especially between international and local call charges. It is the usual consequence of competition, but in few Asian countries has competition yet fully emerged in international markets. In Japan and South Korea, long-distance tariffs have fallen significantly, relative to local tariffs as the entry of private capital has made these services competitive and liberalization of the domestic market in Hong Kong has also resulted in dramatic falls in international charges as the new local operators—including cellular—are able to deliver calls directly to HKTI and pass on revenue-shares (local delivery fees) to their customers. Circumstantial evidence from economies like Hong Kong would suggest that competition has had the effect of improving the quality and range of customer services, but Petrazzini and Clark (1996) find no general evidence to support this contention for either competition or privatization in their survey sample.

A distinctive feature of the approach adopted in Asia toward guarding the welfare interests of stakeholders has been the partial protection afforded to labor. Traditionally, telecommunications staff the world over have been among the most highly organized and well-paid technical workers, enjoying the benefits of state employment or employment by an entrenched private monopoly, with seniority advancement, securely funded pensions, and welfare benefits. The shift from a world in which telecommunications was regarded as a basic utility to one in which it is rapidly acquiring the characteristics of a mass market commodity is perceived by labor unions as a threat to subject their conditions of employment to the vagaries of a commercially aggressive market economy. Privatization in developed economies has everywhere led to substantial staffing reductions, some of it technologically induced, some of it market-driven cost reduction, even at a time when the industry itself was expanding rapidly.

In Asia, however, staff reductions have been more modest and confined to the more developed economies, like Japan, Hong Kong, and Singapore, alongside Australia and New Zealand in the south Pacific. Of course, an obvious part of the explanation lies in the degree of development of the networks. Highly developed networks tend to diminish rather than increase the demand for labor, except perhaps for the most professionally skilled. For less developed areas, part of the explanation may lie with Petrazzini's point that "while privatized firms enjoying monopoly protection have retained most of their labor force, privatized companies facing competitive markets have sharply reduced their personnel" (Petrazzini 1995, 8–9). This applies as well to countries like Indonesia and the Philippines, where until recently there was no competition.[10] But often in Asia it is the state, not unfettered market forces, which determines the course of restructuring. For example, according to the ITU (1995), between 1991 and 1994, a period during which the market was protected, Singapore Telecom shed 30 percent of its employees. Over the same period, when Malaysia was introducing competition, Telekom Malaysia increased staff by nearly 3 percent.

The fact is that in the case of Indonesia, Malaysia, and Singapore, the state remains the major shareholder, and the attitude the state takes toward the trade-off between efficiency and social commitments remains important. In Singapore, the government has adopted the view that the economy's stage of development requires a highly efficient information infrastructure. While the Malaysian government shares the vision—Vision 2020—in practice its populist appeal and commitment to the Malay *bumiputera* (people of the soil) overrides other considerations.

CONCLUSION

Privatization in developing Asian economies is being driven by the same overall considerations as anywhere else, but it has a distinctly local flavor throughout most of the region. The separating line between state and nonstate interests is not rigid, and the state frequently wishes to promote local capital formation as an aspect of nation–state-building, and not infrequently as a way to build local support for the ruling party, military faction, or leading family. A state-sponsored "consensus" is often the preferred approach, especially where the local state is centralized and strong, and the protection of existing stakeholders is therefore given high priority. In these economies development is the key issue facing governments, and the role of telecommunications in development is paramount.

In the more developed Asian economies, the role of information is key to their successful transition to postindustrial societies, and the upgrading of telecommunications facilities and the convergence of information technologies is of paramount importance. Markets rather than consensus politics is the Western model, but even here Asian countries like Japan, South Korea, and Singapore attempt to blend the two. Privatization may be a precondition for the growth of a free market in telecommunications facilities and services and for free trade-in-telecommunications services now being debated in APEC, GATS, and WTO, but in Asia it remains embedded in broader industrial, political, and social aims.

NOTES

1. The IFC lists numerous techniques of ownership transfer, including public offer, closed subscription, joint venture, liquidation, concessions, auctions, voucher- or certificate-based transfers, employee or management buyouts, and combinations of these.

2. Nor is it simply a process of shifting the balance between the state and private capital as if these were always separate entities, since the beneficiaries of privatization may well be the former holders of state power—something not uncommon in Eastern Europe.

3. The PLDT was founded in 1928 under American management, eventually coming under the ownership of the GTE in 1956. In 1967 in a deal for which he was subsequently indicted by the U.S. SEC (for details see Manapat 1993), control passed to a local group headed by Ramon Cojuangco, a close associate of President Marcos. HKT is a holding company of Cable & Wireless Plc. (U.K.), which in 1995 held 57.5 percent of HKT's shares, with China's CITIC owning another 10 percent through its subsidiary CITIC Pacific. HKT owns 100 percent of Hong Kong's dominant domestic carrier, HKTC, Hong Kong's international carrier, HKTI, and CSL, which operates cellular, paging, and value-added services throughout the territory, and roaming services.

4. The principal shareholder in China's new entrants, LianTong (Unicom) and JiTong, is the Ministry of Electronic Industries, together with the Ministries of Railways and Electric Power and several state enterprises, such as the CITIC. The Ministry of Defense is also involved in wireless communications through the PLA. Many ministries run their own private networks. In Vietnam, the Ministry of Defense has set up an Army Telecommunications Company (ATC) to offer services where the public network is not available.

5. NTT was privatized in 1985. According to Naoe (1994), the Nakasone government borrowed ideas from both the Reagan and Thatcher administrations.

6. Prime Minister Thatcher took no risks. Immediately prior to privatization, the Hong Kong government obligingly extended the exclusive operating license of HKTI to the year 2006. HKTI was generating around 70 percent of the revenues and profits of Cable & Wireless.

7. The first is Huamei, a fifty/fifty joint venture between two American companies—SC&M International, a Chicago investment bank, and Brooks Telecommunications, a St. Louis-based builder of advanced telecommunications networks—and Galaxy New Technology, a company controlled by COSTIND, the manufacturing, research, and development arm of the PLA and the key agency overseeing China's aggressive defense conversion effort. The MPT and MEI hold small stakes in Galaxy. Huamei (which means "China America" in Mandarin) has built a US$7-million prototype, state-of-the-art broadband network in Guangzhou. The second is First Star, a joint venture between Singapore Telecom (35%) and subsidiaries of the MPT and the Beijing Municipal Government (as the principal local shareholders). Small stakes are held by the Hong Kong-listed ING Beijing Investment Company and Asia Pacific (China) Electrical Company. First Star is to build a nationwide paging network. (See TIF, 1996).

8. See Petrazzini (1995, 146), but the Malaysian government was encouraged also by the lobbying of local companies eager to enter the industry. Jomo (1994, 277)—referencing Kennedy (1991)—records that in 1983 Sapura Holdings, now a

private telecommunications operator, commissioned a study by Arthur D. Little, "The Advantages and Feasibility of Privatizing Jatan Telekom Malaysia."

9. Deregulation includes moves to free up the use of equipment by nondominant operators and subscribers, the right to install private networks and to bypass public networks, the right to offer a range of services and a range of tariffs without having to seek authorization from the regulator, and so on. Liberalization refers to the opening of markets to new entrants. Often liberalization requires a degree of reregulation to ensure fair and free competition, such as the requirement to interconnect, bans on discriminatory or predatory pricing, revenue-sharing arrangements, and so on.

10. In December 1995, the PLDT made its first announcement of staff reductions, at a time when it was aggressively expanding its build-out plans to fend off competition from the new entrants.

REFERENCES

Hukill, Mark. 1994. "The Privatization and Regulation of Singapore Telecom." *Telecom Journal* 6 (3): 26–30.

International Finance Corporation. 1995. *Privatization: Principles and Practice. Lesson of Experience Series*. Washington, D.C.: The World Bank.

International Telecommunications Union (ITU). 1995. *Asia Pacific Telecommunications Indicators*. Geneva: ITU.

International Telecommunications Union (ITU). 1995. *World Telecommunication Development Report*. Geneva: ITU.

Jomo, K. S., ed. 1994. *Malaysia's Economy in the Nineties*. Petaling Jaya: Pelanduk Publishers.

Kennedy, L. 1991. "Liberalization, Privatization and the Politics of Patronage." Paper presented at the Fourth Annual Conference, International Communications Association, Chicago.

Krzywicki, John. 1994. "Operator Privatization Versus Other (Better) Methods of Restructuring." Paper presented at Developing Asia-Pacific Countries' Pacific Telecommunications Conference, Hawaii. 116–118.

Manapat, Ricardo. 1993. *Wrong Number: The PLDT Telephone Monopoly*. Madrid: The Animal Farm Series, Parque del Buen Retiro.

Naoe, Shigehiko. 1994. "Japan's Telecommunications Industry: Competition and Regulatory Reform." *Telecommunications Policy* 18 (8): 651–657.

Petrazzini, Ben. 1995. *The Political Economy of Telecommunications Reform in Developing Countries: Privatization and Liberalization in Comparative Perspective*. Westport, Conn.: Praeger.

Petrazzini, Ben, and Theodore Clark. 1996. "Costs and Benefits of Telecommunications Liberalization." Paper presented at the Developing Countries Institute for International Economics Conference on Liberalization Telecommunications Services, Washington, D.C.

Smith, Peter, and Gregory Staple. 1994. *Telecommunications Sector Reform in Asia: Toward a New Pragmatism*. World Bank Discussion Paper 232. Washington, D.C.: The World Bank.

Takano, Yoshiro. 1992. *Nippon Telegraph and Telephone Privatization Study: Experience of Japan and Lessons for Developing Countries*. World Bank Discussion Paper 179. Washington, D.C.: The World Bank.

Telecommunications and InfoTechnology Forum. 1996. *"Joint Ventures in China's Telecoms: Background Briefing Paper."* Telecommunications and InfoTechnology Forum (Telecommunications Research Project). Hong Kong: Centre of Asian Studies, University of Hong Kong.

Ure, John, ed. 1995. *Telecommunications in Asia: Policy, Planning and Development.* Hong Kong: Hong Kong University Press.

Wellenius, Bjorn, Peter Stern, Timothy Nulty, and Richard Stern. 1989. *Restructuring and Managing the Telecommunications Sector. A World Bank Symposium.* Washington, D.C.: The World Bank.

World Bank. 1992. *Welfare Consequences of Selling Public Enterprises: Case Studies from Chile, Malaysia, Mexico and the UK.* Washington, D.C.: The World Bank.

THE EVOLVING TELECOMMUNICATIONS ENVIRONMENT IN JAPAN

2

Daniel J. Ryan

As with most developed countries, Japan's telecommunications industry continues to make the transition from government monopoly to rapidly changing competition. The historical monopoly of NTT and its international arm KDD (Kokusai Denshin Denwa Co., Ltd.) are still the dominant telecommunications firms in Japan, but events of the past ten years have eliminated their monopoly position and are now creating significant competitive pressure.

THE NTT MONOPOLY

In the immediate post-war years, there was little concern about NTT's monopolization of the telephone industry in Japan. Of greater priority was the reconstruction of the telecommunications infrastructure, which had been damaged during the war.

In 1953, three laws were passed[1] to clarify the responsibilities and operations of NTT. These decreased the government's role and allowed NTT to manage itself, although it would be regulated by the MPT. The laws prevented new entries into the telecommunications business, and even prevented the establishment of alternative networks. For example, television broadcasters were not allowed to obtain the necessary circuitry for microwave transmission; rather, the appropriate services had to be obtained from NTT. And although the 1957 Wire Broadcasting and Telephone Law allowed some small-scale telephone networks for agricultural cooperatives, these never became serious competitors due to difficulties in connecting with NTT.

The first break in the NTT monopoly came in 1964. This was the period of high economic growth, and NTT was having trouble meeting the rapid increase in demand for telephones.[2] This particular case occurred in Gion, the classic geisha center of Kyoto. The Gion Association, whose history goes back several hundred years, wanted a privately switched telephone network connecting 280 geisha houses in order to facilitate the rotation of geisha girls and to cope with increasing foreign guests due to the upcoming Olympic games. Eventually this system was put into place, although not until after the games. In so doing, the MPT was accused by a government committee of violating the 1953 laws that established NTT's monopoly. The MPT responded that the network was no different than an in-building PBX, and the network remained.

In the following years, gradual changes occurred in the telecommunications industry, parallelling similar events in the United States, albeit at a slower pace. As computers became more commonplace in the late 1950s, the need for data transmission became pronounced. The public telephone network was the logical medium for transmission, but it was not until 1972 that the government gave its approval; by that time the United States had been transmitting data over phone lines for nearly fifteen years. Similarly, VANs were allowed in 1982, nine years after similar events in the United States.

1985: PRIVATIZATION

By the early 1980s, it became clear that maintaining NTT's monopoly position could not be justified. Other firms wanted to enter the telecommunications industry, and NTT's high rates and lack of innovation showed how inefficient a protected monopoly could be. Thus came the impetus for privatization.

There was virtually no opposition to the privatization of NTT. NTT itself wanted to become more independent of government control; other telecom firms wanted the opportunity to enter the industry; makers of telecommunications equipment felt that liberalization would strengthen the market and increase sales; and consumers of telephone services (both households and businesses) hoped to benefit from lower prices as a result of improved efficiency.

The government, in addition to responding to pressure from all these parties, would benefit from the selling of NTT shares; the monies would help reduce deficits accumulated in previous years, especially the 30 trillion yen deficit arising from support of Japan National Railways. Thus in April 1985 the government passed the Telecommunications Business Law and the NTT Law.

The Telecommunications Business Law designated two types of businesses: Type I businesses were facility owners; Type II were facility lessors (i.e., those who leased telecommunications circuit facilities from Type I firms). The former, because of their large investment in equipment, were regulated; most business decisions had to be approved by the MPT. In addition, they had to be at least 70 percent Japanese-owned. Type II businesses had only to notify the MPT at the time of entry; this was done for information purposes and was not used as a barrier to entry; and there were no restrictions on foreign ownership of Type II businesses.

The Type I businesses[3] (see Table 2.1) included local network services, long-distance, international and satellite communications, cellular services, and paging services. The three long-distance competitors entered the market within two years after the law's passage, as did the two satellite competitors. In the intercity market, numerous regional operators began offering leased-line services, mostly utilizing microwave and fiber-optic facilities. The long-distance competition is generally credited with stimulating rate reductions and diversification of services. For example, in 1986 the NTT rate for a 64 kbps Tokyo–Osaka line was 1,100,000 yen per month, whereas the new entrants charged 796,000 yen. By 1995, the rates for all had fallen below 400,000 yen. Note that there is still considerable room for improvement, as the rates for long-distance and dedicated corporate lines in Japan are still 2 to 3 times as much as in the United States.

The Type II businesses were subdivided into two categories. Special Type II are national or international leased line service suppliers; there were forty-three as of February 1995. General Type II are smaller, dedicated networks; there were more than two thousand as of February 1995. The number of Type II firms has been growing rapidly, by more than one hundred per year. As most of these firms are VAN providers, they generally do not specialize in telecommunication service but in related business such as on-line communications, publishing and advertising, and software development and marketing.

The terminal equipment market was also liberalized; users could now install their own telephone sets rather than lease them from NTT. Thus telecommunication equipment manufacturers faced additional competition as consumer electronic firms entered the telephone market. This resulted in a rapid increase in the diversity of telephone sets with multiple functions. Note that the approval of terminal equipment was given to the Japan Approvals Institute for Telecommunications Equipment (JATE), an organization designated by the MPT, which is independent of NTT. This prevented NTT from using technical standards as a barrier to competition.

The NTT Law privatized the monopoly (its official name changed from NTT Public Corp. to NTT Corp.), which then reorganized its structure, including separating its data communication division into a wholly owned subsidiary. Shares were sold to the public in the late 1980s, but even today the MOF still holds two-thirds of NTT's stock.

NTT's privatization and divisional separation meant that procurement became more diffuse and decentralized. Thus, with regards to equipment purchases, NTT sometimes competed with and sometimes bought from other manufacturers. This further enhanced the degree of competition among telecommunication equipment manufacturers.

Table 2.1
Type I Carriers (February 1995)

Type	Company	Types of Services
Long-distance	NTT	Telephone, leased circuit, telegraph, telegram, ISDN
	DDI Corp (Daini Denden)	Telephone, leased circuit, digital data transmission
	Japan Telecom Co., Ltd. (JT)	Telephone, leased circuit
	Teleway Japan Corp (TJ)	Telephone, leased circuit
Regional	NTT	- - see above - -
	Tokyo Telecommunication Network Co., Inc	Telephone, leased circuit
	Osaka Media Port Corp.	Leased circuit
	Chubu Telecommunications Co., Inc.	Leased circuit, digital data transmission
	Shikoku Information and telecommunication Network Co., Inc.	Leased circuit, data communications
	Kyushu Telecommunication Network Co., Inc.	Leased circuit
	Hokkaido Telecommunication Network Co., Inc. (CTnet)	Leased circuit

	Tohoku Intelligent Telecommunication Co., Inc. (TOHKnet)	Leased circuit
	Hokuriku Telecommunication Network Co., Inc.	Leased circuit
	LCV Corp.	Leased circuit
	Kintetsu Cable Network Co., Ltd.	Leased circuit
International*	KDD (Kokusai Denshin Denwa Co., Ltd.)	Telephone, leased circuit, telegraph, telegram, data communications
	ITJ (International Telecom Japan Inc..)	Telephone, leased circuit
	IDC (International Digital Communications Inc.)	Telephone, leased circuit, data communications
Satellite	Japan Satellite Systems Inc.	Leased circuit
	Space Communications Corp.	Leased circuit
Mobile Communications	NTT DoCoMo (9 companies) and 79 others, such as Nippon Isou Tsushin Corp. (IDO) and Tokyo Telemessage Inc.	Cellular phone service, PHS and radio paging

Source: MPT, *Open: Telecommunications Overview of Japan* (Tokyo: MPT, 1995).
*Another firm, Forval International, entered the international market in mid-1995.

POST-PRIVATIZATION

As mentioned earlier, rates have been falling constantly since privatization, with the new entrants leading the way. The increased competition has also led to innovative options (e.g., toll-free numbers; discounts for off-peak calls; call blocking; international calls paid via credit cards; third-party billing). Interestingly, all this has taken place despite a continuing debate over NTT's status.

NTT Divestiture?

When NTT was first privatized, the MPT suggested that NTT's long-distance operations be separated from its local network (as with AT&T in the United States). This view was reiterated in 1989 when the Telecommunications Advisory Council of the MPT issued an interim report. The report recommended divestiture as a means of coping with the serious problems facing NTT (e.g., inefficient management and unfair advantages in the market). The management of NTT expressed opposition to the idea, claiming it would result in reduced R&D spending and rate hikes in expensive rural areas; politicians were especially concerned with the latter point, as rural areas were disproportionately represented in elections. MITI also opposed a breakup, objecting to the fact that divestiture would allow the MPT to appoint its own people to head the new regional companies. MITI also had close ties with telecommunications equipment manufacturers (Fujitsu, NEC, Hitachi, Oki Electric), who in turn worked closely with NTT; none of them wanted to disrupt their relationships.

In the subsequent years NTT has taken the following steps to head off divestiture:

- In April 1992, NTT introduced an independent division system, composed of a Long-Distance Communications division and a Regional Communications division, with their own financial reports
- In July 1992, NTT's mobile communications business (including cellular phone and radio paging) was separated from NTT and named NTT Mobile Communications Network (NTT DoCoMo); one year later it was divided into nine regional blocks covering the entire nation
- In February 1993, NTT announced a rationalization plan that featured a reduction of its workforce to 200,000 by the end of FY 1996 (March 1997), a decrease of 16,000 employees from FY 1993, to be achieved through voluntary retirement
- NTT began to allow competitors to access its network at any point a switch exists, rather than just in one place in each prefecture (as was previously the case)
- NTT continued to lower its long-distance rates

All this suggests that NTT's monopoly in the local market yielded no apparent advantage over the other long-distance firms, despite NTT's controversial access charges. Nevertheless, at the end of FY 1995 (March 1996) the council again recommended divestiture for NTT. Specifically, the following steps would be taken:

- NTT would be split into one long-distance company and two regional companies (East Japan and West Japan)
- The long-distance company would take over NTT's share in the subsidiary companies: NTT Data Communications; NTT DoCoMo; and NTT Personal Communications Network (a PHS operator)
- Long-distance firms would be allowed to enter the international market; similarly, international telephone firms like KDD would be allowed into the long-distance market
- Each of the new regional firms would be allowed to expand into cable television and information services in the other's region, but not its own
- These changes were to take place by the end of FY 1988 (March 1989)

The council also argued that a post-divestiture NTT would still be very profitable, with earnings of 1,000 billion yen (NTT estimated only 260 billion yen).

Not surprisingly, the recommendations were again opposed by NTT and MITI. In addition, the governing coalition of the LDP (Liberal Democratic Party) and the SDP (Social Democratic Party) decided to delay any decisions regarding NTT's status; they were concerned about the effect a breakup would have on NTT's workforce (represented by the powerful and influential Telecommunications Workers Union) in an election year. Incidentally, the coalition's prime minister, Ryutaro Hashimoto, was head of the MOF in 1990, and at that time opposed the council's 1989 recommendation to split NTT. Moreover, the current political environment in Japan is not conducive to decision making; Japan is just now emerging from a four-year recession and is in the process of dealing with a multibillion-dollar bad-loan crisis.

In addition, the public still has hard feelings toward the government as a result of the NTT privatization. When shares were first sold to the to the public, many were bought (with the encouragement of the MOF) by small investors. By 1992, NTT shares had lost seven-eighths of their value compared to the peak price (3.2 million yen) in 1987; most people blame the MOF for this (and for the overall collapse of the stock market).[4] The fact that two former managers and the former chairman of NTT were arrested and charged with bribery and receiving windfall profits did not help the public's opinion of NTT or the government.

The MPT (whose minister, Ichiro Hino, was appointed by the ruling coalition) did not endorse divestiture, despite the recommendations of the council. However, some deregulation was agreed to, including the following:

- KDD would now be allowed into the domestic long-distance market
- NTT would have to provide more interconnections between private leased lines and its public network

• Cellular, paging, and PHS operators would no longer have to apply for rate reductions (though they would still have to notify the MPT)

Access Charges

The MPT also instructed NTT to clarify all details regarding interconnection. It is this question of access to NTT's system, and the access charges that must be paid by competing firms, that will determine whether fair competition can exist in Japan.

In October 1995, NTT reduced access charges to long-distance carriers from 12.57 yen to 10.46 yen. However, the FTC maintains that NTT is still overcharging for access; since the access charge includes NTT's marketing costs, competitors are forced to assist NTT in undermining them. The MPT hopes to have rules in place by the end of 1996 that will allow the true, fair cost of local service to be determined; thus access charges paid by the NCCs will reflect the actual cost of local interconnection and nothing more. But this will be difficult; many of NTT's local and long-distance operations are combined (e.g., billing, attracting new customers), making it difficult to allocate expenses separately to the local market and the long-distance market.

NCC Growth

Despite the fact that roughly half of the NCC's revenues goes to pay the access charges (about the same as in the United States) the new firms have been doing well; this is true in both the relatively stagnant domestic telephone market and the fast-growing wireless and international markets. As Table 2.2 shows, the competing firms have been gaining market share from NTT. This is partly because NTT must subsidize local calls (still only 10 yen from a payphone) and rural areas, resulting in higher rates on NTT's long-distance operations.[5] The new firms' success also reflects their interest in efficiency and cost reduction; revenue per person at the NCCs is about 75 million yen, three times that of NTT. The NCCs are also more willing to buy from foreign

Table 2.2
Telecommunications Market (1995)

	Market Size	NTT-related share (change from previous year)
Domestic	Telephone service: 5,040 b¥	NTT: 90% (-2%)
	Leased-circuit service: 560 b¥	NTT: 84% (-2%)
	Cellular phone service: 600 b¥	NTT DoCoMo: 64% (-3%)
	Radio paging service: 220 b¥	NTT DoCoMo: 64.5% (-1.5%)
International	Telephone service: 270 b¥	KDD: 70.5% (-3.5%)
	Leased-circuit service: 24 b¥	KDD: 77% (-3%)

Source: MPT, Communications in Japan 1995: Summary (Tokyo: MPT, 1995).

suppliers when it is advantageous; for example, NTT buys only 4 percent of its switching systems from foreign suppliers, whereas the NCCs buy 22 percent from overseas.

New Competition

The high cost of connecting a new line to a home or business (more than US$700) has encouraged alternative approaches in the telephone market. Jupiter, a cable television firm, plans to begin telephone service by the end of 1996. And several electric companies have shown interest in entering the market; several have already bought major holdings in regional phone companies.[6] But the biggest new source of competition has been the cellular phone industry.

The cellular phone market, which was virtually nonexistent until the late 1980s, has dramatically increased the level of competition. Although NTT DoCoMo had a head start on the competition, its market share is now 64 percent and falling rapidly (see Table 2.2). NTT DoCoMo's sales have actually increased, but the market has expanded even more rapidly (doubling in the past year) as analog cellular is replaced with digital. The cellular market also got a big push in April 1994, when the MPT began to allow customers to buy cellular phones instead of leasing them from network operators at inflated prices.

Japan has also seen the introduction of the PHS, which began in July 1995. PHS uses small, low-powered base stations sited close together in large cities, so the phone itself is small and light. The battery allows five hours of talking time; airtime charges are a fifth of cellular systems and local calls cost less than payphones. Also, it uses bandwidth efficiently, so it can be used to transmit faxes or multimedia. The only drawback is that it cannot be used in fast-moving vehicles. Although fewer than one million were sold as of early 1996 (approximately one tenth of the mobile market), recent price cuts by NTT and DDI are expected to increase their popularity.

Another source of competition is callback operators. These are foreign firms, usually in the United States, that allow Japanese customers to make international calls at foreign prices. The procedure is as follows: A Japanese person or firm becomes a subscriber to the callback service; when he wants to make an international call, he phones the callback service and hangs up before the call goes through; the callback service then calls him and offers a dial tone originating in the foreign country, from which the customer can call anywhere at the operator country's rates. This is essentially forcing Japanese firms to become as efficient as foreign firms in the international telephone market.[7]

International Effects

Japan continues to be a net exporter of telecommunication equipment (exports: 800 billion yen; imports: 150 billion yen). This is due to Japan's well-known advantage in electronics and to the close (some would say closed) nature of interfirm relationships. But the equipment market has been changing rapidly. Imports of telecommunication equipment into Japan have been rising, while exports have decreased for three straight years. This is partly due to the strong yen, but it also reflects the shift in emphasis from hardware to software. Japan also has a problem in that many of its domestic standards are different from those of other countries. Although this helped to reduce imports of foreign equipment into Japan in the past, it has now become a disadvantage as developing countries begin to adopt the standards used by European and American suppliers. Political pressure has also been a factor, as the United States has demanded greater access to the lucrative Japanese market; Motorola was one notable beneficiary.

Japan is also considering adopting the CDMA standard for its next generation of digital cellular telephony (the current cellular standard, peculiar to Japan, will be incapable of meeting demand if growth continues at the current pace for several more years). This will tend to separate Japan from the European market, which uses GSM. However, the United States uses CDMA and Asia seems to be headed that way; thus a large market with a common standard could be in the making. Whether this will allow Japan to export more or allow foreign firms to sell more in Japan remains to be seen.

International investment has been less pronounced than in other countries. Although many mobile firms (and IDC in the international market) have a sizable foreign ownership,[8] the major telecommunications firms remain largely Japanese-owned. This is expected to change as the NCCs establish stronger links with overseas firms, so as to facilitate technology exchange and enhance efficiency. It also seems likely that the government will eventually ease the restrictions on foreign ownership.

CONCLUSION

The question of whether NTT will be broken up remains unresolved for the time being. But with the intense competitive pressure that currently exists, it may be irrelevant whether NTT continues to supply local service as well as long-distance. Even if NTT were split, regulation would still be necessary to ensure that the new local operators were charging a fair access price to other firms; why not apply that same oversight now to the intact NTT? In other words, deregulate NTT as the British did with BT, not as the United States did with AT&T. This is the argument that NTT executives are making, an argument strengthened by the fact that the former AT&T seems to be reintegrating via mergers.

NTT, with US$60 billion in revenue, remains the largest player in Japan's telecommunication market. And although its market share is dropping, the fast growth of the market has allowed both NTT and the NCCs to generate increased sales. These trends are likely to continue; what is unclear is whether

NTT can match the level of efficiency shown by the new entrants. If not, then NTT may one day become strictly a regional operator by default, as it loses the other markets to the competition.

NOTES

1. The Wire Telecommunications Law, the Public Telecommunications Law, and the Nippon Telegraph and Telephone Public Corporation Law.

2. In fact, not until the late 1970s did NTT finally achieve the two goals it had set for itself: to eliminate the backlog of applications for subscriber telephones; and to provide a nationwide automatic direct-dial network.

3. The non-NTT firms that entered the Type I business market are collectively referred to as New Common Carriers (NCCs).

4. The stock market is still about half of its 1990 peak; NTT stock price is still down about three-quarters from its 1987 high.

5. NTT was given permission to raise subscriber rates by 16 percent in February 1995. This resulted in a 6 percent increase in revenue for the first half of FY 1995.

6. For example, Tokyo Telecommunication Network Co. is a partly owned subsidiary of Tokyo Electric Power Corp.; and the Osaka Media Port Corp. is affiliated with the Kansai Electric Power Co.

7. China, faced with a similar problem, made callback services illegal.

8. Air Touch International, spun off from Pacific Telesis (U.S.) and Cable and Wireless plc (U.K.), have 20 to 30 percent shares of several firms.

BIBLIOGRAPHY

Brull, Stephen V. 1996. "A Free Phone Market In Japan? Don't Hold Your Breath." *Business Week,* March 11.

Economist, The, October 14, 1995, 83.

Economist, The, February 24, 1996, 67.

Far Eastern Economic Review, February 15, 1996, 52.

Gross, Neil. 1994. "Come One, Come All to the Cellular Sweepstakes." *Business Week,* April 25.

Hamilton, David P. 1996. "Japan Struggles to Follow U.S. in Telecommunications Reform." *Wall Street Journal*, February 14.

Hills, Jill. 1992. "The Politics of International Telecommunications Reform." In *The Telecommunications Revolution,* edited by Harvey M. Sapolsky, Rhonda J. Crane, W. Russell Neumand, and Eli M. Noam. New York: Routledge.

Holstein, William J. 1984. "Building The New Asia." *Business Week,* November 28.

Holyoke, Larry. 1995. "Can AT&T Get Through To Japan?" *Business Week,* May 15.

Ministry of Posts and Telecommunications. 1995. *Communications in Japan 1995: Summary.* Tokyo: MPT.

Ministry of Posts and Telecommunications. 1995. *Open: Telecommunications Overview of Japan.* Tokyo: MPT.

Nikkei Weekly, November 27, 1995, 8.

"Survey of Telecommunications." *The Economist,* September 30, 1995.

Tomita, Tetsuro. 1992. "Telecommunications Policy in Japan." In *The Telecommuni-cations Revolution,* edited by Harvey M. Sapolsky, Rhonda J. Crane, W. Russell Neumand, and Eli M. Noam. New York: Routledge.

Williams, Martyn. 1995. "Council Begins Study Into NTT Changes." *Newsbytes,* April 6.

———. 1995. "New Operator in Japan." *Newsbytes,* April 14.

———. 1995. "Profits Surge at Telecom Firms." *Newsbytes,* November 22.

———. 1996. "Telecoms Minister Recommended to Split NTT." *Newsbytes,* February 29.

———. 1996. "Japan Maps Out Plan For Fiscal 1997." *Newsbytes,* March 4.

———. 1996. "Delay in NTT Break Up Decision Called For." *Newsbytes,* March 20.

———. 1996. "Japan Announces Deregulations Plans, Shuns NTT Split." *Newsbytes,* March 29.

———. 1996. "Global Cellular System Waits For Japan." *Newsbytes,* May 8.

THE KOREAN TELECOMMUNICATIONS SERVICE INDUSTRY

3

Privatization and Competition

Jeong-ja Lee

INDUSTRY OVERVIEW

Industry Structure

As in other Asian countries, the South Korean telecommunications service industry has been controlled by the government with regard to who can provide service and what prices they can charge. The three main companies in the industry—Korea Telecom Co. (KT), a general service provider; Korea Mobile Telecom Corp. (KMT), a pager and mobile telephone service provider; and Data Communications Corp. (Dacom), a long-distance service specialist—accounted for about 85 percent of sales in the industry in 1994. However, privatization of the industry has taken place since the early 1980s, when KT was separated from the government as a legal entity. KMT and Dacom started as subsidiaries of KT, but have been spun off as publicly traded private enterprises in recent years. KT itself plans to list on the Korea Stock Exchange by the end of 1996. Figure 3.1 illustrates the industry breakdown, and Table 3.1 includes major telecommunications statistics for the South Korean market.

Three Major Players

The government divides telecommunication service providers into two categories: network service providers and value-added service providers. Network

Figure 3.1
Market Share of KT, KMT, and Dacom

Total Market*: W 7.84t

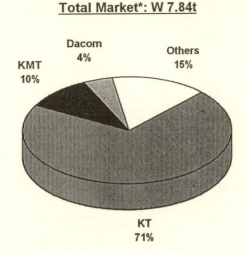

Note: *Dongbang Peregrine Securities estimate.
Source: Korea Telecom, Korea Mobile Telecom, and Dacom.

Table 3.1
South Korea's Telecommunications Industry Statistics

	1989	1990	1991	1992	1993	1994	1995E
Telephone lines installed (000)	13,354	15,293	17,511	19,021	20,223	20,783	21,283
Telephone lines in service (000)	11,792	13,276	14,573	15,593	16,686	17,647	18,075
Lines in service per 100 people	27.8	31.0	33.6	35.7	37.9	39.7	40.3
No. of lines connected to digital exchanges (%)	24.1	33.6	46.5	53.6	58.8	61.8	65.0
Fiber-optic cable (km)	3,260	3,744	4,469	5,476	7,979	10,772	12,616
No. of cellular subscribers	39,718	80,005	166,198	271,886	471,784	960,258	1,630,000
No. of pager subscribers	198,286	417,650	850,515	1,451,710	2,648,754	6,366,921	8,820,000

Source: KT, KMT, Dongbang Peregrine estimates.

service providers own their own circuits, whereas value-added service providers
lease circuits from network providers and may provide only specified service,
such as proprietary database access, data processing, electronic mail, and other
data transmission service. (See Table 3.2.) Network service providers are
subcategorized into general service providers and specific service providers.
General service providers own nationwide circuits and are permitted to provide

all telecommunications services other than those reserved for specific providers, such as regional service or cellular, pager, or marine telephone service. KT and Dacom are classified as general service providers, whereas KMT and ten regional pager service providers are classified as specific service providers.

Until last year, the government restricted general service providers from entering areas of business provided by specific service providers. In other words, fixed-line service providers and mobile phone service providers were kept separate, and this rule forced KT to sell its stake (65% in 1992) in KMT (in addition to privatization) and kept it from entering the cellular business. However, the government changed its policy last year and will allow fixed-line service providers to commence cellular service and mobile phone providers to enter fixed-line service, pending government approval.

KT is South Korea's only licensed supplier of fixed-line service and local and domestic long-distance telephone service and is the principal licensed supplier of international long-distance service. The company owns all domestic public exchanges, the nationwide network of local telephone lines and most public long-distance telephone transmission facilities. Korea Telecom also provides other telecommunication services, including leased circuits, data communication service, telex, telegraph, and satellite communications.

Dacom was established in 1982 to provide data communication service through personal computer networks and to provide software to government offices. In line with the government's plan to introduce competition to the telecommunications industry, Dacom was granted a license to enter international long-distance service in December 1991, and will be allowed to enter domestic long-distance service in 1996.

KMT is currently South Korea's only supplier of mobile telephone service and is the dominant supplier of pager service. The company was set up as a subsidiary of KT in 1984, but Sunkyong Group assumed management of the company in January 1994 as part of a privatization plan. The company introduced CDMA digital service in the spring of 1996 to augment its analog service and raise capacity. (See Table 3.3.)

Table 3.2
Service Provider Classification

Classification	Subclassification	Company
Network service providers	General service provider	Korea Telecom, Dacom
	Specific service provider	Korea Mobile Telcom, 10 pager companies, Korea Port Telephone Co., Shinsegi Telecomm. Inc.
Value-added service providers		About 2,000 companies

Source: Dongbang Peregrine Securities.

Table 3.3
1994 Financials for South Korea's Three Main Telecommunications Service Providers (won billion)

	Korea Telecom	KMT	Dacom
Total sales	5,539.7	782.9	344.9
Telephone business (%)	94.1	0.0	62.4
Data communication + leased circuit (%)	5.9	0.0	36.4
Cellular phone (%)	0.0	58.9	0.0
Pager (%)	0.0	41.1	0.0
Others (%)	0.0	0.0	1.2
Operating income	893.1	287.1	33.6
Recurring profit	761.1	246.4	16.4
Net income	627.1	128.7	13.2
EPS (won)	2,178	23,237	1,094
Total assets	11,298.2	1,540.7	607.3
Total liabilities	6,418.5	1,129.7	387.5
Shareholder's equity	4,879.8	411.0	219.8

Source: Ministry of Information and Communication.
Notes: 1994 figures from annual reports of each company; Korean currency Won/US$ equaled 781 at the end of 1994.

Government Regulation: Rates/License

The government regulates telecommunications service in two ways: the awarding of licenses and tariff controls. The government lifted barriers to enter value-added service in early 1994, but still controls entry into general service.

When general service providers want to increase tariffs or change their tariff structures, they submit proposals to the Ministry of Information and Communication (Ministry of Communication until December 1994), which sets rates following consideration of operating costs, fair investment return on capital employed to provide the service, and inflation. In the past, macroeconomic policy, including strict attention to inflationary indicators, has made the government quite hesitant to grant tariff increases based on increases in operating costs plus a fair rate of return on investment by service providers. This situation, particularly for KT, has kept local telephone service charges quite low, subsidized instead by high rates for international and domestic long-distance service.

LIMITED COMPETITION

As explained previously, the South Korean government announced a plan in 1990 to introduce limited competition in some telecommunications service areas. In accordance with the plan, Dacom was allowed to compete in international long-distance telephone service and started billing in December 1991. In return, Dacom's monopoly on data communication service ended in July 1990 when KT was granted permission to enter that area of business. At the end of 1994, Dacom's market share in international long-distance service was 26 percent whereas KT's market share in data communications was about 10 percent.

KMT enjoyed a monopoly in pager service until mid-1993. The government awarded ten licenses for regional pager service in early 1993, and these ten companies commenced operation in August and December of that year. As of the end of June 1995, KMT's market share in pager service was 56 percent, with the balance shared by the company's ten regional competitors.

In early 1994, when KMT was sold to a private business group (Sunkyong Group) in accordance with the government's privatization plan, a second license for mobile telephone service was granted to a consortium led by POSCO, South Korea's largest steel company. Shinsegi Telecomm Inc. began providing digital mobile telephone service using CDMA technology in mid-1996.

Until new entrants into telecommunications service areas gain a market share of 25 percent or more, the government has set a precedent for allowing a 5 percent price advantage. The price difference for international calling between KT and Dacom, and KMT and the ten regional pager service providers, has since been squeezed to 3 percent as they gained market share. Shinsegi Telecomm will enjoy a favorable 5 percent discount from the tariff structure offered by KMT.

FURTHER COMPETITION EXPECTED

The Ministry of Information and Communication unveiled a package in August 1995 designed to increase competition in present service areas and in service areas that are still being developed. The package is designed to make local service providers better able to compete against foreign entries from 1997 and 1998. The government began accepting applications from private companies in 1995, except for PCS, with awards given in 1996. Table 3.4 outlines the government's plan for granting new licenses.

Personal Communication Service (PCS)

PCS is by far the hottest issue among the new licenses. Korean PCS will be similar to the PHS service in Japan. Since the service is likely to be profitable from the year 2000, South Korea's largest business groups, including Samsung Group, Hyundai Group, and LG Group, are lining up to apply. The government has allocated three additional licenses for bidding in addition to automatic licenses for KMT and Shinsegi Telecom. Although the guidelines for bidding the license have not been released yet, KT will also likely gain an automatic license. The government has promised to foster KT as a representative of local telecommunications industry. A consortium of small and medium-size companies and two or three large business groups will likely compete for the remaining two licenses.

Table 3.4
New Telecommunications Licenses

Business	No. of new licenses	Existing licenses
PCS*	3	None
International long-distance call service	1	2
Domestic long-distance call service	1	2
TRS	1 nationwide operator 9 regional operators	1
CT-2	1 nationwide operator 10 regional operators	None
Mobile data service	3	None
Pager	1 regional operator	11
Line leasing	Qualified companies	3

Source: Ministry of Information and Communication.
Note: *Excludes automatic licenses to KMT and Shinsegi Telecomm.

More Competition in Fixed-Line Service

The government plans to allow one more license in international long-distance service and another in domestic long-distance service, allowing a total of three companies to compete in each area. It is expected that tariffs in the business area will be under pressure in the future as a result of competition and negotiations with the U.S. government to cut rates to North America. The U.S. government reached agreement with the South Korean government in 1988 to promote lower rates for international service and to lower net settlement payments by U.S. carriers to KT. The company expects the per-minute tariff between South Korea and the United States to decline to US$1.00 per minute from the current US$1.50 per minute over the next two to three years. Calling rates to other countries will also fall as a result. Competition in local call service is scheduled to be introduced from 1998 or 1999. Dacom has a plan to provide local call service from 1999 or 2000.

Regulations provide that KT must provide access to all new entrants through its switching stations. Over the longer term, the government will liberalize tariffs in all telecommunications service areas, including local phone service. Currently, the Korea Information Society Development Institute, a quasi-government run think tank, is studying comprehensive liberalization of telecommunications service pricing.

PRIVATIZATION

Dacom Corp.

Dacom Corp. was privatized between the end of 1993 and mid-1994 through the sale of KT's stake in the company and the sale of convertible bonds held by the Mutual Fund of Post Office Employees. Tong Yang Group and LG Group competitively bid for the holdings and purchased roughly 9.99 percent of total outstanding shares. However, because of government regulation that restricts private companies and telecommunications equipment manufacturers from holdings more than 10 percent of a general service provider, both groups failed to take management control. As a result, there is no major shareholder in Dacom at this time.

With rumors circulating that LG Group has collected Dacom shares through relevant networks, but not through members of the group (to avoid possible legal pressure from the government), the government may review regulations regarding ownership of general service providers. Shares have traded at astronomical 1995 price-to-earnings per share multiples of more than 100 in anticipation of a change in ownership. The government is reportedly reviewing ownership regulations and may raise the ownership limit, which could set off a prolonged battle for management control of the company. The National Assembly is expected to approve the regulation sometime in 1996.

KMT

Privatization of KMT started in 1989 when the company listed on the Korea Stock Exchange. KT's holdings in the cellular service provider were diluted by giving up preemptive rights in the initial public offering and subsequent rights issues. In January 1994, KT sold its 23 percent stake in KMT to Sunkyong Group and another 20 percent to domestic institutional investors. As of June 30, 1995, KT held a 19.3 percent stake in the company, while Sunkyong Group's holding stood at 22 percent. The government plans to allow mergers and acquisitions among listed companies, and Sunkyong Group hopes to raise its stake in KMT by another 10 percent.

KT

The privatization of KT has been a significant concern to the government. Since 1988, the government has sold shares of some government-owned companies to the general public as part of an ongoing plan to promote efficiency among state-owned companies. The companies sold in this manner include POSCO and Korea Electric Power Corporation In keeping with its privatization plans, the government announced in 1990 that it was considering selling 25 percent of outstanding common shares in KT in an initial public offering, with an additional 24 percent to be sold in subsequent years to lower the state's holding to 51 percent. However, because of a sharp downturn in the stock market, the government suspended share sales to the general public in late 1993.

In late 1993, the government sold 10 percent of its stake in KT (28,790,000 shares) to a pension fund held by government officials and another 10 percent through a bidding process to domestic institutional investors and individual investors. Still, the government holds 80 percent of total outstanding shares.

The government recently changed its long-term plan for the privatization of KT. It plans to sell off its holdings by the end of 1998, and is preparing to list the company in 1996. However, if the stock market begins to drop, an IPO could be delayed.

MARKET OPENING AND FOREIGN OWNERSHIP

The domestic telecommunications service market is scheduled to open to foreigners in 1997 or 1998. The government plans to allow foreigners to buy interests in domestic service providers at the initial stage, lease circuits from KT, do business in the middle stage, and set up their own telecommunications facilities in the final stage. However, this plan is subject to sudden change.

In addition to lifting ownership restrictions among local shareholders, the government may amend the Korea Telecom Act, allowing foreign portfolio investors to purchase up to 10 percent of outstanding shares in general service providers like KT and Dacom. Current regulations do not allow foreign ownership in the two companies, but allow one-third ownership of outstanding shares in KMT. However, KMT is listed on the Korea Stock Exchange and is subject to internal regulations that limit foreign ownership to 15 percent. The easing of foreign ownership limits is part of a general government policy to allow more foreign participation in the South Korean economy.

DIGITAL SATELLITE TELEPHONY

4

The Right Solution in Developing Indonesia

Bruce Rowe

Developing nations around the world are competing to capture their share of the emerging and expanding world economy. At stake are infusions of foreign investment made possible by privatization and deregulation of many industries. Such investment can lead to new industry, new jobs, and better quality of life.

One constant need for these developing nations is to invest in communications infrastructure in order to show investors that the country can support modern manufacturing plants, reliable phone services, and state-of-the-art information systems.

Indonesia is one nation in the midst of this new competition. The Asia–Pacific region is teeming with countries that want to become the next Japan, Taiwan, or Korea—serving first as a center for low-cost manufacturing and then stepping up to engineering design and product research and development. Malaysia, India, Thailand, and China have all jumped into the arena, with large pools of inexpensive labor and engineering talent. But Indonesia also faces an additional challenge, with its population spread over 13,000 islands.

One major step taken by Indonesia to compete against its regional neighbors is to implement a new telephony system using a thirty-site digital satellite network. Known as the DSC-LBR (for Digital Satellite Channel-Low Bit Rate) network, it connects the capital city of Jakarta and several other large cities in East Indonesia to the outermost of the nation's islands. The success and quality of the network have surpassed everyone's expectations. An average of 12,000 calls per day run smoothly over the network, with peak traffic of more than 15,000 calls per day. Still, the totals represent only 60 to 70 percent of network capacity.

Indonesia is a natural location for communication by satellite because of satellite's inherent ability to connect locations where there is no terrestrial infrastructure (see Figure 4.1). Once the signal is transmitted to the satellite, any location within the satellite beam can be connected quickly and inexpensively. But even satellite technologies are not all created equal; so Indonesia had to step up to a newer, more efficient satellite network.

The new DSC-LBR network is an important link for Indonesia's nearly four million telephone subscribers, connecting medium and small cities to each other, as well as to the nation's major population centers in Jakarta, Surabaya, Ujung Pandang, Manado, and Banjarmasin. From a technology standpoint, the new digital connections fill a gap between a 15-year-old analog SCPC network and newer TDMA trunks used to connect the larger cities. In addition to quality and reliability problems, the old analog network could carry just 10 to 15 percent of the traffic carried by the new digital network. A typical node on the network that may have had five analog channels now is served by thirty digital channels at thirty-two kilobits each.

Implementing all-digital equipment is a key cost-saving advantage because it means less hardware and lower capital costs for the network operator. Most VSAT systems must make a digital-to-analog conversion before calls are transmitted, usually requiring channel banks that convert an E1 (2.048 megabits-per-second) data stream into thirty analog phone lines. Each line then must be sent to its own dedicated SCPC modem for transmission.

Indonesia's new all-digital solution, based on ComStream TDMA DAMA network products, streamlines earth station hardware tremendously. For example, at the DSC Jakarta earth station, 150 analog modems carrying one voice channel each were replaced by one TDMA DAMA modem that carries the same 150 channels on five digital interfaces.

All thirty sites connect directly to local public switched networks to relay calls to individual users. ComStream Corp. worked closely with PT Telkom, the Indonesian phone company, to develop special processing hardware and software that enables the satellite equipment to operate using CEPT protocol—a thirty-channel CCITT standard—and Indonesian R2 signaling. The development allows the DSCM-LBR network to connect seamlessly with the Indonesian public switched telephone network.

Another key benefit of the new digital system is "full mesh" connectivity. Any node on the network can communicate with any other node, without having to pass through a central processing hub, or through another preassigned network connection.

Other VSAT technologies are set up in a "star" network configuration, with a central hub earth station. All network locations are points on the star, and

Figure 4.1
Indonesian Satellite Network

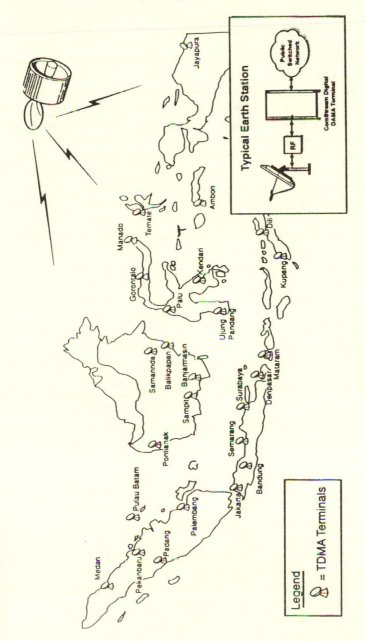

all must send signals to the hub first, which then routes the calls to the proper destination. Star networks are a good solution for data networks, but in voice telephony applications the configuration causes distracting delays and voice echoes in conversations. Star configurations also use the satellite twice for each connection, therefore twice as much space on the satellite transponder is tied up with each call.

Prior to installation of the digital DAMA network, calls originating from some Indonesian cities on outlying islands were always routed to a single backbone destination, for example Ambon. If the outlying city wanted to call Jakarta, then the call would have to go to Ambon first and then take an additional satellite "hop" to Jakarta, reducing quality and making very inefficient use of satellite resources.

The new network is called "hubless" because network processing intelligence is distributed to all nodes rather than being implemented at a single hub. This distributed design increases network flexibility and reliability, with many advantages resulting:

- True point-to-point communication between any two sites, with only a single "hop" from station to station
- Immediate 50 percent reduction in satellite transponder use
- No single point of failure in the network
- No high costs associated with central processing hubs
- No congestion of signals in and out of a central site

Despite the elimination of a central network hub to process calls, network operators can still centralize configuration and control of network equipment using a Sun workstation-based network management system. This central point of control can be located at any network site. PT Telkom monitors the DSC network using a network control center at the earth station in Jakarta.

Efficiency is another advantage that the DSC-LBR network holds over other technologies, even other all-digital networks, because TDMA DAMA allows multiple users to share a common pool of satellite capacity. IDR is an example of a digital solution, but it requires two to four times the amount of transponder capacity because all network connections are preassigned, dedicated circuits that remain open and waiting even when no traffic is passing over them. DAMA technology enables the DSC-LBR network to allocate idle circuits as required to any combination of sites needing a connection. Then, as a connection is broken, the circuit is put back into the pool, available for assignment to a subsequent connection.

Economic benefit from TDMA DAMA technology can be looked at in two ways: as a pure cost savings because it uses less satellite transponder capacity; or as a way for service providers to gain more revenue by using the same amount of space segment to offer more services.

PT Telkom has chosen the latter route in the case of the DSC-LBR network. The Indonesian phone company has continued to use a full transponder for the DSC-LBR network but now completes seven to ten times as many calls and collects a proportionate increase in revenue every day compared to the network when it used the old technology. With the worldwide average annual cost of a transponder equal to US$1 million, the return on investment is rapid, with little time required to recapture the capital cost of upgrading to the new technology.

The Indonesian DSC-LBR network has proved to be a resilient and reliable solution, requiring very little maintenance. Network operation has now been turned over to PT Telkom for routine network monitoring. Traffic statistics, for use in forecasting growth and planning network expansion, are collected and printed easily using the network control center.

With over 15,000 connections daily, this digital network has become an integral part of the infrastructure of Indonesia. The network reduces operating costs, offers more calling capacity, improves transmission quality, and interconnects people across wide areas where terrestrial networks are not practical. This telephone network, using all-digital satellite TDMA DAMA, has proved itself as the right investment for Indonesia's developing economic future.

THE CONTRIBUTION OF FOREIGN INVESTMENT IN CHINA'S TELECOMMUNICATIONS INDUSTRY

5

Meheroo Jussawalla

Most Asian governments today are being driven by the speed of innovations, the flows of capital, and the opportunities for joint ventures to restructure their rigid monopolistic public enterprises and allow the operation of market forces. Economies that in the past considered themselves self-reliant, like India and China, have been forced by the telecommunications revolution to become more open in their trade and investment policies and to forge joint ventures in order to survive in a globally competitive market. The many socialist oriented five-year plans which formed the basis of economic policy had to be abandoned under the driving forces of technology and growing consumer demand. China has been in the forefront of such structural changes. With global connectivity as its goal, China is rapidly removing some of the bureaucratic roadblocks to attract foreign participation in its telecommunications sector.

Accompanying high rates of economic growth ranging between 10 and 12 percent a year, China has had a major problem with inflation. Then in the first half of 1995 it entered a period of recession which has made the government rethink its policy of public enterprise reform. Now Beijing wants to control high inflation, rising debts, poor performance of state-held enterprises, and growing unemployment (*Far Eastern Economic Review,* August 31, 1995, 40). Real GDP growth fell from 11 percent in 1994 to 10.3 percent in the first half of 1995. Grain rationing has been introduced to fight food inflation.

China's foreign exchange reserves have fallen to US$62 billion as of 1995, after the devaluation of the rinminbi by 34 percent in 1994. Exports surged, giving China an export surplus of US$7 billion in the first quarter of 1995.

Many multinationals have set up one or more joint ventures in China and are steadily increasing their market share. However, the frenzied rush is slowing down as China imposes a more restrictive policy and operating costs escalate for foreign investors. Since the telecommunications sector is one of the favored sectors of the government, foreign vendors still compete fiercely to get a foothold in the market. China's telecommunications network has expanded rapidly over the last decade, exceeding the growth of GDP. The telephone sector alone is growing at a rate of 41.6 percent annually since 1993. Government plans call for installing ten million lines per year throughout the 1990s, reaching one hundred million lines by the year 2000. Thus the current teledensity of 4.5 telephones per 100 persons will increase to 8.5 by the end of the decade. According to the Minister for Posts and Telecommunications, Wu Jichuan, between 1991 and 1994 the average annual growth rate of income earned from main trunk lines and long distance lines as well as services reached 41.2 percent in 1992, 57 percent in 1993, and 48 percent in 1994 (*Beijing Review,* July 2, 1995, 8).

In the past, China's telecommunications revenues did not come from products or services but from government subsidies. Consequently, if there was a shortfall in the budget, the telecommunications sector was starved for funds for expansion. Under the new policy, the central and provincial governments are free to make investments in the sector and to negotiate joint ventures for technology transfer and production. Under the Ninth Five-Year Plan, investments in the telecommunications sector will amount to US$100 billion.

Although the financial situation has improved, it is still imperative for China's megaprojects to use a considerable portion of imported technologies. Most of its imports from Japan and Europe are supported by government and bank loans. Some foreign loans are product-tied (e.g., in the case of Sweden, purchases have to be made from Ericsson). Loans from the United States are not tied, which impacts on their market share of equipment sold in China. In 1994, telecommunications companies were advancing low-interest loans to build plants for Chinese-controlled joint ventures.

During 1994, the Chinese telecommunications sector made two major breakthroughs resulting from enhanced competition and deregulation in the services markets. One significant advance was the investment of US$8.5 billion in equipment infrastructure, and the other was the addition of 17 million new lines on the public switched network (Lin Sun 1995). To add to the new services 4.3 million new pagers and 900,000 new cellular phones were added. This makes China the largest market in the world for pagers with a total of 11 million pagers in use and 1.5 million cellular subscribers. Investment in the latest technology of SDH has led to this system being installed for services between Guangzhou and Hong Kong, thus taking China to the on-ramp of the global information superhighway.

The most signficant change has been the emergence of a challenger to the control of the MPT in the form of Liantong (United Communications Corporation, or Unirom). Liantong was established in July 1994 by the Ministries of Electronics and of Railways and the Ministry of Electric Power, together with CITIC. Liantong started by setting up services in four major cities: Beijing, Shanghai, Tianjin, and Guangzhou. While it is not a second carrier, it is leading China in its ambition to start the Golden Projects, which are the Golden Bridge, the Golden Card, and the Golden Customs. These three are China's version of the information highway using speed switching and transmission systems to deliver large quantities of data. With a capital investment of US$1.2 billion, Liantong will need foreign collaboration but will have to appease the MPT for permission in the services sector. GTE is likely to be one of the foreign collaborators.

China spent US$6 billion in 1994 in telecommunications gear, and over the next six years suppliers estimate that the spending will amount to US$90 billion (*Asian Wall Street Journal,* April 16, 1994, 1). In the next section of this chapter, we will examine the role of foreign participation in China's switching and transmission sectors and analyse the market trends in these activities.

FOREIGN INVESTMENT IN SWITCHING AND TRANSMISSION SECTORS

In China, the switching market has always been very difficult to enter because it is highly regulated. The State Council in 1990 gave a directive to equipment purchasers that only Alcatel of France, NEC of Japan, and Siemens of Germany should be considered for foreign collaboration. In 1992, this policy was changed to select suppliers of Stored Program Controlled Switches (SPCs), without mentioning names of companies. AT&T then entered the market with a proposal to start a joint venture for the manufacture of switching equipment. Despite this entry, the primary domestic supplier of central office switches is a joint venture between the MPT and Alcatel. The largest market share for SPC switches of about 30 percent is enjoyed by Alcatel, followed by Ericsson.

Recognizing its mistake in the early 1980s of neglecting the Chinese market, AT&T is now speeding up its provision of its flagship digital switches, the 5ESS series. By 1994, total imports of switch capacity reached 800,000 switches. Demand has driven the market for switches in a highly politically charged environment. The MPT, the State Planning Commission, and the Ministry for Electronics are all key figures in selecting switches; therefore, domestic production of switches is growing rapidly. The major domestic competitors are Shanghai Bell (a collaboration with ITT Belgium) and other smaller companies that have already captured 80 percent of the market. In the market for switches, the hottest competition is between Northern Telecom and AT&T, with Northern having invested in joint ventures up to US$150 million. AT&T has reached a US$1 billion agreement in 1994 to manufacture switches, wireless phones, and integrated circuits. Canada approved a government loan of US$200 million which would help China finance one million lines of switching and transmission gear for the province of Guangdong. Northern will manufacture its own brand of DMS switches and very large-scale integrated circuits for Guangdong and Shanghai. The Chinese investor will control 60 percent of the switching joint venture.

At the same time, multilateral funding agencies like the World Bank gave a US$620 million loan for the purchase of switching and transmission equipment gear for three Chinese provices. AT&T also set up a branch of its Bell Labs in Shanghai in 1993. As far back as 1989, AT&T started a joint venture with Shanghai Optical Fiber Communications Corporation and the Shanghai Telecommunications Equipment Factory, each of these having a 22 percent share in the joint operations. By October 1992, AT&T Network Systems had established two more joint ventures in China, bringing the total investment to US$20 million. This was done despite the handicap of being shut out of China's market when, after 1989, the U.S. government placed sanctions on trade with China as a reprisal for the Tiananmen Square events (Warwick 1994). During 1993, AT&T had installed 200,000 5ESS trunk lines, 900 transmission systems, and 9000 kilometers of fiber optic cables. AT&T now has a 20 percent market share of the transmission systems in China. In collaboration with Japan's KDD and China's MPT, AT&T Communications Services Group have undertaken a US$70 million digital network project for private line services in Beijing and Shanghai. The project includes AT&T's Skynet satellite service and extends an optical fiber cable linking Japan with China. In February 1993, AT&T signed a memorandum of agreement with the State Planning Commission to do business with China, identifying certain areas of business such as switch manufacturing, Very Large Systems Integration (VLSI) manufacturing, wireless systems manufacturing, and R&D with Bell Labs. In addition, AT&T created a China business unit called AT&T China. AT&T's China business was delayed because of COCOM and by the MFN status of China; these export controls cost AT&T about US$500 million in business with China. Even so, AT&T sells more than US$100 million a year of telephone equipment to China. By 1997, the company expects to sell US$1 billion of telecommunications products to the exploding Chinese market.

By the year 2000, China hopes to tap US$7 billion worth of foreign capital for aggressively leapfrogging its way onto a futuristic information superhighway. In 1993, overall investment in China's telecommunications fixed assets was US$4.7 billion according to Reuters news service, as cited in the *Asian Wall Street Journal* (June 22, 1994, 4). If China is to keep its promise of installing ten million lines a year up to the year 2000, it will need a large infusion of foreign capital; only for developing a new generation of its network switching gear it will require US$2 billion. With the surge in China's telecommunications market, there is an intense scramble among global suppliers to snatch as much market share as possible, even if it involves staking their own capital.

MOBILE SYSTEMS

Despite the fact that the Chinese are smitten by the telephone revolution, there are vast tracts of the country that are still lacking basic services. The cost of laying land lines over difficult terrain is high, and households in some of the remote areas must pay the equivalent of US$900 (two years salary) for a regular telephone and wait a year to receive the service; thus many people use public telephones operated from window sills of shops. It is in such areas that mobile services offer the most economic alternative. These include cellular telephones and (for those who cannot afford the up-to-US$5,400 cost of a cellular phone) pagers and CT2 mobile systems supplied by Motorola, for a one way connection.

The cellular telephones market in China is growing at a rate of 100 percent per year. There are more than forty cellular switches and 500 base stations which proportionately are relatively few to the density of the population in cities like Beijing, Shanghai, and Guangzhou. The Total Access Communications system (TACS) has been adopted in China for its cellular services. It is also used for police and emergency services; in 1994, public paging was introduced in Guangzhou province for this purpose. Now more than forty cities and all thirty provinces have taken to cellular systems. So far, penetration of pagers has been higher in the urban areas; remote regions have been neglected even though their potential is higher. China imports one million pagers a year, mostly from Motorola, Panasonic, OKI, and NEC. In addition, one hundred brands of pagers are domestically produced and sold that are cheaper than the imported ones. The provincial governments are planning to subsidize their use in order to save the costs of land lines for their budgets. The MPT projects that usage will grow significantly in three regions, namely the Beijing–Tianjin–Tiangshi corridor in the north; the Yangtze Delta in central China; and the Pearl River Delta in the south. China uses the European standard for equipment and service, the GSM. The handset costs the equivalent of US$2,200, the hook-up cost is another US$1,000, which MPT charges, and the monthly service charge is US$27, which the average Chinese (monthly income: US$30) cannot afford to pay.

Beginning in 1994, foreign equity participation in the cellular market has been considered by the MPT. For the Liantong new non-MPT cellular project, the government and the Ministry of Electronics refused to permit foreign capital but allowed foreign companies to build networks in those areas where there are too few phones. Currently, there are forty cellular phone switches and 500 base stations which are inadequate for the density of population in cities like Beijing and Shanghai and Guangzhou. If roaming facilities are to be provided to their users, the cellular systems will have to rely on foreign equity or joint-venture participation as provided by the Iridium project of Motorola, the Inmarsat P, or the Globalstar systems, all of which are being offered to the MPT by its suppliers. In fact, China has agreed to take an equity stake in Motorola's Iridium system of LEOs, in which the signals will move from the satellite to the user (a "message hopping" technology).

Taking a cautious approach, Motorola in 1992 constructed a plant in the northern city of Tianjin to manufacture pagers. By 1994, Motorola started to sell 10,000 units per week at a retail cost with service of US$200. By 1993, the demand for pagers was four million, and Motorola's Tianjin factory could hardly keep up. This demonstrates how investment in the Chinese telecommunications market has paid off for the U.S. leader in cellular systems. Now Motorola has started a first phase for a joint venture in the Tianjin Economic and Technology Development zone to make pagers, along with integrated circuits and cellular phones. In the second phase, Motorola will manufacture automotive electronics and advanced microprocessor systems. In total, Motorola will invest US$400 million. This marks a new conceptual approach among multinationals as they are now looking at an integrated approach that involves manufacturing, sales, and R&D. In order to train Chinese engineers for its new ventures, Motorola is sending them to its own facilities in Schaumberg, Hong Kong and Singapore.

Liantong was set up by the Ministry of Electronics in conjunction with the Ministry of Railways and the Ministry of Power. It provides domestic long-distance services and is now beginning to permit limited foreign equity participation (as it urgently needs capital investment to expand its cellular systems and permit roaming facilities throughout the vast interior, rather than just the coastal provinces). In July 1995, Liantong started to supply cellular services in four Chinese cities, breaking the monopoly of MPT. The latter immediately lowered its tariffs to counteract competition from Liantong. Even if China commits its total foreign exchange reserve of US$46 billion to the development of modern systems of telecommunications, it will still have a shortfall of US$35 billion. Vendor financing may be available up to US$25 billion, and fianancing may be available from the IFC (an arm of the World Bank), yet there would still be a deficit for the cellular systems that China needs (like the Iridium project from Motorola, or the Inmarsat P, or the Globalstar system now being offered to China on a joint venture basis).

JOINT VENTURES IN SATELLITE COMMUNICATIONS

The vast area, varied terrain, and spread of populaton make it incumbent upon China to opt for satellite communications. These services are cost insensitive to distance and provide instant and reliable service.

Just as the MPT and the Ministries of Electronics, Railways and Power Supply and other ministries have a stake in the telecommunications sector, so also the Peoples Liberation Army (PLA) has been very active in its control over satellite communications, both fixed and mobile, and is a major supplier of VSATs for accurate reception of satellite-based programming for television along with voice and data signals. These receiving dishes are supplied by the PLA to the rural areas; and because the MPT mandate that their use should be strictly controlled could not be enforced and had to be operated in the breach, satellite communications has become one of the more progressive sectors of China's communications industry.

Interestingly enough, China's satellite communications got started after the visit of the late President Richard Nixon in 1972. The American visitors left behind a satellite dish as a gift to the Chinese. Since then, China has made impressive strides in both the technology and the services. It built, with indigenous equipment, one of the most successful launch rockets, called the Long March II and III, which competes with American, French, and Russian systems and offers competitive prices. While the Chinese charge US$45 million per launch, the other systems charge US$90 million. While not all its launches are sucessful, this is equally true of some of the launches by the others.

Although the satellite market in China did not take off until the mid-1980s, it has witnessed rapid growth due to foreign collaboration in both capital equipment and supplies, especially from Hughes Space Corporation. The MPT itself, which had a monopoly over the PSTN for decades, has simultaneously encouraged the use of satellite technology.

China initiated satellite communications in June 1986, when it leased transponders on Intelsat and imported earth stations from abroad (Swensrud and Huafeng Xu 1995). By the end of 1994, 85% of all international switched circuits were satellite-based and the transmission for all local and central television broadcasts was by satellite. This was also true of broadcasts to the remote areas and for long-distance traffic (both public and private). The operating arm of the system is Chinasat (China Telecom Broadcast Satellite Corporation) along with the DGT. During the Eighth Five-Year Plan, the MPT established twenty Standard A earth stations in nineteen provinces. One of these, in Beijing, provides national emergency services. China has been using transponders on Intelsat both over the Pacific and Indian Ocean regions and pays lease rent to the international cooperative as a member signatory. It has now leased its orbital slot at 87.5 degrees East to Intelsat for its 805 satellite in return for ownership of 45 percent of transponders on the sophisticated digital communications system plus an upfront payment of US$21 million. Another Intelsat service now used, called the IDR, provides hundreds of multiplexed voice circuits. This shows that while China keeps its satellite communications market exclusively for domestic ownership, it still uses international suppliers for newer technologies and services.

As China is unable to construct its own satellites with Ku band transponders, a second-hand satellite was purchased from GTE Spacenet in 1992, now called the Chinasat V. China also is one-third owner of the Asia Pacific's most successful commercial satellite system called Asiasat that has the largest viewership in the world for its Star TV network. CITIC along with Hutchison Whampoa of Hong Kong and Cable & Wireless of the United Kingdom are the principal shareholders of the system. The stunning success of Star TV induced China to lease six transponders on Asiasat for its government and business users who receive the northern beam of the satellite's footprint. It has a strong customer base in China composed of banks, securities houses, publishers, and the oil industry to link remote sites with central headquarters. Currently, there are 500,000 dish antennas in China's major cities receiving television programs. However, with the purchase of the Hong Kong share by Rupert Murdoch, the Chinese government insisted that BBC broadcasts should not be received within the country to preserve cultural integrity. Murdoch complied, and mostly Chinese language broadcasts are now transmitted.

Further foreign participation was established when three ministries in China collaborated with Hong Kong, Thai, and Taiwanese capitalists to launch another satellite, called Apstar-2 (backed by APT Satellite Co.), with Apstar programming. Many foreign broadcasters like CNN, ESPN, MTV, and HBO had signed up for transponders on Apstar-2, but in 1995 the Long March launched it and within sixty seconds the satellite exploded, landing the investors with a total loss of US$250 million. The foreign investors are claiming a refund of their shares, and China has agreed to some arbitration procedure.

Another foreign collaboration is the Bank of China's VSAT network for its many branches for electronic funds transfer, which it gets through an agreement with Asiasat. The Great Wall Corporation also has become a partner in a teleport venture with the government of Macau, called Teleset and offers access to the ill-fated Apsat system.

To meet the fast growing market demand for various satellite communications services, China has recently launched the first of the Chinese-made DFH (Dong Fang Hong) Three series which is designed with a life span of eight years. Since the early 1990s, China has emphasized digital technologies and Ku band transponders, deploying foreign data-voice integrated VSAT systems. Such an earth station has been opened in Guangzhou. China is still relying on foreign technology and equipment through joint ventures for equipment manufacture with Hughes Space Corporation and VSAT terminal suppliers like ComStream and Scientific Atlanta. China has imported virtually all of its major earth stations from the United States, Canada, Japan, and Germany. China's current Ninth Five-Year Plan attempts to meet the growing demand for satellite communications, now increasing at 12 percent a year. This is particularly true of long-distance transmission service. Now the MPT faces competition in the satellite market from new entrants Liantong and Ji

Tong. Liantong is planning to construct its own satellite infrastructure, for which it is seeking foreign collaborators. Ji Tong is planning to use satellites for its Golden Bridge Project, which will provide voice, video, and data through a broadband integrated communications system. If the Chinese government allows the satellite networks to engage in the competitive leasing of international satellite transponders, China will become a more cost-efficient consumer of satellite networks.

CABLE TELEVISION AND FOREIGN COLLABORATION

It has been suggested that cable television provides a back door to the Chinese telecommunications market (Schoenfeld 1995). While China's telephone penetration rate is 2 percent, its penetration rate for television is 90 percent. Most of the viewership is based on satellite or microwave broadcasts, but in the future cable television will have a prominent role to play in China's market. The reasons are that cable provides a cost-effective mode of convergent technology, including mutimedia services to reach subscribers' homes. Wharf Cable TV in Hong Kong (as cited by Schoenfeld) estimates that using revenues from cable television could save China US$30 billion in its telecommunications infrastructure costs. However, the Chinese government does not permit foreign participation in its television programming. In March 1995, the Agreement on Intellectual Property Rights was signed between the United States and China, which, if implemented, will make the Chinese cable television market more accessible to U.S. companies. This is because the agreement allows joint ventures to be established for the production and coproduction of films and television programming. Revenue sharing is also allowed under the agreement. For rural areas, however, cable television would be costly to install, so direct broadcast satellites offer a viable alternative, which is preferred by the Chinese government. In the cities, the government can control the quality and contents of the programming by filtering and censoring programs offered by cable television, which is not possible with satellite technology, as the latter relies only on rooftop antennas.

JAPAN'S INVESTMENT IN CHINA'S TELECOMMUNICATIONS SECTOR

From the early 1980s, Japan has been investing approximately US$9 billion overall for the economic development of China. Its OECF has been the principal investor in areas other than telecommunications. It has offered concessional yen loans for a number of infrastructure projects. American firms are able to bid on OECF development projects in China. OECF loans now account for 60 percent of Japan's total bilateral assistance for development (Clifford 1993). The rate of interest charged to China varies between 2.5

and 3.5 percent, with repayment spread over thirty years. It is the largest foreign lender to China, with unfettered loans, providing more financing than the World Bank or the Asian Development Bank.

Among its loans, the OECF has financed a scheme under the Eighth Five-Year Plan to install computer-driven price information networks and data banks in Beijing, Shanghai, and Guangzhou to assist the State Economic Planning Center in developing integrated planning. Likewise, IBM Japan has bid for major projects funded by the OECF and supplies mainframe computers to China. Telecommunications loans under the OECF rank third in the amount of lending, following transportation and power. These untied loans offer significant opportunities for U.S. companies in the teleommunications sector to win bids advertised by the China Technical Import Export Corporation; so far, the number of U.S. bidders is small. Over the past decade, Japanese firms have won 37 percent of the total contracts awarded for China, whereas Hong Kong and Chinese firms have won 42 percent of the contracts; firms of U.S. origin have won only 3 percent of the total contracts. It has been noted that joining forces with a Japanese or Chinese partner helps to secure bids more successfully; Hewlett Packard did this with Nichimen Corporation in supplying workstations and PCs to the Beijing Institute of Technology.

CONCLUSION

Despite the many handicaps of bureaucratic regulations and frequent changes in policy decisions in the Peoples Republic of China, foreign investors have succeeded through flows of technology and capital to advance the modernization of China's telecommunications industry and bring China into the global information infrastructure and the age of multimedia channels of transmission. The streets criss-crossing China's version of Silicon Valley in Western Beijing's university neighborhood are lined with shops displaying the posters of equipment supplied by IBM, DEC, Microsoft, and Intel. At stake is one of the world's fastest growing computer markets. Compaq expects that during this decade its sales will reach US$1 billion a year. Computer companies find that low-cost labor and engineering and programming talent make it possible not only to supply the domestic market but perhaps to export as well. The demand for personal computers in China was 650,000 in 1994, largely due to affluent urban dwellers. Added to this is the potential of supplying computers to government offices. At present, China's PC market is dominated by three companies: These are the domestic supplier Legend Holdings Limited with a 40 percent share; AST based in Irvine, California, with sales of 140,000 in 1994; and Compaq with a 22 percent share.

With the spurt in computer ownership, the next step has been the proliferation of Internet usage by the Chinese. Even though the language of the Internet is English, its Chinese users are surfing the various bulletin boards, news reports, and sports information available on the Net. In the cities, satellite communications, cable television, pagers, cellular phones, and the Internet have all become a part of the daily lives of the upper-income Chinese, and their numbers are growing. Chinese subscribers can now choose between two telephone companies plus the cellular facilities. There is more fiber-optic cable linking Chinese cities than most other countries in Southeast Asia. Both AT&T and KDD of Japan have provided submarine cable to link China's coastal provinces and China with other countries like Japan and Korea.

While China still does not permit foreign ownership of telecommunications services, we have seen that it permits nonequity investments and joint ownership in equipment manufacture. Foreign firms have been aggressively pursuing deals to build, operate, and transfer the ownership of networks in China. Multinationals like AT&T, Ericsson, Alcatel, Motorola, Scientific Atlanta, and Sprint are strongly entrenched in the Chinese telecommunications market, selling billions of dollars worth of equipment and establishing joint ventures to ensure long-term contracts.

One of the bigger projects proposed by AT&T is to build and operate a broadband network for fifty office buildings in the new financial district in Pudong in Shanghai. Another such proposal has been made by Singapore Telecom International for building a fixed-line network in Shanghai but has not yet received the sanction from the MPT. The Minister for Telecommunications is optimistic about the future of the telecommunications sector and expresses hope that China will learn new ways of experimenting with foreign capital (*Far Eastern Economist,* October 5, 1995, 56). With growing demand for foreign investment funds in Indonesia, India, and the Philippines, the competition for foreign capital has intensified. Hence, China will soon have to rethink its policy of restricting foreign capital and will have to permit a fair rate of return on investments. Already the MPT finds itself challenged by the new competitors like Liantong and Ji Tong, both of whom have made many deals for foreign participation in their networks. Ji Tong plans to run value-added services in the form of the Golden Card, a national credit card clearance system, Golden Bridge, a national information network, and the Golden Gate, which will connect all customs and trade-related activities.

On the whole then, China is profiting greatly from the infusion of capital and technology in its newly liberalized telecommunications sector. As the MPT's grip over the operations and equipment manufacturers weakens, and as technology overtakes the regulators, China will move from centralized control to a free market, purely in its own self-interest. In the current information age it is not possible for any country, even one with a Communist government, to remain isolated from the global economy as it rides along the information superhighway.

BIBLIOGRAPHY

Clifford, Bill. 1993. "Japan's Lending Program in China." *The China Business Review* 20(3): 30–34.

Jussawalla, Meheroo, and Lin Sun. 1994. "Contenders for China's Telecommunica-
    tions Market." Paper submitted to the U.S. Department of Commerce for
    Briefing Book on China's Telecommunications Industry, March.
Schoenfeld, Susan. 1995. "Cable Television: A Back Door to China's Telecommuni-
    cations Market." *Intermedia* 23(3): 18–20.
Sun, Lin. 1995. "Western Misconceptions About China's UNICOM." *Intermedia*
    23(1): 25.
Swensrud, S. Blake, and Huafeng Xu. 1995. *Satellite Communications* 19(5): 31–33.
Warwick, William. 1994. "A Review of AT&T's Business History in China: The
    Memorandum of Understanding in Context." *Telecommunications Policy*
    18(3): 265–274.

NYNEX's EXPERIENCES IN THAILAND WITH TELECOMASIA

6

An Example of Foreign Cooperation in the Opening Up and Expansion of the Telecommunications Sector in Asia

Maureen D. Piché, Ben Park, and Roger Carlson

KEY TRENDS IN WORLDWIDE TELECOMMUNICATIONS

Scarcely a day passes without some development in the rapidly changing global communications industry. The pace of technological change has started to drive the convergence of the telecommunications, entertainment, and computer sectors. The Global Information Infrastructure (GII), the Internet, and a host of other advanced applications under development will soon have the ability to span the world.

And yet in many parts of the world, the majority of people still have no access to basic telephone service. What telecommunications infrastructure exists, is often poorly maintained and unable to support the kinds of services that are taken for granted elsewhere. A recent World Bank[1] estimate suggests that emerging economies will require US$40 billion in investment each year over the next five years just for their telecommunications sectors to close the gap with developed countries. To date, much of the investment in the expansion of telephony infrastructure has taken place in the developed nations of the world. As the data in Figure 6.1 indicate, there continues to exist a major imbalance by regions of the world between the distribution of telephone lines relative to population.

Figure 6.1
Comparison of Percentage of Global Population and Telephone Lines

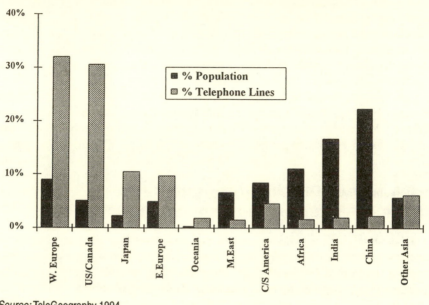

Source: TeleGeography 1994

A disproportionate amount of global telecommunications infrastructure and investment is concentrated in a few developed countries. For example, the nations of western Europe, the United States, Canada, and Japan account for a little more than 16 percent of the world population of 5.5 billion but are served by almost 75 percent of the 575 million global telephone lines. This contrasts with India, with a similar proportion of world population, yet which has only 2 percent of the world's telephone lines. The differences are even greater from an investment standpoint, in light of the fact that only ten countries in the world account for nearly 70 percent of the value of telecommunications infrastructure investment.

Much research has also focused on the linkage between the level of economic development of a country and the scale of the telecommunications network serving it. A direct correlation has been established between a country's penetration of telephone lines per 100 people (this measure is often referred to as teledensity) and per capita GDP. ITU has found that an increase of approximately 2.2 telephone lines per 100 population is generally accompanied by an increase in GDP per capita of US$1,000. The data on Figure 6.2 show this correlation illustrated by major regions and select countries of the world.

Figure 6.2
Correlation between Teledensity and Economic Development

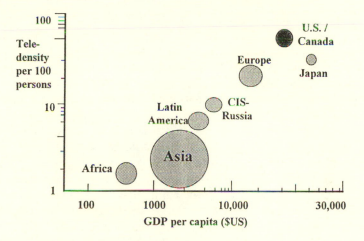

Source: International Telecommunications Union (ITU), World Bank
Note: Size of circle approximates to population.

THAILAND—SETTING THE SCENE

Thailand is emblematic of how a developing country can efficiently manage the growth of its telecommunications network. In the early 1990s, Thailand, like many other nations, was faced with a difficult set of issues. Over the period from 1986 to 1992, Thailand's average annual GDP growth was almost 10 percent, as a concerted effort was made to improve the country's economy and standard of living. However, concern was also growing that the poor quality of the country's infrastructure (and the telecommunications network in particular) would act as a bottleneck to future economic growth.

The telecommunications network was limited in its coverage (greater in urban areas and less in rural areas), with a low overall teledensity rate of around 3 lines per 100 people. This is in sharp contrast to a country like the United States, which achieved an equivalent teledensity level back in the year 1902 and now benefits from more than 56 telephone lines per 100 people. The Thai telephone network had a number of other problems: Waiting lists for telephones were long (more than one million persons and up to seven years), and the quality of existing services was often poor, as evidenced by a low call-completion rate. From a regulatory standpoint, Thailand's domestic telecommunications network was the exclusive preserve of a state-owned body—the Telephone Organization of Thailand (TOT).

Estimates indicate that to keep pace with every 1 percent increase in a country's annual GDP, a matching increase of more than 1.2 percent in spending on its telecommunications infrastructure is required. This represents a huge investment commitment, one that Thailand is not alone in facing. There are many other Asian nations where all types of infrastructure improvements, including telecommunications, have not kept pace with the needs resulting from the rapid economic growth in the region.

The political challenge faced by many governments is how best to advance development in a balanced manner without diverting limited resources away from one sector by investing in another, and all without exceeding debt ceilings. As an example, Figure 6.3 indicates that the level of telecommunications infrastructure spending in a country such as Indonesia must be balanced by the needs of other competing sectors of the economy, as shown in the latest national five-year planning period, *Repelita VI*. Telecommunications networks are certainly expensive, but the ability to communicate is an important element in any business decision related to investing in a new country. The better the telecommunications infrastructure, the more attractive a country becomes to foreign investors, a factor that is vitally important for export-driven economies such as those in the Asia–Pacific region.

Another example of the pressures caused by the need to fund massive infrastructure investment programs can be found in China. A 1993 *Asia Week*[2]

Figure 6.3
Indonesia Infrastructure Spending by Sector (1994–2000)

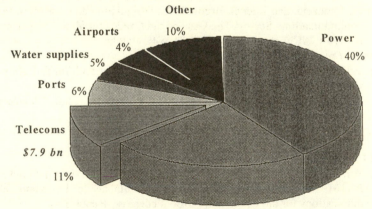

1994 - 2000
Total - $75 billion

Source: Hoare Govett

article citing Salomon Brothers noted that China's plans to add up to one hundred million new telephone lines will cost at least US$100 billion up to the year 2000. Financing from equipment vendors of up to US$25 billion is likely to be available, but even if China spends all of its hard currency reserves (estimated at more than US$45 billion) on telecommunications, there still will be a capital shortfall of at least US$30 billion.

Other nations in the Asia–Pacific region are facing similar issues. The 900 million people of India are served by only 8 million telephone lines, and similarly low teledensity rates are experienced throughout the region. The level (or shortfall) of investment capital needed to provide basic telecommunications service is only part of the problem. The *Far Eastern Economic Review*,[3] referencing the World Bank, recently estimated that between 20 and 50 percent of network equipment already in place in many areas of the world is not working because of lack of funds for maintenance and upgrades. Vendor financing is readily available to assist with new equipment purchases but is often lacking with respect to the provisioning and maintenance of established telecommunications networks.

BOT/BTO SCHEMES—VEHICLES FOR INFRASTRUCTURE AND MARKET DEVELOPMENT

In Thailand, the TOT faced significant problems in maintaining the level of network growth needed to accommodate the requirements of a rapidly expanding economy. These difficulties and others are typical of those facing many telephone network operators in emerging economies throughout the world and include the following:

* Outdated and poorly maintained networks
* A lack of expertise in areas of modern technology and services
* A shortage of capital
* Government debt ceilings
* Foreign ownership restrictions

Expansion of the telecommunications infrastructure was a key element of Thailand's seventh National Economic and Social Development Plan, which ran between 1992 and 1996. The government has set a teledensity target of 10 lines per 100 people by the end of the plan period. To meet this goal, it was recognized that a new and innovative approach to growing the telecommunications network was needed. In the late 1980s, reinterpretation of legislation that had originally created the TOT resulted in decisions which began to allow for some private participation in the telecommunications sector. However, a mechanism for achieving this had to take into consideration the TOT's legal monopoly in areas related to the provision and ownership of basic telephone services in Thailand.

This was achieved by adopting a variation of the Build–Operate–Transfer / Build–Transfer–Operate schemes (BOT/BTOs) that allow for the utilization of private-sector funds and business expertise for network buildouts. Since its adoption, these types of investment approaches have become increasingly popular for infrastructure development projects in many emerging economies. As in Thailand, many of these new approaches also have been customized to address unique legislative and/or regulatory conditions in their host country.

In a typical telecommunications BOT/BTO scheme, a network is *B*uilt by a concession holder, and then in return for financing and building the network, the BOT/BTO concession holder will *O*perate the network for a specified number of years, sharing in the revenues generated from the project. The private investor recoups their investment, earns a return, and in the process puts in place a modern telecommunications network. The local licensing authority will generally have a minority share in the revenues from the project over the life of the concession. At the end of the concession period, ownership of the network is *T*ransferred to the government or appropriate local licensing authority. In the case of Thailand, legal considerations require the network assets to be transferred to the TOT as soon as they are ready for operation.

TelecomAsia (TA)

Many BOT/BTO concession holders are partnerships between local–national and foreign companies. The local company brings knowledge of the market and how business is conducted in the host country, while the foreign company generally brings the necessary sector expertise. In 1991, the Thai agro-industrial conglomerate CP Group was awarded a concession to construct a two-million line telecommunications network in the Bangkok metropolitan area, requiring an estimated investment of several billion dollars. Measured in terms of line size, the project is roughly equivalent to the number of telephone lines currently operational in New York's Manhattan. Plans call for constructing the two-million line network over a five-year period, which is an extremely ambitious undertaking considering that over the previous forty years only two million lines were added to the telephone network throughout the entire country of Thailand.

The CP Group established a subsidiary company, TA, to operate the concession. Early the following year, NYNEX Network Systems Company, a subsidiary of NYNEX Corporation of the United States, was selected by TA to be its strategic partner, bringing with it the necessary technical and operational expertise for the implementation of the project. The CP Group is the majority owner of TA, while NYNEX is the minority partner. The TA concession runs for a period of twenty-five years, expiring in 2017. TA builds the network, transfers the assets to the TOT immediately, and then operates the network for the TOT over the remainder of the concession period. In order to earn a return from participating in the project, TA retains 84 percent of revenues, with the remaining 16 percent due to the TOT.

Shortly after the award of the two-million line Bangkok concession, a similar one-million line provincial network concession was awarded to TT&T, a consortium led by Jasmine International. Under the terms of the original agreements, both concession holders were also protected from the development of other networks while the three million new lines were under construction. In a recent development, TA and TT&T were granted additional lines by the Thai government. TA was granted an additional 600,000 lines, bringing its total to 2.6 million lines, and TT&T was granted an extra 500,000 lines. As part of the agreement, TA will forego its construction period exclusivity and the TOT will be allowed to install another 800,000 lines, mainly in the Thai provinces.

THE BENEFITS OF BOT/BTO SCHEMES—HOW TA HAS
HELPED THE DEVELOPMENT
OF THE THAI TELECOMMUNICATIONS SECTOR

BOT/BTOs bring a wide range of benefits to emerging economies while also providing companies with the opportunity to invest in new markets. The benefits to the host country go far beyond the expansion of the telecommunications network and can be felt across a range of sector-specific, business, social, and economic areas:

Infrastructure Investment. TA is installing a state-of-the-art network using the latest fiber-optic and digital switching technologies. As a result, more than US$2.5 billion in privately accessed funding is being invested in the development of Thailand's telecommunications infrastructure through the TA project. It is doubtful whether the government could (or would) have allowed the TOT to source this level of funding to expand its network. Removing expansion of the telecommunications network from the long list of other infrastructure upgrades has allowed limited government resources to be deployed elsewhere.

Network Expansion. As a result of the two BTO concessions, Thailand's teledensity is forecast to rise to 10 per 100 by the end of 1996, while teledensity in the Bangkok metropolitan area will rise to nearly 40 per 100. Before the recent addition of 600,000 new lines, the TA network build was on target to be completed one year in advance of the mid-1997 milestone set by the government. From waiting lists of many years in areas of Bangkok where network construction is complete, service is now available in days. TA is currently connecting an average of 1,000 new lines every day.

Technology Leapfrog. It is also important to note that in the field of telecommunications there is currently a unique opportunity, due to the advent of new technologies, for nations with underdeveloped networks to leapfrog a whole technological generation. Investments in state-of-the-art technology made now will in many cases serve a nation's telecommunications needs for the next twenty-five years.

Technology and Management Expertise Transfer.   The transfer of technology to developing nations is an issue that is receiving more and more attention. As TA's strategic partner, NYNEX has provided detailed assistance in all aspects of the establishment of the organization, implementation of the network, and day-to-day operations of the company. This includes technical assistance in the selection of equipment and the management of relations with vendors to ensure that the most appropriate equipment is selected at the best price, as well as the establishment of marketing and sales procedures and organizations for customer service.

In addition to providing a chief operating officer, since the start of the concession NYNEX has seconded on a short- to medium-term basis more than fifty carefully selected and highly qualified staff to TA. The majority of these secondees have backgrounds in operations and network services and engineering. At all times, the emphasis has been on the transfer of management and technical skills and the gradual phasing in of local responsibility, thereby releasing NYNEX expatriates to work on other projects. NYNEX has also established a research and development laboratory in Bangkok which is working on network design and applications tailored to the regional marketplace.

Creation of New Jobs.   TA directly employs approximately 3,000 people in Thailand. This does not take into account the new jobs and skills that also have been created in the construction and equipment sectors that provide services to TA.

Introduction of New Services.   In addition to making basic telecommunications services available to a wider cross-section of society, TA is planning to introduce services comparable with those that are available in other major international cities, including Centrex, voicemail, and ISDN. Through a concession that was granted to a subsidiary of TA, Universal Cable Television Network (UTV), an overlay is being added to the TA network. This will deliver the first true cable television and interactive entertainment services in Thailand to selected markets in Bangkok and ultimately to the provinces. Through another subsidiary, Telecom Holding Company, TA is seeking to expand into other growing markets in the Asia–Pacific region.

Expansion of the Telecommunications Market.   Through the revenue-sharing elements of the TA and TT&T concessions, the TOT has been able to benefit from the expansion of the Thai telecommunications sector. In 1995, for example, Salomon Brothers[4] estimated that TT&T will pass almost baht 3.5 billion (US$140 million) in revenue sharing to the TOT. Under the add-on program where TA will build out the additional 600,000 lines, TOT will also now derive an overall higher percentage of the revenue than previously existed under the original two-million line concession agreement. Through local content requirements, Thailand has also been able to expand the national telecommunications equipment manufacturing sector along with associated financial, technology transfer, and job creation benefits.

Investment Opportunities. The liberalization of the telecommunications sector through the licensing of TA and TT&T has ultimately resulted in the widening of investment opportunities for private investors. The national public telecommunications operator (PTO) often has one of the largest market capitalizations on a country's stock market. The successful IPO of TA shares in late 1993 represented the first major chance that investors had to participate in the growth of Thailand's telecommunications sector. With 60 percent of the IPO shares reserved for local nationals, TA now represents the second largest company (in terms of market capitalization) quoted on the Stock Exchange of Thailand.

Market Liberalization. TA and TT&T represent the first step in Thailand's move toward full liberalization of basic services. The two concessions effectively broke the monopoly of the TOT for the first time and have opened the door for future liberalization moves. There has been considerable speculation about the future structure and responsibilities that the TOT will ultimately have under Thailand's proposed master plan for the liberalization of the domestic telecommunications industry.

Overall, the success of the TA project has helped to enhance the competitiveness of Thailand's capital and economy. While other infrastructure problems remain, Bangkok at least will have a state-of-the-art network and telecommunications operator to rival that of any other important city in the world.

APPLICABILITY ELSEWHERE IN ASIA AND BEYOND

The TA model is certainly transferable. The same market and environmental conditions that led to the creation of the TA concession can be found elsewhere. For example, the economies of China and Indonesia have been among the fastest growing in the world over the last decade, but both have phone densities of no more than 2 per 100 people. BOT/BTO type projects offer a means to address these infrastructure difficulties, while providing benefits to all parties concerned.

Other nations in the Asia–Pacific region have been monitoring the success of the BTO concessions in Thailand and are now adopting similar schemes tailored to the individual requirements of their own countries. A recent survey by Salomon Brothers, highlighted in Table 6.1, shows some of the designs used to extend and apply the BOT/BTO theme in specific Asian countries. In certain cases, a country may use more than one structure, depending on the nature of the project.

Beyond Asia, new approaches are also being explored to find ways to improve access to telecommunications services and help close the gap between

Table 6.1
BOT/BTO Designs

Structure	Country	Key Elements
Build–Transfer–Operate (BTO)	Thailand	- Asset transfer after construction - Operated by concessionaire - Revenue sharing - Finite concession period
Build–Own–Operate (BOO)	Australia Hong Kong, India, Japan, Philippines	- Most common - Few restrictions on ownership - Government license required - May have limited life
Business Cooperation (BCC)	Vietnam	- Agreement to cooperate in a particular project - An element of revenue sharing
Build–Maintain–Transfer (BMT)	Philippines	- Vendor financed network build - Vendor builds, finances, maintains - Network leased to operator - Limited life lease
Joint Operating System	Indonesia	- Private consortium builds and operates network for PTO - Keep majority of revenues - Finite concession period

Build–Transfer	PRC, Indonesia	- Equipment supply
		- Network may be implemented by
		  vendor/outside party
		- Possible revenue sharing instead
		  of direct payment

Build–Lease–Transfer	PRC	- Networks built by private cos. - Lease to local PTTs - Revenue sharing - Possible deferment of payments for future conversion to equity

Source: Salomon Brothers, *Asia–Pacific Telecommunications—An Industry in Transition* (Hong Kong: Salomon Brothers, 1994).

the developed and emerging economies. To that end, the ITU, with backing from the United Nations has put forward its *WorldTel* proposal. This is probably the most ambitious and far-reaching proposal yet in terms of seeking to establish a public–private partnership to promote telecommunications infrastructure development. *WorldTel* seeks to identify profitable telecommunications investment opportunities and bring together governments, private investors, and telecommunications operators to form long-term partnerships to benefit the 80 percent of the world's population that currently does not have access to basic telecommunications service.

CONCLUSION

The experience of TA shows that there is much for a nation to gain by pursuing liberalization policies which encourage private-sector participation in key industries such as telecommunications. In five short years, Thailand will have deployed a state-of-the-art network along with the technology and potential to offer the latest in advanced telecommunications services to its citizens. Managerial expertise has been transferred, new and sustainable jobs have been created, and the revenue and support base for an entire industry has been greatly expanded. From an investment point of view, new opportunities have been created for private investors and companies such as NYNEX, which not only provide attractive financial returns but also support continued economic growth and overall market development.

NOTES

This chapter is included here by permission of the NYNEX Network Systems Company, © NYNEX Corporation 1995.

1. World Bank, *Telecommunications Sector Background and Bank Group Issues*, Seminar to the Executive Directors of the World Bank and International Finance Corporation, Washington, D.C., February 16, 1994.

2. *Asia Week,* "A Phone in Every Home," August 18, 1993.

3. *Far Eastern Economic Review,* "Calling Out to Growth—Asia Demand for Communications Gathers Pace," April 8, 1993.

4. Salomon Brothers, *Thai Telephone and Telecommunications Report*, May 26, 1995.

BT's EXPERIENCE OF PRIVATIZATION

7

Marcus Brooks

BT was the first major British industry to be privatized. This marked the end of a long process whereby the organization gradually moved away from direct government control. It also marked the beginning of a transformation in customer service and business orientation for the company and the general transformation of the U.K. telecommunications market.

In 1984, at the time of privatization, BT, or British Telecom as it was then known, operated almost entirely in the United Kingdom, where it enjoyed a virtual monopoly. This situation has been completely transformed. In the United Kingdom, BT faces the most competitive telecommunications market in the world and also one of the most detailed regulatory regimes. Every sector of the U.K. market—apparatus supply, local networks, long distance, international, and mobile—is competitive. There are over 160 licensed competitors to BT and many others whose operations do not require individual licenses. BT has changed its network and management processes to respond to this challenge. In addition, BT is now a major international company which has adapted to the challenges of operating on a global scale.

BT's experience of privatization, therefore, involves more than the mechanics of selling shares and facing different accounting requirements. In particular, BT's experience has to be placed in the context of the regulatory regime that was created in 1984 to manage the transition to a competitive market and the immense changes in the U.K. telecommunications market that have occurred over the last twelve years, as the competitive market has become a reality. Accordingly, this chapter is organized into seven sections:

- the reasons for privatization
- the road to privatization
- the regulatory structure
- liberating the market
- the development of competition
- the transformation of the business after privatization
- the challenges now facing BT

WHY PRIVATIZE?

It is worth spending some time considering the motives behind privatization. Clearly, on one hand, the government was concerned with raising revenue for the Treasury and had an ideological commitment to private ownership; but there was also a desire to liberalize the telecommunications market in order to better meet the needs of customers and in the belief that a competitive market is a more efficient one. Thus the government went down the road of privatization on the premises that the purpose of telecommunications is to serve customers; that operators are likely to have the best incentive to serve customers where there is competition, and that proper competitive conditions are not feasible with BT retained in public ownership. This was strongly stated in the 1983 White Paper on telecommunications, which concluded that competition was unlikely to emerge while the monopoly provider remained in the public sector.

This philosophy strongly informed the way the telecommunications regime in the United Kingdom was initially structured and has largely determined how telecommunications policy has been conducted from 1984 to date. Thus there has been an emphasis on promoting the interests of consumers and promoting competitors as the best means of securing these interests

THE ROAD TO PRIVATIZATION

Before 1969, telecommunications in the United Kingdom was the responsibility, and monopoly, of the general post office, a government department whose activities included the royal mail. Its head, the postmaster general, was a government minister. The post office's budget was established by the usual procedures governing public expenditure, and its employees were civil servants who might, at some stage in their careers, move to other government ministries.

The 1969 Post Office Act modified the relationship of the post office and the government. The post office, which retained its monopoly on telecommunications services, became a public corporation. It was still owned by the state, but instead of being headed by a minister, it had a chairman appointed by the government.

Under the British Telecommunications Act of 1981, British Telecom was separated from the Post Office. Although British Telecom remained a public corporation, its monopoly started to erode. The 1981 Act empowered the government to grant licenses to competitors. BT also lost its monopoly on the supply of customer premises equipment—retaining exclusivity on provision of the first telephone in a set of premises for a limited period.

The decisive step came in 1984. The Telecommunications Act of that year transformed British Telecom into British Telecommunications Plc—which has traded under the name BT since 1991. Becoming a "plc" (Public Limited Company) meant that BT was obliged to meet the legal requirements of private-sector companies, including such matters as the presentation and filing of accounts.

In 1984, 50.2 percent of BT's shares were sold to the public. At the time, this was the biggest company flotation which had been carried out on the London stock market. All employees of the company were entitled to receive fifty-four free shares with a face value of 25p—the price at which the government sold shares to the public was £1.30. In 1992, the government sold a further quantity of its shares, reducing its holding to approximately 22 percent. In 1993, virtually all the remaining government-owned shares were sold. The British government now owns less than 1 percent of BT's shares. Despite the sale of shares, the government retained certain rights in connection with the company which were written into its Articles of Association—in effect, BT's constitution.

The first of these concerned takeovers. BT's Articles of Association require the BT board to oblige any person holding more than 15 percent of the shares in the company to sell them. This limit on share ownership effectively prevents any attempt to take over the company. The "Special Share" gives the government the right to veto any change to this provision. In other words, the BT Articles of Association contain provisions to safeguard the control of the company. Through its Special Share, the government can veto any change to these arrangements.

The second right which the government retained was the power to appoint two directors to the BT Board. These directors were not allowed to hold executive office in the company or to be its chairman or deputy chairman. Unlike other directors, however, they could not be dismissed by a general meeting of shareholders. In 1994, the provision for government-appointed directors was abolished, as the government felt that it was inappropriate as it no longer owned shares in the company—although its other powers in connection with the "Special Share" remain unchanged.

There were several other residual government rights, including a veto over any change to the provision in the Articles of Association that the chairman and chief executive must be British citizens.

It is worth noting that although the government retained these residual powers it did not make extensive use of them. The government-appointed directors were all leading businessmen—typically chairmen or chief executives of major British companies. They were not politicians, civil servants, or academics, and they functioned in a way virtually indistinguishable from ordinary non-executive directors. Indeed, the government-appointed directors, like all directors, owed a statutory duty to the shareholders as a whole and not to any segment of them. There was never a sense that there was a "Government lobby" within the BT board. The government chose, instead, to influence the company through the regulatory system which the 1984 Telecommunications Act also established.

THE REGULATORY STRUCTURE

The government recognized that simply transferring the incumbent operator to the private sector, while an important first step, was not going to be enough to secure a competitive market. While the introduction of private ownership did introduce discipline via the capital markets it did no more. It was realized that competition would take some time to develop and that in the intervening period a substitute for competition was required to control the incumbent and provide an appropriate climate to nurture new entrants until they were able to fend for themselves.

One of the main issues to be addressed in approaching the issue of regulation was to ensure that the regulatory system was independent of government and politics. This led to the establishment of Oftel, a nonministerial government department, modeled on the U.K.'s Office of Fair Trading, headed by a director general appointed by the government for a fixed term.

The director general's duties and powers are established under the 1984 Telecommunications Act, and while most of his powers are specifically drawn from this, he also has certain powers under general competition law in respect to telecommunications. However, the principal way by which the director general exercises his authority is via his duty to enforce telecommunications licenses (under the act, to operate any telecommunication system requires a license) and also his ability to amend them in certain circumstances. To amend a license, the director general either requires the agreement of the licensee or failing this he may make a reference to the MMC and amend the license on the basis of a favorable report. If the licensee accepts the proposed amendment, the director general may implement it following a statutory consultation period. If the licensee objects, the director general may refer the proposed amendment to the MMC. If the MMC concludes that the proposed amendment is in the public interest, the director general may amend the license accordingly.

BT was issued a license in 1984 to run for twenty-five years with a requirement for ten years notice of revocation. Attached to the license are sixty-three conditions, which principally serve to place obligations on and control BT's exercise of market power. The number of conditions has expanded over the years, as the license has become longer and more complex as it has been amended.

The conditions cover a variety of issues, but there are three key categories: those which impose service obligations on BT; those which assist competitors; and those which control BT's principal prices.

BT's Service Obligations

BT is obliged to provide telecommunications services throughout the United Kingdom. A distinction is drawn between "voice telephony" and "other services." There are very few qualifications to the "voice telephony" obligation. The only significant exception is if "any reasonable demand is . . . met by other means and . . . it would not be reasonable . . . to require the Licensee [BT] to provide the services requested." "Other services" are subject to more qualification, the most significant being that if the revenues expected to be received from service provision to particular customers would be unlikely to cover the cost of provision, BT is not obliged to make the service available to them.

"Voice telephony" is not defined. This reflects the fact that what is understood by such a service changes over time. Customers today assume that voice telephony includes the ability to dial directly all U.K. calls, which was not available in the 1950s. Again, itemized billing and access to services such as call waiting and caller display are increasingly taken for granted.

"Other services" is taken to mean private circuits and other services clearly not "voice telephony." BT has made little use of the qualification on its obligation to provide such services. It should, however, be noted, that while other PTOs have universal service conditions in their licenses—which usually come into force once market share thresholds have been met—all take the more relaxed form of BT's "other services" obligation.

BT also has obligations in respect to public call boxes although this does not take the form of a requirement to provide them but instead to not remove or relocate those in situ without going though extensive consultative procedures. There is a revenue threshold from the removal of boxes (£185 pa, which has remained unchanged since 1984), an interesting example of the tightening of a license requirement through inflation.

Fair Trading and Competitor Assistance

Those conditions which constrain BT's exercise of market power fall mainly into three areas: interconnection; information; and cross-subsidy.

Interconnection. BT is obliged to allow other licensed operators to interconnect with its network, and where commercial terms cannot be agreed to Oftel is empowered to determine the terms on which interconnection takes place.

Unsurprisingly, interconnection has become an increasingly important consideration as the number of competitors has increased since 1984. It was with this in mind that Oftel brought forward proposals on interconnection and accounting separation in 1993, leading to the amendment of BT's license in 1995. These amendments were designed to produce standard charges for standard interconnection services, to reinforce the principle of no undue discrimination by BT among operators or between BT's retail operations and other operators with respect to both price and quality of service, and to produce published, audited accounting separation statements for a set of regulatory businesses (access, apparatus supply, network, retail systems, supplemental services, and residual). BT is required to publish these full accounting separation statements each year. The costing and pricing of interconnection services is currently undergoing further consideration, as are the proposals for a separate price control for network services.

Information.   BT is obliged to control the distribution of information it obtains in the course of operating its network, so that information obtained as part of BT's monopoly activities may not be used to benefit BT's operations in competitive markets.

Cross-subsidy.   The rules on cross-subsidy are designed to prevent BT from using profits from the exercise of market power in one area to cross-subsidize its activities in others, where competition maybe stronger. BT is divided into three units for the purpose of the rules:

- The systems business (BT's network services)
- The four restricted areas, namely,
  land mobile radio services (e.g., paging and cellular)
  apparatus supply business (selling equipment)
  apparatus production business (making equipment)
  supplemental services business (value-added services)
- Nonlicense activities (any other aspects of BT's business)

These are illustrated in Figure 7.1.

BT must not *unfairly* use resources from any part of its business, including those of another of the four restricted areas, to cross-subsidize any of the four restricted areas. BT has to keep its accounts in such a way that transfers between any part of its business and each of the four restricted areas may be identified; the cost basis of transfers has to be identified. This is to prevent the transfer of valuable resources at an artificially low price.

Cross-subsidy as such is not forbidden—it is a normal business practice when, for example, a new product is being launched—but the rules prevent cross-subsidies which would distort the working of a competitive market, such as funding a loss-making activity for an extended period until the competition quit.

Figure 7.1
Areas to Which Cross-Subsidy Rules Apply

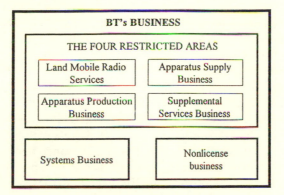

Further assistance to competitors is given by BT's exclusion from certain markets. Thus, under its license BT is not allowed to provide broadcast entertainment services to the home. The company is also prevented from providing mobile services under its license and is restricted in its ability to make use of fixed radio in the access network.

Pricing

Perhaps the most important license requirement is that relating to price control, under which changes in many of BT's prices are controlled by a price cap.

Price caps control the average movement of prices. If some move by more than the specified limit, this must be offset by reductions elsewhere so that the average movement is within the permitted boundary. BT's price cap is based on three elements—the basket, the standard, and the variable. The *basket* is the list of services which are subject to price control. Although this is not exhaustive, all BT's main network services are now included. The *standard* is the Retail Price Index (RPI)—a general consumer price index published by the government. The *variable* is known as "X." Hence the formula is known as "RPI-X." The power to set "X" gives the regulator a wide measure of control. It enables him to decide whether the average movement of prices should be above or below the rate of inflation. In BT's case, the "X" factor for the general formula has always been negative, reflecting the view that BT had scope for cost savings—through technology and improved management—which should be passed on to the consumer. It also means that the RPI-X formula embodies a view of the level of profit which BT is entitled to make. The price cap formula is embodied in a condition in BT's license which remains in force for a defined period, usually four years. When the current arrangements are about to expire, new provisions are made.

There are two main price controls, one on public switched telephony services and one on private circuits, though there are a number of subcaps within these (see Table 7.1).

The first price cap on BT's main services was set at 3 percent less than inflation in 1984. Since then, however, there has been a tightening and expansion of the cap. The cap became 4.45 percent less in 1988, then 6.25 percent in 1991. The current cap which runs until 1997 is set at 7.5 percent. Over the years, what started as a fairly simple cap has become increasingly complex (as well as becoming increasingly severe), as more activities have been included within it and more detailed controls applied, with a proliferation of subcaps.

Until recently, one of the most important subcontrols within the overall cap on switched telephony services was the limit on exchange line rental charges, which were not allowed to increase by more than RPI+2 per annum.

Historically, BT has underpriced its line rental charges, and they did not fully recover their costs of provision and maintenance. This underrecovery was known as the "access deficit." In a monopoly, this underrecovery is sustainable, since the losses can be subsidized from call charges, but in a competitive market where customers are able to use BT to make calls over competing networks and where competitive pressures push call prices downwards, there is a need to match prices more closely with costs. The RPI+2 cap was designed to prevent BT from engaging in substantial line rental increases (or price rebalancing) and to protect consumers from rate shock. At the same time, Oftel introduced a system known as the Access Deficit Contribution (ADC) scheme, whereby other operators would make a contribution to BT's losses on exchange line services. The system was set whereby other operators would, once certain market share levels had been met, make a contribution based on market share. In practice, most ADC payments from other operators were waived by Oftel, and the only payments made were by MCL in the final years of the scheme. Oftel abolished the ADC scheme at the same time as it removed the constraint on line rental price increases.

One of the consequences of this policy has been that competitors were deterred from competing in local access but concentrated on high-use business customers, undercutting BT's calling rates, which were kept artificially high because of the constraint on rebalancing. There are also a number of structural controls on BT's prices which affect the company's ability to offer discounts and to provide packages combining goods and services. BT is not permitted to link the provision of service to the purchase of equipment, but it is obliged to publish the prices, terms, and conditions of its main network services and may not deviate from the price list for particular customers.

The principal effect of these rules is that BT is not permitted to charge extra to people who live in areas where it is costly to provide service or to offer special discounts for heavy users. Although a condition was added to the license in 1991 permitting special pricing packages, these must be available to all

Table 7.1
Changes to the Price Control Mechanism (1984–1993)

PERIOD	'x'	BASKET CONTENTS	SUB-CAPS	OTHER REMARKS
1984 - 89	3.0	Exchange line rentals and dialed domestic calls		BT observed a voluntary RPI+2 cap on residential exchange line rentals.
1989 - 91	4.5	Exchange line rentals, dialed domestic calls, and operator-assisted call charges.		Voluntary RPI+2 cap on residential and business exchange line rentals. Additional (involuntary) caps - co-terminus with main price cap: RPI+2 - connection charges RPI-0 - connection and rental of domestic private circuits .
1991 - 93	6.25	Domestic and (outgoing) international switched calls and the contents of the subcaps.	RPI+5 - rentals of lines for multiline businesses and other operators. RPI+2 - connection charges and other exchange line rentals.	10% reduction in international call charges. Provision for flexible tariff packages (subject to detailed rules). IPLCs included in separate private circuit price cap.
1993 - 97	7.5	Domestic and (outgoing) international switched calls and the contents of the subcaps.	RPI+5 - rentals of lines for other operators. RPI+2 - exchange line rentals. RPI-0 - rental of hard-wired lines.	Standard connection charge cut to £99 ex VAT. Detailed changes to Supportline low-user scheme. Special packages excluded from basket calculation. All prices subject to RPI limit unless higher increase permitted by subcap.

customers rather than being offered on an exclusive basis. In addition, limits were set to the size of discount which could be offered, and all such packages are subject to approval by Oftel after an evaluation of their likely impact on competition.

The impact of price controls on BT's business is clear. Table 7.2 shows how the percentage of BT's turnover has steadily increased since the inception of the system. It has been claimed that the price control system has successfully met its objectives in protecting customers and competitors. Customers benefitted from price reductions. From 1984 to 1996 the weighted average of BT's controlled prices fell (in real terms) by 42 percent.[1] The system helped BT's competitors to launch their businesses. It gave them a head start in competing with BT for the businesses of large organizations who sought to negotiate special contracts for their business. In addition, the imbalance of BT's prices, perpetuated by the price controls, limited BT's ability to cut its call charges, thus making it easier for competitors to offer lower prices. It is, however, arguable that the system has had some less desirable results. The delay in solving the rebalancing problem made it unattractive for others to compete in the provision of local networks. Competition has been confined to those who enjoy peculiar cost advantages, such as cable television operators who are able to recover costs on their entertainment and telephony businesses, and Ionica, which uses low-cost radio technology. Thus the price controls held back the development of competition in what is probably the most important part of the market for residential customers. A further consideration is that the price-cap regime effectively fossilized the precompetitive pricing structure. It tended to create an environment where pricing was considered largely within the constraints it imposed. The result has been that the pricing of fixed telecommunications services still largely follows the pattern established in the 1920s—a fixed rental charge and further charges based on use, distance, and duration. The mobile operators, unconstrained by a price control regime, were the first to introduce packages offering varying combinations of fixed charges,

Table 7.2
Percentage of BT Group Turnover under Price Control

Date	Value of X	Turnover under price control
1984 - 89	-3.0	48% - 53%
1989 - 91	-4.5	55% - 56%
1991 - 93	-6.25	64% - 66%
1993 - 97	-7.5	64% - 67%

Source: Oftel, *Pricing of Telecommunications Services from 1997, Annexes to the Consultative Document,* (London: Oftel, 1995, 5, Annex B1).

"free" call allowances, and differing prices for calls. Customers could select whichever package best met their needs. The price cap regime may have delayed similar flexibility and responsiveness to customer needs in the fixed telephony market.

LIBERATING THE MARKET

Moves toward a liberalized and competitive market began in 1981 when BT was separated from the post office and the government liberalized the markets for terminal apparatus and value-added services. Then in 1983 MCL was established as a full competitor to BT, providing various fixed network services throughout the United Kingdom. It actually commenced service in 1986, constructing its own fiber-optic network across the United Kingdom.

At the time of MCL's creation, the government also established the duopoly policy, to run for at least seven years, which stated that only BT and MCL would be allowed to provide fixed network services and public telephony during this period. This was needed to allow MCL to establish itself and for BT to bring its operations up to an acceptable commercial standard.

From 1984 on, however, the drive for liberalization has gathered ever more speed. It is possible to break the quantum changes in the U.K. telecommunications market and the regulatory and competitive environment to date into three phases.

The first phase took place over the years from 1984 to 1990, during which there was a progressive liberalization of peripheral markets, while the basic BT/MCL duopoly was left intact. One of the key liberalizing developments was the licensing of two operators, Cellnet (60% owned by BT) and Racal Vodafone, to provide analog cellular services. Then in 1989 four public telepoint operators were licensed, providing one-way standard CT2 radio services direct to the handset. This service, however, proved something of a failure, and there are now no telepoint services in operation.

In 1989, in a further liberalization of the mobile market, the government licensed three PCN operators to provide microcellular GSM-based services in the 1900 GHz band. Following a merger, there are now two PCN operators in the market, Mercury One to One and Orange, owned by Hutchison. Also in 1989, the government permitted the provision of "simple resale" services; that is, the renting by a new operator of a circuit from BT or MCL to be connected by the operator to the public network at one or both ends, enabling a bypass service to be provided to the public. Finally, throughout this phase licenses were granted to run cable television networks in various local areas, almost exclusively to companies other than BT, now mainly dominated by U.S. telephone and cable companies.

The second phase of privatization and liberalization began with the expiry of the seven-year duopoly period in November 1990 and the announcement of the government's new policy on telecommunications in March 1991 after a period of intensive public consultation. The outcome of the review was that the U.K. domestic market should, generally speaking, be totally open to competition, with licenses being available to all applicants with the means and skills to provide service. On the international market it was concluded that the duopoly should end, though the government said it was unlikely to grant licenses for some time. This now remains the only area where competition is restricted, though Oftel recently undertook a consultation on opening up this market further. The government also concluded during the review that the restrictions on BT entering the cable television market should remain and would not be reviewed until at least 2001.

The third phase can perhaps be said to date from the consultation Oftel launched in 1994 on "Effective Competition." In this, Oftel recognized the rapid development of competition and raised the possibility of a move away from the detailed regulation to which BT had been subject since 1984. Issues addressed by the document included interconnection charging and pricing, access deficit charges, price rebalancing and pricing flexibility for BT, measures to prevent anticompetitive behavior, treatment of service providers, and the universal service and its funding. There has been a variety of further consultations on these various issues, and the document has marked the start of a major debate on all aspects of U.K. telecommunications regulations. Although an adequate treatment of all the areas currently under discussion is not possible here, certain of the issues are, however, of particular importance.

Oftel has brought forward proposals to replace a number of detailed license conditions and replace them with a new license condition in all operators licenses, giving the director general power to act against anticompetitive behavior. Under this condition, the director general could take action to require a "dominant" operator (which would nearly always be BT) to stop or start doing something, as the director general sees fit; there would be right of appeal. BT has raised objections to this proposal out of concerns about the concentration of sweeping discretionary powers in the hands of one individual.

Oftel is currently consulting on the form of the next BT price cap and has already published two consultative documents. The current price cap will expire in July 1997, with agreement on a new price cap to be reached by mid-1996, in order to allow time for an MMC reference if agreement proves impossible. A particular concern for BT regarding Oftel's proposals has been that while Oftel has recognized the case for deregulation they are proposing continuation of a harsh price control. BT believes that this will prove a disincentive to investment and competition and a threat to the longer-term interests of consumers.

The outcome of these regulatory debates will inevitably determine the nature of the U.K. telecommunications industry for many years to come.

DEVELOPMENT OF COMPETITION

It is worth considering just how much the U.K. telecommunications market has been transformed since 1984, and just how far competition has developed.

MCL, the company originally licensed to compete with BT, has attracted large numbers of customers in those market areas which it has chosen to target, and in March 1995 it had 2.5 million installed lines. Since 1991 and the end of the duopoly policy, DTI has issued more than 150 new licenses to provide telecommunications services. Those operators that have been licensed cover most sectors of the U.K. telecommunications market. At the local level, many more cable companies have been licensed to provide telecommunications services, and they have experienced rapid growth in demand (see Table 7.3).

Fourteen of the licenses issued have been PTO licenses, which empower the licensee to install their systems in other persons' land, dig up the streets, and largely enjoy much the same rights as have been granted to BT and MCL (though without the obligations imposed on BT). The companies granted licenses include the following:

- Energis (owned by National Grid), which is building a network using the Grid's ducts and pylons to carry the cables and which started providing direct and indirect service to business customers in 1994

- MFS, which began to provide direct services to large business customers in the City and certain other parts of London in 1994 and plans to expand into other urban areas

- COLT, which began operating in 1993 and targets similar customers to MFS

- AT&T, which is the largest carrier of switched telephony traffic in the world, handling a high proportion of long-distance and international calls in the United States and which is targeting mainly large, multinational companies

- Ionica, a business start-up enterprise which intends to provide direct fixed connections using new radio technology (thus avoiding the expense involved in installing telephone lines to each of its subscribers)

Table 7.3
Cable Growth

	January 1996	**January 1995**
No. of operating franchises	105	80
Franchises providing telephony	97	63
Telephone lines installed	1,419,819	717,586
- residential	1,287,248	649,350
- business	132,571	68,236

Source: Independent Television Commission.

While BT retains a large share of the national market for telecommunications, in particular in the access market with 95 percent of direct fixed connections at the end of March 1995, it is misleading to take this at face value. In those segments of the market that have been targeted by competitors, a different story emerges. Such segments include the following:

- Areas where cable television is available and where cable companies have gained 24 percent market share;
- Business long distance calls, where BT's competitors have gained 22 percent market share;
- Business voice revenue in the City of London, where BT's competitors have gained 43 percent of the market;
- Business international calls in the City of London where as much as 61 percent of the market is now served by operators other than BT.

THE CHALLENGE OF THE COMMERCIAL ENVIRONMENT

In 1984, BT faced a series of major challenges. It had to provide its customers with the quality of service they required at competitive prices—otherwise it would lose business to competitors. BT also had to provide its shareholders with a suitable return on their investment—otherwise the share price would fall and the company would be locked into a vicious circle of increases in its cost of capital, forcing it to forego the investments needed to become more competitive, leading to further decline in competitiveness.

The newly privatized BT initiated a major program of network modernization. During the period from 1984, more than £20 billion has been invested in BT's network (see Table 7.4). The result of this program, which reached a peak in 1990 when over £3 billion was invested in a single year, was that the United Kingdom now has one of the most modern networks in the

Table 7.4
Investment in BT's Network

Year	£ million	Year	£ million
1984	1,530	1990	3,103
1985	1,836	1991	2,875
1986	1,973	1992	2,565
1987	2,140	1993	2,148
1988	2,361	1994	2,161
1989	2,877	1995	2,671

Source: BT Report and Accounts.

world. BT's trunk network is fully digital. More than 98 percent of BT's customers are connected to digital or modern electronic exchanges which have been adapted to provide equivalent functionality, and the number continues to increase.

The fruits of this investment have been passed on to customers. Trunk network faults are now approaching the practical limits, running at less than one per thousand calls. Customers now have the benefit of facilities provided by new technology such as itemized bills and innovator services developed by BT, such as caller display and Chargecard.

Customers, however, are also interested in low prices. BT has been able to reduce the costs of telecommunications for all its customers. Figure 7.2 shows that both business and residential customers have felt the benefits of the cost savings brought about by investment and improvements in operating efficiency. BT has also provided a suitable return to its shareholders. Since 1984, the company has been consistently profitable. Shareholders have experienced a steady increase in the dividends received from their investment and the earnings per share have remained at a healthy level (see Table 7.5).

When BT was privatized there were fears in some quarters that profitability for shareholders and low prices for customers would be pursued at the expense of employment. Table 7.6 shows that these anxieties were misplaced. In the years immediately following privatization, the number of people working for BT remained stable; if anything there was a trend for numbers to increase slightly. This is not surprising as the modernization of the network required the contribution of many people in planning as well as the installation of new equipment. It is only since 1990 that numbers have fallen. The reduction in the number of employees has nothing to do with privatization but

Figure 7.2
Average Business and Residential Customer Bills

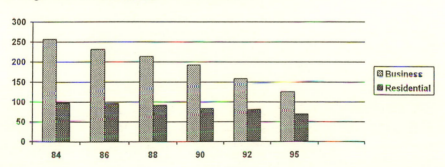

Source: BT figures, various years.
Real prices (£) including VAT. Figures are for the month of March, except for 1992 (July) and 1995 (February).

Table 7.5
Earnings (EPS) and Dividends (DPS) per Share (pence)

Year	EPS	DPS	Year	EPS	DPS
1984	-	-	1990	25.0	11.8
1985	14.8	3.9	1991	34.0	13.3
1986	17.1	7.5	1992	33.2	14.4
1987	20.9	8.45	1993	19.8	15.6
1988	23.6	9.5	1994	28.5	16.7
1989	25.9	10.5	1995	27.8	17.7

Source: BT Report and Accounts.

Table 7.6
Number of People Employed by BT (at year end)

Year	Number of people (thousands)	Year	Number of people (thousands)
1984	241.1	1990	245.7
1985	235.2	1991	226.9
1986	236.0	1992	210.5
1987	234.4	1993	170.7
1988	237.2	1994	156.0
1989	244.4	1995	137.5

Source: BT Report and Accounts.

is the result of factors affecting all operators, irrespective of ownership. Modern telecommunications equipment simply requires fewer people to operate it. Because of its commercial success, BT was well placed to deal with the challenge by establishing a series of early retirement and voluntary redundancy schemes which have enabled nearly 100,000 people to leave BT without compulsion. This dramatic reduction in the number of employees has been achieved without a single compulsory redundancy. The conclusion is that during this period BT responded strongly to the challenges and both its customers and shareholders have benefited.

THE WAY AHEAD

The telecommunications industry does not stand still, and BT must continue to develop if it is to succeed. The two key driving forces are technology and the globalization of the industry.

Developments in technology are of clear importance. The past twenty years have seen the supersession of electromechanical switching by digital techniques, and of copper cable by optical fiber. Networks continue to be able to do more in less time and at less cost. For an operator to be able to provide its customers with the best which modern technology can offer and to survive in an increasingly competitive business, it must keep abreast of technology and be able to decide which development path to follow.

A key element in BT's planning is a commitment to world-class research and development. The laboratories at Martlesham, in which £265 million was invested in the last financial year and which employ more than 3,500 people, enable BT to keep abreast of the fast-moving technology of telecommunications. Martlesham has become a center of excellence for software development, especially the complex systems used to control large, international networks.

One of the consequences of both the technology and the worldwide appreciation of the benefits of competitive markets is that the telecommunications industry is becoming global at a rapid pace. BT has pursued with energy its goal of providing service to its major customers wherever they are located. BT now runs the world's largest data network, with nodes in thirty-nine countries and offices in more than twenty.

BT's alliance with MCL broke new ground for a major telecommunications partnership in that it resulted in the establishment of networks, facilities, and services for customers rather than just the promises which tend to be the sole output of such ventures. BT has recently concluded alliances, for example with Banco Santander in Spain and Viag in Germany, to develop its position in the continental European market. BT however still remains dependent on the United Kingdom for 98 percent of its revenue, and this will remain its main center of operations for some time to come. Therefore, what happens in the United Kingdom will be of vital importance to the company's continuing success.

CONCLUSION

The privatization of BT was part of two processes that were inextricably linked—the removal of direct government controls over the company and the development of competitive telecommunications markets. BT has responded positively to this new environment and has been able to meet the needs of both customers and shareholders.

The revolution in the U.K. telecommunications market since 1984 as a result of these processes cannot be overstated. The United Kingdom has become a world leader in telecommunications, with among the lowest prices in the world. BT is one of the world's most efficient operators. The market is fully open to competition. Customers enjoy a wider and more broadly based choice of services and operators than is available anywhere else. Investment is at an all-time high. The United Kingdom is becoming more competitive, more attractive to inward investment, and BT, toughened by exposure to competition, is now a leading world player. The achievements of privatization and liberalization and, indeed, the operation of the regulatory regime thus have been substantial. The key issue now though is how these achievements are carried forward, and in particular how the regulatory regime evolves to respond to the new competitive era.

NOTES

This chapter is included here by permission of the author and BT, © British Telecommunications PLC 1996.

1. *Pricing of Telecommunications Services from 1997, Annexes to the Consultative Document,* Oftel, December 1995, 7, Annex B, Table B2, (b).

TELECOMMUNICATIONS IN THE CZECH REPUBLIC

8

The Privatization of SPT Telecom

Maria Michalis and Lina Takla

INITIAL CHARACTERISTICS OF THE CZECH TELECOMMUNICATIONS INDUSTRY

As was the general case in previous centrally planned economies, telecommunications in former Czechoslovakia was a neglected sector. Broadly speaking, the low prioritization and the underdevelopment of telecommunications in the former Communist countries mainly was due to security concerns and the fact that services, in general, were excluded from the definition of the "productive" sector and, consequently, "their provision was just tolerated as a burden to the national economy" (Laska 1991).

It is estimated that from 1978 to 1989 limited investments took place in telecommunications. It was mainly in the provision of new lines rather than in the areas of maintenance or infrastructure, and growth rates in investments were below 3 percent (Noam 1992, 279). Under Communist rule, more than half of the net profit of the state's telecommunications and postal operations were redistributed to unprofitable economic activities, whereas the federal MPT[1] was subject to 70 percent tax on profits (Bright 1991, 160). Within SPT Praha, the profitable telecommunications activities cross-subsidized the over-burdened postal ones. As a result, the ratio of telecommunications investment to total telecommunications revenue in the mid-1980s in former Czechoslovakia was just 21 percent (Beale and Ypsilanti 1993, 42). Doyle, Hruby, and

Muller (1993) reveal how a ministerial directive dating back to the 1970s precluded investment in the telecommunications industry if such investment were to lead to a network carrying more than 5 percent excess capacity.

In 1990, there were 420,000 pending applications for telephone lines, whereas the waiting time was several years (Bright 1991). The poor quality of infrastructure meant that only basic data services and low transmission rates were feasible. The outdated and worn out infrastructure also resulted in the absence of value-added services. The network was of low quality, and consequently many lines were overloaded. In 1990, about 30 percent of direct exchange lines (DELs) were business lines and 70 percent were residential (see Erbenova and Hruby 1995). This contrasts with OECD averages, where around 20 percent of DELs are for business use and 80 percent are for residential use.

In 1991, there were 14.9 main lines per 100 inhabitants in former Czechoslovakia, with significant regional disparities. This situation, although better in comparison with Hungary (9.1) and Poland (8.7), contrasted sharply with the OECD average of 43.3 and the EU average of 40.9 (data from Beale and Ypsilanti 1993). The same year, call completion rates were between 45 to 48 percent. The limited switching facilities (about two-thirds of which were installed in the Czech Republic and the remaining in the Slovak Republic) were of very poor quality: Half of them were more than thirty years old and of Strowger technology; 47 percent were Crossbar; and just 3 percent were digital (data from Zehle 1993, 95).

Historically, the state enterprise SPT Praha s.p. (Správa pošt a telekomunikace Praha) was responsible for both the telecommunications and the postal sectors in the Czech Republic. Although SPT Praha was one of the largest and most profitable enterprises in former Czechoslovakia, the country's telecommunications sector did not receive the needed financial capital to implement investments. The network was operated under a federal institutional framework which can be mapped as shown in Figure 8.1.

Until 1992, the regulation of tariffs was complex and involved numerous layers of administration (see Figure 8.2). In former Czechoslovakia, telecommunications tariffs remained unchanged from 1979 up until 1992. In 1979, tariffs were increased by two- to threefold. More specifically with regard to tariff structures, telephone rates for business and residential users were 40 percent or less of the OECD 1992 average. Similarly, fixed charges accounted for 23 percent of the residential bill, contrasting with the OECD 1992 average of 40 percent. Finally, there were no off-peak discounts (data from Jajszczyk and Kubasik 1993, 69). Tariff structures were uniform across time (no off-peak discounts), and there was no difference between residential and business charges. Tariffs for international calls were high; although international calls accounted for only 25 percent of traffic impulses, they represented 26.8 percent of total revenue in 1991 (Hruby 1992).

Figure 8.1
Institutional Structure of the Telecommunications Sector up to the End of 1990, Former Czechoslovakia

---

Central Organ of the Federal Level

Federal Ministry of Post and
Telecommunications

SPT Praha s.p. (Správa pošt a telekomunikace Praha)
Správa Radiokomunikace Praha
Proposed tariffs and consulted with the following three ministries

SPT Bratislava s.p (Správa pošt a telekomunikace Bratislava)
Správa Radiokomunikace, Bratislava
Proposed tariffs and consulted with the following three ministries

---

Tariff Setting Step 1

Federal Ministry of Communication
Approved international tariffs

Czech Ministry for Economic Policy and Development

Slovak Ministry of Communications and Transport

Tariff Setting Step 2

Federal Ministry of Finance
Approves domestic tariffs proposed by the Federal Ministry of Communications

Czech Ministry of Finance

Slovak Ministry of Finance

Figure 8.2
Institutional Structure of the Telecommunications Sector, Czech Republic (1993)

DESCRIPTION OF THE PRIVATIZATION PROCESS

There was thus a perceived need to revamp the telecommunications sector as part of the general move toward a market economy. Figure 8.2 maps the structure of the sector after the break-up of the federation. From January 1993, the Czech Ministry of the Economy assumed the responsibility for the sector. Post and telecommunications were separated, and gradually the company was partially privatized. While the federal PTT Ministry was engaged in the administration of the sector, the Ministry of the Economy had set up the Czech Telecommunications Office, which deals with both administration and regulation. The Czech regulator is the Ministry of Finance.

In 1992, the Czech Republic government started preparing to split state-owned SPT Praha into two distinct companies. On January 1, 1993, the separation of postal and telecommunications activities was officially concluded with the creation of two new entities: Ceská pošta s.p. and SPT Telecom. Equally, the traditional cross-subsidies from telecommunications to postal activities ended. The company was restructured, with peripheral plants and activities sold separately.

The privatization of the telecommunications activities of SPT was started under the framework of the second wave of the Czech voucher privatization scheme in March–December 1994 (see Takla 1994 for a description of Czech privatization) and under the guidelines of the Telecommunications Privatization Project. The management of the company prepared and submitted a privatization proposal to the Ministry of Economy of the Czech Republic, in June 1992. The project proposed the transformation of the company into a joint stock company from January 1, 1994, with a minimum state shareholding of 51 percent. By government decree, 26 percent of the shares were transferred into vouchers and distributed among individual investors and Investment Privatization Funds (IPFs). Vouchers were converted into shares in 1995 and started being traded on the Prague Stock Exchange from June 22, 1995.

As a result of the first stage of SPT's privatization, the state maintained a 74 percent stake (distributed among the Czech National Property Fund (NPF), 70%; the Restitution Investment Fund, 3%; and the Endowment Investment Fund, 1%). After the second stage (i.e., that of the selection of a foreign partner), 27 percent of SPT's shares was sold to a strategic investor and IPF's share fell to around 16 percent and individual owners' to around 3 percent. The NPF's stake fell to 51 percent (see Seda and Hruby 1995).

The choosing of a strategic investor was a long process. The debate about the future of the telecommunications industry included both the privatization and regulation aspects needed for the envisioned structural changes and modernization plans. In August 1994, the Czech government passed through the regulatory and operational framework for the Czech telecommunication industry a document entitled "The Main Principles of the State Telecommunication Policy." The main issues addressed by the document are: (1) investment; (2) technology; and (3) the transfer of managerial know-how. This was to be achieved by allowing for a "strategic" investor and was administered by the Ministry of the Economy. The selection of this strategic foreign partner was lengthy and politicized, as the government met with some opposition from local operators and already existing private investors (i.e., IPFs). Nevertheless, the government emphasized that the company's investment needs were best met by such a partner and that the pursuit of restructuring was best achieved through equity injection rather than debt financing. The government drafted a list of invited participants in the tender, in spring 1995. The strategic partner was required to be a network operator.

Five international companies were invited to bid for SPT Telecom. They are the following: (1) Danish operator TelDanmark supported by BT; (2) U.S. Ameritech, with Deutsche Telecom as junior partner; (3) an alliance between Bell Atlantic and France Télécom; (4) a Swiss–Dutch consortium, TelSource; and (5) the Italian operator STET. The strategic investor was offered an initial ownership stake of 27 percent (with the possibility of more later). The price of that stake was valued at US$1 billion and the strategic investor was required to spend US$3.5 billion to modernize the network and double the number of lines by the year 2000. The bidding process was closed in mid-July 1995. The state managed to sell the 27 percent stake for US$1.45 billion.

The winning consortium was the TelSource consortium, which placed the second highest bid (the highest bid was placed by STET). TelSource is made up of the following partners: PTT Telecom Netherlands, KPN's telecommunications division, and, the minority partner, Swiss Telecom with AT&T as a nonequity partner. "It was chosen for the price, its plans for modernising SPT's network, and the operational experience of the bidders." ("Record Dollars 1.45 bn bid secures stake" 1995). In addition, both partners in the

TelSource consortium are considered relatively small operators, thus SPT's own future regional strength is expected not to be threatened (Boland 1995c). The contract signed between the Czech government and TelSource caps the consortium's ability to increase its SPT share on the Prague Stock Exchange.

Broader political considerations also played a role in the selection of the Dutch–Swiss consortium. More specifically, the government was afraid of becoming too economically dependent on Germany and, following a bad experience, it was reluctant to get involved with France Télécom (Robinson 1995). In addition, a 1992 resolution passed in the Czech Republic concerning the prospective sale of 27 percent of SPT confined the involvement of state-owned operators at 15 percent. This measure deterred the German (Deutsche Telekom) and the French (France Télécom) operators from bidding together (Telecommunications Survey 1995, 42).

The great interest in the privatization of the public operator of the Czech Republic can be explained by the fact that SPT's network was relatively better than others in the region (Boland 1995c). In addition, the smooth introduction of economic reforms, political stability, the successful completion of one of the most ambitious mass privatization programs, and the geographical location of the country at the center of Europe all helped SPT to attract many potential investors. The only comparable experiment in central Europe to date is the one of the sale of 30.3 percent of the Hungarian telecommunications operator (see Table 8.1) to MagyarCom, a U.S.–German consortium. The difference between the Czech and Hungarian privatizations is that Czech privatization receipts have gone toward modernizing the company, while Hungarian revenues were aimed at reducing Hungary's foreign and domestic debt.

MODERNIZATION OF THE NETWORK—WHAT IS EXPECTED FROM THE STRATEGIC INVESTOR?

"By the year 2000, SPT must become a customer friendly, world class, financially sound, competitive company and be strong enough to survive as part of the global telecommunications market, albeit small by world standards" (Karel Dyba, the Czech Minister of the Economy, responsible for the partial privatization of SPT Telecom).

The First Telecommunications Project (FTP) was developed in 1991 by a group of experts from SPT Telecom, Bell Atlantic, US West, and the German consulting firm Detecon. It outlined a package of qualitative and quantitative improvements up to the year 2000. The government early on suspected that economic liberalization and transition to a market economy would lead to a surge in demand for DELs by the growing small-business sector as well as by the old-state sector, which was increasingly open to competition from abroad on both domestic and international markets. The rapid economic change led to a surge in demand for telecommunications services.

Table 8.1
Comparing Czech and Hungarian Privatization

	Private Stake (%)	Type of strategic partner offer	Amount (US$)
SPT Telecom	49%	27% strategic stake end of June 1995	US$1.321 billion in foreign direct investment, US$131 million managerial software and other investments
Matav Hungary	40%	30% stake sold through public offering to Amertitech & Deutsche Telecom in 1993	US$875 million

At the end of 1992, there were 1.8 million main telephone lines (a penetration rate of 17.65 percent per 100 inhabitants, up from 15.1 per 100 inhabitants in 1989, see Hruby 1992), representing an increase of 6.52 percent from the previous year. The waiting list for a telephone connection reached 490,300, the average waiting time being around four years (ranging from a fortnight up to sixteen years). Only 5.63 percent of exchanges were digitalized (SPT annual report 1992, 20–21). This surge in demand continued well into 1994, with "the estimate of cumulative number of requests by the end of 1994 at 650,000" (Erbenova and Hruby 1995).

The bulk of both switching and transmission technologies in the telecommunications network was very old. This situation resulted in the poor quality of services offered as well as the overloading of the network. Under these circumstances, the need for quick modernization was resolved by the development of a digital overlay network rather than an increase in the capacity of the existing analog network. The implementation of the digital overlay network started in 1993 as part of a Kcs 130-billion modernization plan which is expected to be fully completed by 1997 (around US$4.8 billion) (Telecommunications Survey 1995, 47).

Under the FTP, the penetration rate was planned to increase to nearly 34 by the year 2000. This target was later revised to 40 as the number of DELs actually installed exceeded targets. The goals set by the plan are mainly geared toward satisfying business customers' demands, as they are the main providers of revenue. By the end of September 1994, the total number of DELs (2.1 million) implied a penetration rate of 21. By the end of August of that same year, the overrepresentation of business customers with respect to the OECD average was even more pronounced: 32 percent of DELs were business and 68 percent were residential (Erbenova and Hruby 1995).

The guarantee of (near) monopoly provision of services until the year 2000 was the incentive the Czech government employed to encourage high bids from strategic investors. The main aim of the government, as repeatedly stated, was network upgrade and expansion. One of the obligations of the strategic partner is that of accelerating the development of the telecommunications industry. On top of the privatization proceeds, the winning consortium will have to invest around US$3.5 billion to contribute to SPT's modernization plan. Unlike other sales of assets by the state, none of the proceeds will enter the state or the NPF's budget. They will, however, be reinvested in the company.

The Deal

SPT is maintained as the major carrier; it will retain its monopoly of voice telephony until 2000 (on international and most local calls) and it has already established a significant presence in other markets such as mobile and data communications (see below). A process was introduced in February 1995 under which a second company will be able to bid for the operation of local telecommunications networks in sixteen selected regions of the country, which are considered particularly underserved. This introduction of limited competition in the operation of local networks will attack SPT's monopoly.

The privatization agreement includes a number of quantitative and qualitative targets. Under the terms of privatization, telephone line density must double, reaching 40 per 100 population by the turn of the century ("Phone Firms Czech In" 1995); the level at the time of the privatization being one line for every five people, or around 19 per 100 inhabitants (Boland 1995d). The new chairman, following privatization, said that more than two million new lines will be installed by the year 2000 (The European, August 17, 1995). At the time when the privatization agreement was concluded, there was a waiting list in the range of 600,000,[2] with a waiting time of up to two years ("Phone Firms Czech In" 1995). TelSource and SPT have to fulfil the following requirements (Seda and Hruby 1995; and Telecommunications Source 1995, 47):

1. By the end of the first year of operation of the partnership, 35 percent of requests for a line must be satisfied
2. 95 percent of requests should be satisfied by the end of 2000
3. The call completion rate should rise from its current rate of 60 to 65 percent to 97 percent by 1998.[3]

THE REGULATORY ISSUES

Corporate Governance

SPT's foreign partner will take three seats of the five-seat executive committee of SPT ("No Other Way" 1995). This exceeds the partner's entitlement as reflected by its 27 percent stake. However, this decision was made in order to grant the foreign partner greater management prerogative and to enable it to forge on with the implementation of the FTP. The strategic partner will nevertheless be controlled by the NPF through its 51 percent majority shareholding and its possession of a "golden" share.[4]

Regulation

The initial condition of the telecommunications industry was characterized by both "long-term under-development and under-investment . . . accompanied by deformations in the level and structure of prices for telecommunication services" (Erbenova and Hruby 1995). The inherited price structure required a specific design of the regulatory environment.

Changes were introduced on the regulatory front from early on. Since the beginning of 1990, SPT funds ceased to cross-subsidize other activities, and the company became subject to tax on profits in line with the situation of other enterprises in the country. Moreover, that same year the telecommunications terminal equipment market was liberalized, subject to type approval.

The 1992 Telecommunications Act of the Czech and Slovak Federal Republic (March 12) largely embraced the EU's sectoral policy framework, opening the way for the introduction of competition. "The Act separated regulatory and operator functions and established the possibility to open telecommunication services for competition" (Erbenova and Hruby 1995).

As Figure 8.2 shows, the task of regulating the industry is shared between the CTO and the Ministry of Finance. The CTO prepares the tariff structure in coordination with the operator, but the final decision lies with the Ministry of Finance. Proposals for refining the regulatory procedures and better defining the respective roles of both state organs are currently being debated and could lead to an amendment of the Telecommunications Act.

Although the network is operated by a monopoly provider, the Telecommunications Act does not imply any assumption of monopoly provision of services. In fact, the document entitled "The Main Principles of the State Telecommunication Policy" envisages further demonopolization. Although long-distance voice telephony is scheduled to remain a monopoly at least until the year 2000, the government's principles envisaged the establishment of sixteen "local" networks in which entry of new operators will be enabled. The new entrant can either create a joint venture with SPT or operate by its side in a duopoly. The tender aimed at selecting these sixteen operators was expected to be completed by December 1995, and the new licenses will be operational from September 1996. Two pilot projects by two cable companies, Dattel in Prague and Kabel Plus in Liberec, led the way for this experiment and have received a license from the Ministry of Economy to provide local voice telephony networks as other cable television services.

Cellular phone provision is also run as a monopoly. In June 1990, agreements for the creation of two joint ventures were signed between US West International Inc. and Bell Atlantic Inc. with the Czech MPT. The first joint venture involved the creation of EuroTel Praha and was awarded a twenty-year license for the construction and operation of an analog cellular network, Nordic Mobile Telephone (NMT) 450i, operating in the 450 MHz frequency range). The majority (51%) of EuroTel Praha is owned by SPT Telecom, and the remaining is equally divided between US West International Inc. and Bell Atlantic Inc. (i.e., 24.5% each) through a Dutch-based holding company, Atlantic West BV. The system was officially launched in September 1991, and after a slow take-up in the end of 1995, there were 30,000 subscribers.

The second joint venture between US West International Inc. and Bell Atlantic Inc. with the Czech MPT concerned the development of a packet-switched public data network (PSPDN) by EuroTel Praha enjoying exclusive rights until 1996. In December 1991, an X.25 PSPDN was put into operation by EuroTel Praha (Zehle 1993, 95).

Currently, the process of awarding two GSM digital cellular mobile licenses is under way. One of the licenses has already been set aside and will be awarded to EuroTel Praha whereas the next one is at the stage of evaluation. With regard to the award of the second license, the winner of the tender, with a 49 percent stake, will form a joint venture with the state radio transmission company Ceská Radiokomunikace a.s.

Indirect competition, therefore, has been introduced, and will increase with the award of two GSM licenses, on the basis of competing technological provision of services. The provision of other services and networks, sale of terminal equipment, and the installation and maintenance of such equipment are regulated by the conditions in the issued licenses with no monopoly restrictions. About fifty licenses have been granted since 1992 (Erbenova and Hruby 1995).

Entry is the first area of oversight for the regulator; the regulation of tariffs is the second. When setting tariff policy, Czech regulators could opt for one of three procedures: (1) maximum price-setting; (2) rate of return regulation; and (3) price-capping. Maximum price-setting is the method currently in use. This method is viewed as flexible, since the regulator decides on the level of "appropriate" profits and adapts the tariff for next period according to current period results.

Charges are to be price-capped from 1997 to 1999, and there will be a virtual monopoly on voice telephone for the following four years. Price-capping, or RPI-X regulation, was promoted in U.K. utility privatizations as a regulatory tool that promotes competition, curbs monopoly power, and increases cost efficiency. Tariffs for different telecommunications services are treated together as a weighted basket of goods, with the weights being revenue shares.

The Path of Tariff Regulation since 1992

A first set of tariff changes was introduced in September 1992: The tariff of a pulse was increased by 50 percent while off-peak discounts were decreased by 50 percent for direct-dialed long distance calls. Further changes were introduced in April 1995. Nevertheless, the new tariff structure is a long way from a fully cost-oriented one. Tariffs for public mobile and public data services, together with some additional value-added services, remain unregulated and are relatively higher than the respective tariffs in OECD (data from Hruby 1995, 46). Tariffs for the public mobile service and the public data service are *de facto* not regulated. Erbenova and Hruby (1995) state that "these tariffs are subject to the regulation as well, however in practice so far any tariff proposal by the operators has been accepted by the regulator."

The formulation of SPT's future tariff policy raised conflicts between the Finance Ministry and SPT and as a consequence the privatization process was delayed. More specifically, the SPT wanted significant increases in local call charges as a way to help generate revenue for its Kcs 130 billion modernization plan up to 1998. The Finance Ministry, responsible for formulating the tariff policy, estimated the cost of SPT's modernization plan at only Kcs 70 billion and therefore argued that a steep increase of local call charges was not necessary (Boland 1995a). The tariff policy is now designed by both the Ministry of Finance and SPT Telecom.

In January 1995, a price regulation framework for the telecommunications sector was approved. The Ministry of Finance would follow a maximum price rule for the period 1995 and 1996, the rule being that the "average price increase weighted by the revenue shares of the regulated services will not exceed the agreed rate of 7 percent in 1995 and 3 percent in 1996" (Hruby 1995, 46). Peak-load pricing for local calls was introduced in 1995, international tariffs fell and rental charges rose by more than 62 percent. Public payphone tariffs and connections, however, were frozen by the government for fear of political public opinion reprisals.

The government will switch tariff setting techniques in 1997 and move away from maximum price-setting. Tariffs will be price-capped from 1997 to 1999. In devising the price-capping formula, the Czech regulator first chose the producer price index as its inflation index. It then chose its x-factor (a number reflecting the difference between total factor productivity growth in the economy and total factor productivity growth in the telecommunications operator). The government has decided to set this number at 2 percent reflecting the 100 percent expansion plan (compared to 3% in France and Germany and 5% in Italy and Spain). Other factors entering the formula include allowances for institutional and economic policy changes, such as modifications in the accounting rules, VAT one-step jumps, social security reform, and a move toward a floating exchange rate.

CONCLUSION: THE REGULATORY CHALLENGE

In conclusion, many changes have beset the telecommunications sector in the Czech Republic, in a condensed period of time. The rationale behind the partial privatization of the operator and the granting of monopoly position to the incumbent operator SPT Telecom was to allow the company room to strengthen the domestic network of the company through modernization and expansion investments. The main question left unanswered by this chapter is whether such modernization could have happened only under the guarantee of monopoly power and at the demise of competition.

However, a well-defined, effective, and transparent telecommunications regulatory framework is needed irrespective of the ownership status of the PTT (i.e., fully state-owned or fully/partly privatized) and irrespective of the market structure of the relevant sector (i.e., competition or monopoly). Equally, the role and competence of the regulatory authority should be clearly defined, especially in the case of Eastern Europe, where countries have had no regulatory experience. This contrasts with the restructuring, privatization, or liberalization of telecommunications in the United Kingdom and the United States, where the institutions favoring a regulatory framework were easily put in place. In addition, the regulatory body should be given sufficient powers and it should not be confined solely to the formulation of regulations, but must be powerful enough to ensure implementation. This should tip the balance away from the operator and in favor of the regulator. As Beale and Ypsilanti (1993, 46) observe commenting on the situation in former Communist countries: "Operators are too powerful in terms of influencing the emerging policy framework and market structure. As well, although a de jure separation between operational and regulatory functions often exists, there is still little de facto separation." The issue in Eastern European states is not just one of simple transfer of ownership or one of rapid liberalization. Eastern European states have the compounded challenge of developing and modernizing the network and of offering new services, all under tough financial conditions and limited management and marketing skills. In addition, there is a lack of accounting and financial capabilities which play an important role in laying down the regulatory environment.[5]

The exact regulatory framework has played an important role in the privatization process. Even a couple of months before the eventual strategic sale of 27 percent of SPT, prospective bidders were claiming that the sector-specific regulatory framework was still unclear (as cited in Boland 1995b). More specifically, the degree of monopoly that the SPT would enjoy following privatization as well as the future tariff policy played a central part in the determination of the value of its equity. In general, the higher privatization proceeds realized in the Czech Republic in comparison with Hungary has been attributed, among other factors, to the more comprehensive and more monopolistic regulatory framework (Telecommunications Survey 1995, 39).

NOTES

1. In former Czechoslovakia, the overall control of the telecommunications network and services was assumed by the Federal Ministry of Posts and Telecommunications (MPT). Its structure was federal, with different operators in the two republics: SPT Praha and SPT Bratislava.

2. According to the winning TelSource consortium, the waiting list could be a high as 1.5 million (as cited in "Telecommunications Survey," 1995, 47).

3. In the summer of 1995, the successful connection rate for local calls was just 74 percent ("KPN Finds a Czech Mate," 1995).

4. This share has a nominal value of Kcs 1,000 and was transferred to the NPF in September 1995 following a decision by the Czech Ministry of Privatization.

5. For example, accounting and financial skills are vital in determining tariff regulation. On top of the scarcity of such skills and the conflicting definition of "cost," the task itself of adopting cost-oriented tariffs in networks of outdated technology is very difficult, if not impossible, due to the lack of appropriate and sufficient cost data.

REFERENCES

Beale, Jeremy, and Dimitri Ypsilanti. 1993. "Raising Revenue in Eastern Europe." *Telecommunications* (International edition) 27(1): 40–46.

Boland, Vincent. 1995a. "Dispute on Tariffs Delays Flotation of Czech Telecom." *Financial Times,* January 5.

———. 1995b. "Survey of Czech Finance, Industry and Investment: Deals on a Daunting Scale. The Sales of SPT Telecom and Two Oil Refineries." *Financial Times,* June 2.

———. 1995c. "Western Europe Telecoms Look East. Saturation Prompts Search for New Markets." *Financial Times*, July 4.

———. 1995d. "PTT heads list of SPT bidders." *Financial Times*, June 28.

Bright, Julian. "Czechoslovakia." *Telecommunication* (international edition) 25(10): 160–162.

Doyle, Christopher, Zdenek Hruby, and Jurgen Muller. 1995. "Czech Telecommunications and Transition: How Fast and What Form Should Deregulation Take?" DAE Working Paper, Department of Applied Economics, University of Cambridge.

Erbenova, Michaela, and Zdenek Hruby. 1995. "Regulation and Tariffs in the Telecommunications Sector: The Case of the Czech Republic." Paper prepared under EC ACE grant No. ACE 92-0405-R, October.

European, The. August 17, 1995.

Hruby, Zdenek. 1992. "Telecommunications Investment and Tariff Policy in the CSFR." Paris: OECD.

———. 1995. "Czech and Slovak Republics. After Czechoslovakia." *Telecommunications* (international edition) 29(10): 46–48.

Jajszczyk, Andrzej, and Jerzy Kubasik. 1993. "Telecommunications Tariffs in Central Europe." *IEEE Communications Magazine* 31(10): 68–73.

"KPN Finds a Czech Mate." *Investors Chronicle*, July 7, 1995.

Laska, Ivan. 1991. "Laska Sets Priorities." *Telecommunications* (international edition) 25(10): 163. (I. Laska was the First Deputy Minister for Posts and Telecommunications for the Czech and Slovak Federative Republics).

Noam, Eli. 1992. *Telecommunications in Europe.* New York: Oxford University Press.

"No Other Way: Business in the Czech Republic." *The Economist,* March 25, 1995.

"Phone firms Czech In." *Daily Telegraph*, July 19, 1995.

"Record Dollars 1.45 Billion Bid Secures Stake in Czech Telecom Group." *Financial Times,* May 29, 1995.

Robinson, Anthony. 1995. "Survey of International Telecommunications: Race to Update National Networks." *Financial Times*, October 3.

Seda, Richard, and Zdenek Hruby, 1995. "Czech Telecommunications: Financing of Network Expansion and the Choice of Strategic Partner." Paper prepared under the EC ACE grant No. ACE 92-0405-R, August.

Takla, Lina. 1994. "Privatisation in the Czech Republic and Slovakia." In *Privatisation in Central and Eastern Europe*, edited by Saul Estrin. London: Longman.

Telecommunications Survey. *Business Central Europe,* September, 1995, 38–52.

Zehle, Stefan. 1993. "Telecoms in Eastern Europe: Investing for Growth." *Telecommunications* (international edition) 27(11): 85–96.

PRIVATIZATION AND COMPETITION IN HUNGARIAN TELECOMMUNICATIONS

9

Anna Canning

Somewhere in the towering historical shadow of Americans Bell and Edison stands an equally pioneering Hungarian: Tivadar Puskás, inventor of the telephone exchange. Turn-of-the-century Hungary was at the forefront of technological development, most notably in telecommunications and transportation infrastructure. The telephone network laid in Budapest as part of a massive program of development during the 1880s was one of the most modern in Europe; by the early 1890s the city had the most advanced wired broadcasting system in the world, and it boasted the first underground railway on the Continent.

The decrepitude of these same networks a century later, at the time of the collapse of Hungary's socialist state, was no less remarkable. Hungary, widely regarded as economically advanced and politically "progressive" among the former socialist countries of Central and Eastern Europe (CEE), was one of the most backward in terms of telephone density. In 1990, Hungary had fewer than 10 main lines per 100 inhabitants, and potential subscribers could expect to wait, on average, twelve years for a connection to be installed; around 10 percent of its exchanges were still operated manually, and as many as 30 percent of villages had no private telephone lines at all. Only Poland, the former Soviet Central Asian republics, and Albania outdid Hungary regarding dearth of telephone lines, with penetration rates of 9 percent, 5 to 8 percent and 1 percent, respectively. Countries such as Bulgaria (22%) and Slovenia (21%) had teledensities comparable to the less developed EU member states, such as Portugal (see Table 9.1.), although such quantitative

Table 9.1
Selected National Penetration Rates (main lines per 100 inhabitants, 1990)

Poland	9	West Germany	49
Hungary	10	UK	44
Czech Republic	16	Greece	36
Slovakia	13	Spain	33
Slovenia	21	Portugal	18
E. Europe average (incl. FSU)	11	EU average	40

Sources: National statistics; Okolicsanyi, Károly. 1992. "Telecommunications in East Central Europe." *RFE/RL Research Report* 1(37): 55–60; *Heti világgazdaság* October 10, 1992, 53; Hunya, Gabor. 1995. "Transport and telecommunications Infrastructure in Transition." *Communist Economies and Economic Transformation* 7(3): 369–384 (1995).

comparisons are a poor indication of their relative level of development; telephones may have been more widely available in Bulgaria than in Hungary, but antiquated technology and aged installations ensured that even a brief shower of rain could render them both equally unusable.

The necessity of efficient, flexible telecommunications networks and services for the smooth functioning of a modern (and increasingly globalized) market economy is axiomatic. Lack of these placed severe constraints on the post-war economic development of the former socialist countries and even, ultimately, contributed to their economic and political decline.

The endemic nature of shortage in the communist command economies is now well known,[1] but shortage as manifested in the service sector, and particularly in telecommunications provision, had special features distinguishing it from shortages of, say, consumer goods or manufacturing inputs. Nor was the lag in development of these areas of the service sector in the CEE countries merely the consequence of economic policy errors on the part of successive governments. Rather, it was the result of chronic underinvestment and systematic neglect which reflected the ideological bias of socialist central planning in favor of "productive" activities (and "material" production in particular). The allocation of investment resources was prioritized accordingly— to the detriment of the services sector and infrastructure development.[2] Politically driven pricing policy was another factor contributing to the backwardness of all the network utilities by the time of transition. Under socialism, connection fees and call tariffs generally did not cover the costs of providing the service; tariff structures were highly distorted by a system of cross-subsidization whereby revenue from some services (e.g. international calls) was used to provide others, and charges to certain consumer groups, particularly domestic users, were kept artificially low. Underpricing resulted in increased demand, inadequate levels of maintenance, and outmoded, run-down capital stock.[3]

In the case of telecommunications, underdevelopment also reflected the power structure of the Communist party-state, in which political control over information was crucial and both public and entrepreneurial access to information strictly regulated in conformity with the top-down hierarchy of the party and its "nomenklatura."[4] In addition, the tendency of these countries toward autarkic development, in isolation from the world economy, prevented technology transfer and thus contributed to widening the gap in technological development between CEE and the West (Bicanic and Skreb 1991; Cave and Valentiny 1994). This gap quickly became a chasm during the 1980s, when active restriction of technology exports to CEE imposed by COCOM (Coordinating Committee for Multilateral Export Controls) prevented the former socialist countries from participating in the revolution occurring in Western telecommunications and information technology as a result of advances in microelectronics. Compared with the other CEE countries, Hungary recognized relatively early on—in the early 1980s—the negative economic impact of underdeveloped services, and telecommunications in particular. Political constraints on the reform of this sector also eased from the mid-1980s (perestroika), but Hungary declined to waste precious hard currency resources on the low-grade technology available to it. Finally, in 1986, Austria Telecom—in defiance of COCOM—agreed to sell Hungary a license for the manufacture of digital exchanges, but the damage done was already considerable.

Hungary's history of economic reform prior to 1989 is well documented, and a wealth of literature analyzing the achievements and shortcomings of successive reform attempts exists.[5] While the relationship between infrastructural development and economic growth is widely known, few analysts have investigated the specific role of poor telecommunications in undermining efforts by the Hungarian administration, especially from the early 1980s, to decentralize economic decision making away from the central planning authorities to the firms. The obligation to communicate via the vertical hierarchy was removed (at least to a degree), but the means to develop flexible, multilateral networks of communication among the economic actors, essential to a decentralized economy, are not available to replace it. More clearly quantifiable, however, is the economic damage inflicted; one estimate puts the annual loss of GDP in Hungary attributable directly to inadequate telecommunications at 4 to 5 percent (Major 1992).

THE CHALLENGES OF ECONOMIC TRANSFORMATION

When Hungary began the process of transformation to a market economy in 1989, with high aspirations of "leap-frogging" directly into the world of fiber optics, satellites, and multimedia communications, bypassing several generations of technology development in the West, the problems the sector faced were not only severe shortages and backwardness. There was no money for modernization on the scale required to meet even existing demand, and telecommunications found itself in competition for resources with other sectors whose need for finance to cope with the demands of adjustment to the new economic circumstances was equally pressing.

- In the first phase of transformation, domestic investment resources shriveled because of the rapid fall in GDP (–3.5% in 1990 and –11.9% in 1991) and to the imposition of tight monetary and fiscal controls in order to curb inflation and stabilize the economy.[6]
- Hungary was internally and externally indebted (it had the highest per capita external debt in the region), and the additional burdens on the central government budget as a result of privatization and restructuring (e.g., unemployment) placed further constraints on investment.
- Rapid liberalization of charges for telecommunications services as a means of raising revenue for investment was not politically feasible, due to their high subsidy content, particularly in the case of household users.

At the same time, the need for rapid infrastructural development—both quantitative and in terms of the quality and range of services offered—became all the more acute as a direct result of the process of economic liberalization.

- The collapse of the socialist trading bloc, the CMEA, shifted trading links toward hard currency markets and thereby changed the geography of demand for infrastructure services. Deficient road and rail networks and telecommunications links with the West became a serious obstacle to competitive foreign trade and the integration of business into the world economy.
- Domestically, the emergence of private-sector business and the resulting explosion in the number of economic organizations, especially smaller firms operating in the service sector, created more sophisticated interfirm relations and thus more flexible transport and communications requirements.

Inadequate telecommunications were also the main technical impediment to the development of other institutions and services essential to a market economy (e.g., banking and financial services, business information services, data processing), as well as to the modernization of state administration. Besides opening the way for crucial development in these areas, investment in telecommunications has other externality effects which are of particular significance to an economy in transition:

- Network development would create significant new employment in the short to medium term, thereby absorbing some of the unemployed labor resulting from privatization of state-owned enterprises and reducing the need for state spending on welfare provision.

- It is a growth industry,[7] resilient to recession and attractive for investors. Privatization of the state-owned telecommunications provider and the opening up of other segments of the market (e.g., equipment manufacture) would generate substantial sale proceeds and attract inward investment, thereby boosting foreign exchange revenues and releasing the state from significant capital expenditure burdens.
- It would bring technology transfer, with all its attendant benefits (increasing R&D, improved products and processes).
- It would improve the value of human capital through training in new technical and management skills.
- It would have significant multiplier effects (e.g., create new service industries and businesses), ultimately enhancing overall prospects for economic growth.

Infrastructure, therefore, and telecommunications in particular, was both an objective of economic regeneration in the transition economies and a barrier to it. For all the reasons previously outlined, reform and privatization of telecommunications has received priority over that of other utilities in the majority of CEE countries, an approach supported by the big international aid-finance institutions, such as the European Bank for Reconstruction and Development (EBRD), which spent almost one-third of its loan budget on CEE telecommunications development projects in its first year of operation (Telecommunications Survey, 1993).

TOWARD PRIVATIZATION

By the time of Hungary's first democratic elections in 1990, initiatives had already been taken to separate and corporatize telecommunications, postal services, and broadcasting, which had until then operated as departments of the Hungarian Post Office, a state-owned monopoly (not dissimilar in structure to the classic PTT model in existence in most countries until relatively recently). Under the reformist government of Miklós Németh, regulatory functions were first of all separated from operations, with the former being transferred to a newly created Ministry for Transport, Telecommunications, and Water Management (MTTW) in January 1989. The operations of the old Hungarian Post were divided into their main components in January 1990, and three new entities were founded, the Hungarian Telecommunications Company (Matáv), the Hungarian Post, and the Hungarian Broadcasting Company (later renamed Antenna Hungária). Existing legislation governing post and telecommunications dating from the 1960s was amended, creating the possibility of joint ventures with Hungarian or foreign partners and permitting the use of a range of investment finance options, including equity capital and debt issues. Following a period of consultation with foreign advisors, corporatization of Matáv was completed in July 1991, with its registration as a joint-stock company wholly owned by the state, which exercized its ownership rights through the State Property Agency (SPA), set up in 1990 for that purpose.[8] The SPA in turn delegated back to the MTTW responsibility for managing telecommunications assets.

Corporatization of Matáv was a necessary prelude to privatization, but it took a further eighteen months of parliamentary and public debate before any consensus was reached with regard to the nature, objectives, and extent of privatization. It was clear that investment on the scale required to bring Hungary's telecommunications up to the average 1990 level of the EU countries by the end of the century was beyond the scope of domestic investors and the hard-pressed central budget. A ten-year development program embarked upon by Matáv in 1990 envisaged an annual increase of 10.8 percent in the number of telephone lines (to bring the penetration rate to almost 38 percent by the year 2000), and estimated that the capital investment required to implement this program for the first three years (1990–1993) would be HUF 160 billion (US$2 billion at 1990 exchange rates). According to a 1992 survey by the International Telecommunications Union, the total investment required in Hungary from 1992 to the end of the decade is estimated at almost US$3.5 billion (*Heti világgazdaság,* April 29, 1993) Even development loans from multilateral organizations such as the World Bank and the EBRD (which provided loans of US$150 million and ECU 90 million respectively to Hungary in 1990 specifically for telecommunications development) could at best provide only a fraction of what was needed for infrastructure development projects of this order of magnitude—and indeed such aid-finance was often conditional upon other targets for sectoral adjustment being met.

Despite the odds, Matáv made tangible progress between 1990 and 1993 with its program for revitalizing Hungary's telephone networks (Tables 9.2 and 9.3). A series of commercial bond issues—mostly subscribed by domestic institutional investors—raised around HUF 2 billion. Additional private

Table 9.2
Number of Telephone Lines in Hungary, 1990–1994

	1990	1991	1992	1993	1994
Domestic	704,738	818,831	951,429	1,134,884	1,355,447
Business	265,418	282,546	311,383	332,062	343,103
Public	25,683	26,752	28,321	30,631	32,952
Budapest	459,058	496,550	539,063	578,278	662,814
Rural areas	536,781	631,579	752,070	919,299	1,067,688
TOTAL	995,839	1,128,129	1,291,133	1,497,577	1,731,502

Source: Béla Weyer, "Matáv-privatizáció—Kétszer ad, Kilassan ad," *Heti világgazdaság,* August 12, 1995, 52.

Table 9.3
Data on Telecommunications in Hungary

	1991	1992	1993	1994
Main lines	1,128,129	1,291,133	1,497,577	1,731,502
Main lines per 100 inhabitants	10.92	12.52	14.57	17
Public payphones	26,725	28,321	30,631	-
Card phones	300	1,218	8,500	-
Exchanges	1,710	1,680	1,735	-
automatic (%)	93.2[a]	95.2	96.5	-
of which digital (%)	7.4[a]	16.5	33.0	47.0[b]
Telefax stations	14,580	24,721	29,388	-
Telex stations	14,213	13,296	11,664	-
Waiting list (potential subscribers)	657,796	753,079	771,873	-

Sources: Matáv Rt.; UK Government OTS, "Telecommunications in Hungary," Sector Report, Department of Trade and Industry; Gabor Hunya (1995), "Transport and Telecommunications Infrastructure in Transition," Communist Economics and Economic Transformation 7(3): 369–384 (1994).
a. 1990
b. 1995; Business Central Europe (1995), 43.

funds, although less substantial, were raised through investment funds set up to channel money from potential subscribers into local network development.[9] Partial liberalization of its pricing regime in 1991, including raising consumer charges on some services to bring them more into line with actual costs, not only increased the company's revenues but also helped to open new external credit lines for development (e.g., a DM 185 million loan from EBRD). More rational pricing also enhanced the sector's attractiveness to foreign investors, particularly the big multinational telecommunications corporations, which were poised to enter the potentially lucrative CEE markets once the appropriate conditions were in place. In 1991, in an innovative move, Matáv launched its own investment company, Investel, a joint venture with the investment arm of Ireland's Telecomm Eireann, in which the latter took a 25 percent stake.

Enticing major foreign investors into other segments of the Hungarian telecommunications market which were less dependent on the resolution of regulatory uncertainties was relatively easy; in late 1990 the German giant Siemens and Ericsson of Sweden set up joint ventures for the manufacture of telephone equipment, including digital exchanges, with promises of substantial government procurement orders[10] for the development of the national trunk network. Siemens also bought a 46.8 percent stake in the Hungarian Cable Works and 60 percent in an equipment manufacturing firm, Telefongyár. The easing of COCOM restrictions on Hungary from February 1992 opened the way for further advances. By 1993, more than half a million new lines had been installed, waiting times had been reduced to six years in many areas, a new digital overlay backbone network was in place, and a considerable number of the old mechanically-switched exchanges had been replaced by digital equipment (see Table 9.3). The company decentralized its operations, setting up a number of subsidiaries and joint ventures to carry out activities such as network construction, maintenance, and planning, and entered into a joint venture with a U.S. regional telecommunications firm, US West, to form Westel, which began to offer mobile telephone services in summer 1991, the first such initiative in the CEE countries.

Attracting development finance nevertheless remained a primary objective of privatizing Matáv, and it was clear that only a foreign strategic investor could provide the requisite capital, along with the technical know-how and management expertise. Other motives also played a significant role, not least the Hungarian government's need to raise revenue—a key feature of the overall privatization strategy adopted by the Hungarian government in 1990. Government policy concerning the privatization of state-owned corporate assets slowly matured, bringing with it the realization that privatization of the network utilities, including telecommunications, would require revision of existing sectoral legislation and establishing regulatory provisions, along with the institutions to oversee their implementation. Legislation on privatization passed in the summer of 1992 thus separated the manangement of state-owned "entrepreneurial" assets which could be disposed of straightforwardly from assets which were to remain wholly or partially in state ownership in the longer term, or until appropriate regulatory mechanisms were in place. The role of the SPA was accordingly streamlined to manage only the former, while the utilities, along with industries deemed to be of national or strategic importance, were transferred to a new body, the State Holding Company (SHC).[11] The stake to be retained by the state in the companies managed by the SHC varied considerably. In the case of Matáv, the longer-term prospect of sharing in the profits from this lucrative sector (revenue to the state budget from telecommunications in 1990 alone amounted to HUF 8 billion) and the perceived "strategic" importance of maintaining national sovereignty in telecommunications led the government to opt to retain a majority stake (51%) in state ownership.

Financial and technical preparations for a partial privatization of Matáv were already well advanced in the hands of the consultants N.M. Rothschild and Sons and Salomon Brothers, but the debate on telecommunications legislation and regulation had meanwhile shifted onto altogether more difficult terrain: that of Matáv's monopoly position as the national services provider. Various lobbies exerted influence in different directions; the government at first bowed to pressure from the telecommunications industry and put forward draft legislation envisaging the introduction of competition only in the field of value-added services, allowing Matáv to retain its exclusive rights over the use of the base network, considered a natural monopoly. Opposition parties and many economists advocated greater liberalization of the telecommunications market and the abolition of Matáv's monopoly. The outcome of the protracted wranglings was inevitably a compromise.

THE LEGAL AND REGULATORY FRAMEWORK

The Telecommunications Act was passed in November 1992 but did not come into force until July 1993, following the passage in parliament of companion legislation on frequency management (April 1993) and the publication of a national Telecommunications Policy document setting out development plans for the various segments of the telecommunications market, defining policy principles with regard to the granting of concessions for telecommunications services, outlining the regulatory regime and policy concerning the partial privatization of Matáv. A principal feature of the policy document was to accelerate implementation of the national telecommunications development plan, moving the deadline forward from 2000 to 1997. More significant, the document envisaged the liberalization of a wide range of telecommunications services and introduced the possibility of competition in the regional telephone markets. Matáv would, however, retain its monopoly over the national network (on grounds of "obligation to supply" and to preclude "cherry-picking" in the development and provision of services). In addition, its monopoly in the domestic long-distance and international market would not be phased out until after 1999, in order to secure (via continued cross-financing) revenues for "stable" completion of the national network and, it was argued, to enhance the company's privatization (and thereby the government's revenue-earning) prospects.[12] Although Matáv's monopoly was thus no longer absolute, it remained substantial, particularly considering that many value-added services also depend on access to the backbone network.

Under the Telecommunications Act, the market is divided as follows:

- *Services subject to concession agreements* (in accordance with the provisions of the 1991 Act on Concessions[13]). These included public telephony services, public mobile telecommunications services, public national paging systems, and both national and regional radio/television broadcasting (i.e., all services which the state has an obligation to supply). From April 30, 1994, public telephony services could be provided only by concession-holders. The Act also stipulated that local concessions be put up for tender if a local government majority (more than 50%) so requested. Matáv would be permitted to bid on the same terms as other bidders.

- *Services subject to license*. These included public switched data transmission and cable television.

- *Services not subject to authorization*. These included proprietary, private, and closed-group networks within the premises of any company or organization (this service could be extended, subject to license, to a specified group of users beyond the premises of the organization).

The Act does not provide for a unitary regulatory authority. Instead, different functions are assigned to different bodies:

- The *Communications Supervisory Authority*, with regional offices nationwide, is responsible for issuing authorization (licenses) for the provision of telecommunications services.
- The *Telecommunications Conciliation Forum*, a nonprofit, nonpolitical council funded partly from member subscriptions and partly from the Telecommunications Fund (TF).[14] Its main function is to "protect the public interest," liaising between national and local government bodies, industry organizations and consumers and arbitrating in the case of disputes between them.
- Both of these are accountable to the ministry MTTW, which retains overall responsibility for formulating and implementing policy and regulating prices.

Price regulation also required a radical overhaul. A new tariff regime was introduced by joint decree of the MTTW and the Finance Ministry in 1993, taking effect from January 1, 1994 (see Table 9.4). The most significant

Table 9.4
Telephone Tariff Regulatory Regime

Tariff	Pre-1994	Post-1994
Connection	administratively fixed charge	administratively set maximum charge
Repair	based on actual cost	unrestricted
Line rental	administratively set maximum charge	price cap
Local calls	administratively set maximum charge	price cap
Domestic long-distance calls - zone I	administratively set maximum charge	price cap
Domestic long-distance calls - zones II and III	administratively set maximum charge	price cap
International calls	unrestricted	price cap

Source: MTTW; *Heti világgazdaság,* Supplement: Telecommunications, August 7, 1993, 45.

change was the introduction of a price capping system for most tariffs to replace the maximum charges set by ministerial decree for each individual service. Akin to the system in operation in the United Kingdom, the cap applies to the rate of increase in total revenue earned from a group of services; in Hungary this is indexed to producer prices (PPI). In order to bring charges—especially for local calls—into line with costs by the end of the 1990s, the decree provides for a maximum annual price increase of PPI+7% for local and zone I calls (estimated to mean an increase of 15 to 20% in real terms), but limits the annual rate of increase for domestic long-distance and international calls to PPI-4% (a reduction of around 10% per annum in real terms).

PARTIAL PRIVATIZATION OF MATÁV

The tender for the privatization of a significant minority stake (at least 30%) in Matáv, along with a concession for the provision of public international and domestic long-distance services, and local telephone services in twenty-nine areas (see Table 9.5), was issued by the ministry and the SHC in August 1993. The twenty-five-year concession, renewable for a further twelve-and-a-half years, included an eight-year exclusivity clause and committed the successful bidder to increase telephone lines by a minimum of 15.5 percent per year and eliminate the waiting list by 1997. In accordance with

Table 9.5
Matáv Indicators Prior to Privatization (December 1992)

Telephone penetration rate (lines/100 inhabitants)	12.52
Per capita GDP (U.S.$)	3,400
GDP/telephone line	27,156
Matáv annual revenue (U.S.$ millions)	646.4
Profit after tax (U.S.$ millions)	15
Revenue per employee (U.S.$)	31,596
Revenue per main line (U.S.$)	500.7
Lines per employee	63
Profit as a percentage of revenue	2.32
Debt:equity ratio (% of registered capital)	46

Source: Salomon Brothers, cited in Tamás Szalai, 1993, "Várjon a tárcahangra!" *Heti világgazdaság,* November 27, 1993, 105.

the government's policy decisions regarding the type of investor and commitment sought for Matáv, bidders (or, in the case of consortia, at least one member with a minimum of 40% interest) had to fulfill the following requirements, in addition to demonstrating the financial capability to execute the transaction:

- operating experience (already serving at least one million subscribers)
- solvency (gross revenues of at least US$1 billion from public telecommunications services in the previous two years)
- network development experience in the previous five years

The initial round attracted interest from fourteen major telecommunications companies or consortia worldwide, including six European, four U.S., and three Asian operators. Four bidders were short-listed to participate in the second round and invited to submit detailed proposals by November 1993:

- Euro Telecom Hungary: STET (Italy) and Bell Atlantic (United States)
- Duna Telecom: France Telecom and US West
- Telefonica International (Spain)
- MagyarCom: Deutsche Bundespost Telekom, Ameritech (United States), Cable and Wireless (United Kingdom)

In a deal which made international headlines, and the first of this scale in the region, the ministry announced in late December 1993 that the German–U.S. consortium MagyarCom (the U.K. partner withdrew at the last minute) had won a 30.2 percent stake, along with financial and operational control of Matáv, for the sum of US$875 million. The German partner's experience of network modernization and expansion in its eastern territories, likewise a former centrally planned economy, is said to have played a significant role in MagyarCom's selection, although Hungary's interest in maintaining strong economic and political ties with Germany may also have been a factor.[15]

Although not the highest, the winning bid exceeded most analysts' expectations,[16] considering Matáv's poor financial indicators (see Table 9.5); in 1992, its productivity was well below that of telecommunications providers in many developing countries, while its debt ratio (long-term debt alone amounted to US$670 million) was equivalent to almost half of its registered capital, resulting in a very low level of profitability. The company's finances were given a timely facelift (less than one month before the privatization deal) by a capital injection of HUF 8.55 billion (around US$86 million at the end of 1993 exchange rates) from the IFC and the EBRD, which gave the two organizations an equity stake of 10 percent in Matáv, partially substituting earlier loan agreements. Added risk factor facing potential investors was the lack of clarity regarding telecommunications regulation; pricing mechanisms and regulatory institutions were not yet fully in place; and the general elections scheduled for spring 1994—which the former communist party's successor, the Hungarian Socialist party, was tipped to win—further increased uncertainty with regard to the future regulatory environment.

Hungary's favorable geographic location undoubtedly helped to secure such a high price for Matáv; "transit" telecommunications traffic presumably accounts for a substantial proportion of revenues from international calls (which made up 28 percent of total revenues in the first half of 1993). The advantages of gaining a significant foothold in the region, particularly at a time when international competition in telecommunications markets is set to intensify as the EU prepares to open its telecommunications borders and do away with its remaining state-owned monopolies, hardly need to be enumerated here. Successful conclusion of the privatization deal before the end of December also brought advantages for MagyarCom. Under the Hungarian tax legislation in force until the end of 1993, the new owners were eligible to claim significant tax benefits applying to new joint ventures with foreign participation—a 100 percent tax holiday for the first five years and 60 percent for the next five.[17]

Of the total paid by MagyarCom, US$400 million was to be used to raise the company's equity; the remaining US$475 million was earmarked as follows:

- US$335.25 million to be paid to the SHC in exchange for Matáv shares (most of this was ultimately destined for the Treasury, to finance the budget deficit)
- US$133.25 million, the concession fee, was to be paid into the Telecommunications Fund
- US$6.5 million to cover the privatization consultants' fees

Following privatization, the company's registered capital amounted to HUF 104 billion, and its assets were estimated to be worth some HUF 200 billion (see Table 9.6).

The concession agreement committed the new owners of Matáv to a development program including installation of at least 250,000 new lines per year until 1996, as well as modernization of exchanges, billing, and enquiry systems, all involving an annual investment of an estimated HUF 60 billion

Table 9.6
Post-Privatization Ownership of Matáv

MagyarCom	30.2% (Deutsche Telekom 15.1%; Ameritech 15.1%)
EBRD	1.98%
IFC	0.99%
SHC	67.83%

(approximately US$600 million at end of 1993 exchange rates). Of this amount, 40 percent was to be self-financed from company revenues, the rest from international loans. Partial privatization and the implementation of a new tariff regime conforming to international practice rapidly boosted the company's creditworthiness, and attracting the requisite development finance has not posed a problem. In 1994 a DM 85 million loan was proffered by the Export—Import Bank of Japan, an international consortium of 27 banks granted a five-year syndicated loan of US$150 million, while the European Investment Bank (EIB) provided the equivalent amount in ecu. During 1995 the company's investment arm, Investel, secured a further loan of US$300 million—the biggest loan granted to a CEE enterprise without the backing of a government guarantee—from a consortium comprising the EBRD, the IFC, and Deutsche Bank, along with thirty-five commercial banks (including Credit Suisse, First Boston, JP Morgan, and the Japanese bank Sumitomo) (*Figyelö*, October 20, 1994; *Heti világgazdaság*, December 9, 1994; U.K. Government OTS 1995; Budai, September 14, 1995). The loan, to be disbursed in several tranches (i.e., installments), will be used to finance telecommunications development during 1995–1996 and to replace earlier, less favorable credit agreements. Matáv's total credit commitments to date amount to HUF 100 billion. Intensive investment during 1994–1995 has meant that network development so far is ahead of target.

Decisions expected in late 1995 or early 1996 concerning the fate of the remaining state-owned shares in Matáv will be crucial for the company's future development. Following the election of the socialist/liberal coalition government in the summer of 1994 and changes in key personnel at the relevant ministries, Hungary's progress with privatization slowed noticeably and the government's strategy with regard to the future of the utilities became clouded with uncertainty. Privatization of the gas and electricity utilities seemed to have stalled, and although the sale of a second tranche of shares in Matáv appeared to have support in principle from the end of 1994, when plans were announced to reduce the state-owned share in Matáv to 25 percent plus one share, the government's actual policy only emerged gradually. A portion of the state-owned shares (about 10%) was to be allocated in accordance with other (social) policy objectives, as follows:

- HUF 0.5 billion to employees in exchange for property vouchers issued in the early 1990s (Neumann 1994)
- HUF 2.6 billion in the form of employee shares payable in installments over five years at preferential interest rates
- HUF 1.6 billion to local governments
- HUF 5.8 billion to be offered in exchange for "compensation vouchers" issued to members of the public whose assets had been confiscated for ideological or political reasons under the earlier regimes[18]

Progress was delayed by the government's decision in early 1995 to merge the two bodies responsible for privatization and management of state assets (the SPA and SHC) to form the State Privatization and Holding Company (SPHC). Opinions regarding the nature and timing of the second phase of privatization were divided: Matáv/MagyarCom representatives favored postponement until the company was in a stronger financial position, in order to boost share prices; the government's need for privatization revenue, however (HUF 150 billion is the ambitious target for 1995), to keep the budget deficit under some semblance of control, make it likely that a decision is imminent. Uncertainty also surrounded the question of whether the sale should be targeted at portfolio investors or strategic investors, and, in the case of the latter, whether or to what extent the incumbent MagyarCom consortium should be allowed to increase its stake. Privatization consultants Credit Suisse, First Boston, and Deutsche Bank have submitted proposals to the SPHC and the government; reports emerging from Hungary indicate that the stake to be offered will be 34 percent, and the sale is expected to fetch around HUF 110–112 billion.[19] It appears increasingly probable that MagyarCom will be invited to turn its present 30.2 percent stake into a majority one, which is likely to have a positive impact on the value of Matáv shares[20] ahead of the anticipated flotation of Matáv on the international stock market, notably in Frankfurt and New York, as well as Budapest, in 1996.

LOCAL NETWORKS

In accordance with the Telecommunications Act, the MTTW divided Hungary into fifty-six (later reduced to fifty-four) primary regions in which a local telephone service could be offered and, in April 1993, invited local governments to notify the ministry of their intention to apply for independent concessions for the operation of local telephone networks. Any not applying would automatically remain in the hands of Matáv. In July the MTTW published a list of twenty-five regions which had satisfied the financial and technical requirements for eligibility to tender for local concessions, and in September 1993 tender prospectuses were issued. The concessions offered were for an initial period of twenty-five years, with the possibility of a one-off extension of twelve-and-a-half years, and granted the concession-holder a monopoly of eight years for the provision of services in the given region. Eligibility to bid was restricted to companies set up exclusively for the purpose of operating the concession and having at least 25 percent plus one share in Hungarian ownership. The number of regional concessions for which a company could bid was not restricted, providing the company could guarantee to service each region. In addition to payment of a concession fee (which varied according to the region), successful bidders committed themselves to the following:

- to begin supplying services within one year of signing the contract
- to increase the number of telephone lines in the given region by 15.5 percent per year and reduce the waiting time to six months for a minimum of 90 percent of applicants and twelve months for all by January 1997
- to ensure compatibility of regional systems with those operated by Matáv
- to pay an annual royalty amounting to 0.1 percent of their gross turnover

The tender attracted considerable interest from foreign investors, many of whom were already active in local network-building projects in partnership with local governments and Hungarian entrepreneurs. When the results were made public at the end of February 1994, it was revealed that forty-one bids were received for twenty-three primary regions (two attracted no offers and thus reverted to Matáv); eight concession contracts were awarded to Matáv, and fifteen to other operators, predominantly U.S.- and French-led consortia and a number of local government companies, some with foreign partners. According to a ministry estimate, the investment required by the regional companies in the first two years of operation, in order to provide the 700,000 new lines pledged in the concession contract, was in the region of HUF 150 billion (US$1.5 billion). Table 9.7 gives details of non-Matáv regional concession-holders' investment commitments and ownership.

Overall, the outcome of the regional concession tenders means that Matáv remains the dominant supplier of local telephone services in Hungary, with exclusive control in thirty-nine of the total fifty-four primary areas until 2002. Moreover, the twenty-nine primaries uncontested by local governments, and therefore "automatically" granted to Matáv were among the most developed, accounting for around 60 percent of the country's population and some 75 percent of existing telephone lines.[21] Many of the areas put up for tender, by contrast, were some of the poorest, not particularly attractive in terms of economic potential; many were badly hit by unemployment and the worst served with regard to telecommunications.[22] While development of telecommunications infrastructure in these areas would undoubtedly benefit the population (and prove politically worthwhile for the local governments concerned), the capital investment required was likely to be proportionately higher and returns on the investment a more distant prospect, especially if rising charges stifled consumer demand. With the 10 regional concessions gained by Matáv in the tender process, the company extended its control to around 80 percent of Hungary's local telephone market.

Regional telecommunications development has been far from smooth, however, blighted by evidence of corruption in the awarding of concessions[23] and by a prolonged dispute over the value of the physical assets to be taken over from Matáv by thirteen of the fifteen independent regional concession-holders. These assets had originally been valued at a total of HUF 20.4 billion by Coopers and Lybrand, but independent valuations commissioned on the insistence

Table 9.7
Regional Concessionary Telephone Companies Independent of Matáv

Primary region	Concession-holder	Ownership	Concession fee (HUF mns)	Investment plan 1994-96 (HUF mns)	New lines planned 1994-96 ('000s)
Békéscsaba	Hungarotel Rt.	CET (U.S.)	1008	7,350	22.0
Dunaújváros	Dunatel Rt.	UTS (U.S., Fr)	170	5,646	35.0
Esztergom	Egom-Com Rt.	UTS (U.S., Fr)	390	4,118	24.0
Gödöllő	Digitel Rt.	local gov., Israel, Fr.	340	4,370	34.0
Jászberény	Jász-Tel Rt.	JászCom (local gov., NL, CH)	65	2,200	30.0
Monor	Monor Telefontársaság Rt.	Tápiótel (U.S.); Detcom	200	6,007	46.0
Orosháza	Hungarotel Rt.	CET (U.S.)	78	1,655	15.1
Pápa	Pápatel Rt.	CET (U.S.)	165	6,516	17.0
Salgótarján	Kelet-Nógrád Com Rt	HTCC (U.S.)	215	4,627	25.7
Sárvár	Rába-Com Rt.	HTCC (U.S.)	275	2,465	10.6
Szeged	Déltáv Rt.	CGE (Fr)	1,300	13,500	80.0
Szentes	Déltáv Rt.	CGE (Fr)	100	3,500	60.0
Szigetszentmiklos	Kisduna-Com Rt.	UTS (U.S., Fr)	130	3,495	19.6
Vác	Digitel Rt.	local gov., Israel, Fr.	510	3,048	27.0
Veszprém	Bakonytel Rt.	UTS (U.S., Fr)	560	9,497	44.0

Sources: Matáv Rt.; Béla Weyer, "Matáv-privatizáció—Ketszer ad, Kilassan ad," *Heti világgazdaság,* August 12, 1995, 65.
Abbreviations: CET = Central Euro Telecom; UTS = United Telecom Services; CGE = Compagnie générale des eaux; HTCC = Hungarian Telephone and Cable Corporation.

of the regional companies set their value at less than HUF 15 billion, an average of 67 percent of the earlier value. In one region, Sárvár, the new assessment was as low as 37 percent of the original (*Figyelö,* February 2, 1995, 23). Failure of the regional companies to reach agreement with Matáv over the transfer of assets by the February 1995 deadline could have resulted in the concessions being withdrawn. Although this risk was averted, the dispute had two serious consequences: huge unexpected losses (in excess of HUF 5 billion) to Matáv and the potentially damaging effect of the affair on the company's second phase of privatization; and the postponement of regional development targets by a year. Considering the losses caused by the delay to the regions involved, and the fact that resources from the TF—set up primarily to support modernization in Hungary's less developed regions—were used to compensate Matáv,[24] the real losers in the dispute were undoubtedly the regional consumers.

MOBILE TELEPHONY IN HUNGARY

Mobile telecommunications have proved especially attractive to users in the economies in transition and are playing a vital role in the development of business communications, since in many areas it can still take years to obtain a fixed-line connection. Three companies operate mobile services in Hungary: Westel Radiotelefon (operating an analogue system and 51% owned by Matáv) was launched in 1991; in October 1993 its sister company, Westel 900, and the Pannon GSM consortium (comprising four Nordic telecommunications companies, PTT Telecom Nederlands, and three Hungarian firms) won fifteen-year concession contracts to provide digital GSM communications services on 900 Mhz.

In all three cases, the number of subscribers has surpassed expectations, making this the most rapidly-growing segment of telephone market, despite the fact that both the equipment and the subscription charge are expensive relative to fixed-line connections. By autumn 1995, Westel 900 GSM had become the market leader, with just over 100,000 subscribers; Westel Radiotelefon had nearly 70,000, while subscribers to Pannon GSM numbered around 50,000. The launch of GSM in spring 1994 brought rapid expansion in mobile use; the number of new subscribers more than doubled in the first eighteen months up to September 1995, bringing the total to 230,000. The number of mobile users in Hungary already outstrips that in EU countries such as Portugal and Greece (see Table 9.8), and the total figure is expected to reach more than a quarter of a million by the end of 1995. Figures relating to investment in network development are equally impressive. Including the concession fees (approximately US$50 million each), the mobile sector in Hungary attracted inward investment amounting to more than US$0.5 billion in the period up to September 1995 (most of this, US$450,000 million, in the eighteen months since the launch of GSM). By autumn 1995, Hungary had GSM "roaming" agreements with twenty-two countries (Budai 1995).

Development has not been completely problem-free, however. Westel Radiotelefon was dogged by high call failure rates, poor sound quality, and frequent interference.[25] This was in part because network development was unable to keep pace with rapidly growing demand, but also because the 450 Mhz frequency overlapped with the proprietary telecommunications network of the Hungarian Railway Company (MAV). Hungary's two digital mobile systems still do not offer the quality of fixed-line digital systems, and neither GSM company has yet been able to fulfill its promise of a 95 percent call-success rate.

Table 9.8
Mobile Phone Use in Selected European Countries (per 1000 inhabitants)

Sweden	159
Finland	128
Denmark	99
Great Britain	61
Italy	39
Austria	35
Germany	31
Ireland	24
Netherlands	22
Hungary	20
Portugal	19
Greece	16

Sources: *Figyelö,* Telecommunications Supplement (Tantusz), August 24, 1995, 21.

Competition between the two companies is heated, and both have pursued relentless marketing campaigns to win subscribers. In terms of subscriber numbers, Pannon, which offers a wider range of services, currently lags behind Westel GSM, whose development strategy gave priority to building national coverage (as regards both reception and availability of end-user equipment). Westel may not keep its competitive advantage, however, if Pannon succeeds in offering more choice in the longer term. Competition from GSM has made Westel Radiotelefon improve the quality of its service and keep its call tariffs competitive.

Paging services in Hungary are provided by three companies: Operátor Hungária, the first to begin operations, offers a national service (with 12,000 subscribers in 1994); two companies, Euro Paging Hungary and EasyCall Ermes Hungary, hold fifteen-year renewable concessions (granted in 1994) to offer ERMES services. The Hungarian ERMES systems began to come on stream in mid-1995 and, like GSM, will eventually enable subscribers to be reached throughout Europe, wherever equivalent systems are available. Besides their regular commercial uses, paging systems have an additional appeal in economies in transition such as Hungary as a "quick-fix," cheap alternative to mobile phones.

CONCLUSION

Telecommunications development in Hungary is proceeding rapidly, spurred partly by the post-Communist governments' fairly enlightened approach to the need for partial liberalization of telecommunications markets in order to foster development of a market economy and enhance Hungary's prospects of economic and political integration into the EU. This approach was, however, also determined by necessity, which led the government to renounce tariff revenues and absolute sovereignty in telecommunications in favor of privatization revenues and inward investment. The overall policy adopted by Hungary is roughly in line with the sequencing of liberalization set in the EU: Elements of competition were introduced first in equipment manufacture and in the retail market for end-user appliances, followed by liberalization of data transfer and other value-added services. As in the majority of EU member states, Hungary's main telecommunications provider will retain its monopoly over national services for a set period, after which the monopoly will be phased out. Uncertainties persist: Government secrecy over plans regarding the second phase of Matáv's privatization, the row between Matáv, the ministry, and the local concessionaries over asset valuation, and lack of clarity in the regulatory environment have all been damaging, though evidently not sufficiently to undermine investor confidence in Hungarian telecommunications. The regulatory environment is evolving, although it will be some time before it is clear how well consumer interests will be served.

Development plans so far are on target, and in some regions, despite setbacks, supply already exceeds demand (e.g., Sopron). The state-of-the-art networks being installed will facilitate development in areas such as ISDN (launched in Hungary by Matáv in May 1995) and enable Hungary to keep pace with advances in telecommunications technology now coming to the fore in Western Europe and worldwide. The business telecommunications environment in Hungary has improved radically; most of the options available elsewhere are also available in Hungary, although the cost to the customer remains high relative to the cost of other services and commodities. Prices should become more competitive as telecommunications services providers complete their network development programs, thus eliminating supply problems, and a "buyers' market" is generated. Mobile telecommunications have played a special role in Hungary (and in the other transition economies of CEE), often substituting rather than complementing fixed-line services, a trend due largely to the lack of availability of the latter, but also to the wider range of value-added services immediately accessible to mobile customers. With improving quality and an ever-expanding range of services, mobile telecommunications are likely to continue to provide stiff competition to Matáv even after 1997, when network development is completed, although it is not clear that the present rapid rates of mobile growth can be sustained.

While Hungary is unique in the region in introducing competition in local public telephony services, the national provider, Matáv, remains in control of 80 percent of the country's local networks. There is therefore a risk that it could eventually use its dominant position to initiate a price war and thereby squeeze smaller competitors out of the market. With the state retaining a substantial ownership stake in Matáv, the company also has a powerful ally. This was manifested, for example, in the ministry's decision to support Matáv's bid to outlaw "call-back" services via the United States on the grounds that they violate the company's exclusive concessionary rights over the international and domestic long-distance network. In the longer term, however, Matáv will face challenges from the introduction of wider competition both at local and international levels, following the expiry of monopoly rights in the various segments of the Hungarian telecommunications market. The company still has a long way to go in building consumer confidence. As a result of its legacy from the past, Matáv inspires little "brand loyalty." Efforts are underway to shake off the company's notoriously consumer-unfriendly image by means of improvements in customer support services and aggressive marketing, but only time will tell whether these efforts have been effective in enabling Matáv to retain its present degree of market dominance in the future.

Regional competition within CEE is also likely to intensify. Most of the transforming former socialist countries in CEE concentrated initially on their own development and enhancing international links with the West; thinking with regard to the need to develop regional links is catching up. The Czech telephone company, SPT, which was partially privatized in autumn 1995, is likely to prove a tough rival in the emerging battle in the CEE region for supremacy as an international hub.

One criticism which could be leveled at the Hungarian government's strategy with regard to competition in telecommunications is that the gradualist approach, which has characterized Hungary's transformation process as a whole, may not have been the most advantageous approach for this sector. While the objective of eventual integration into the EU guided policy making and development of legislation in many spheres, alignment in telecommunications policy may prove to have been neither wise or necessary. Europe, still dominated by state-owned monopolies, already lags behind the United States in terms of competitiveness; if Hungary expects to reach only 1990 EU levels of provision and efficiency by the time the EU opens its markets in 1998, then Hungary and other countries in the region are likely to find themselves trailing when telecommunications markets go global.

NOTES

The author is indebted to Professor Paul Hare and Dr. Junior Davis of CERT for comments and suggestions on earlier drafts of this study. For the purposes of this chapter, telecommunications is used to refer principally to telephone services, rather that in its wider meaning of "electronic transmission of impulses by telegraphy, cable, telephony, radio or television" (Okolicsanyi 1992).

1. It is beyond the scope of this chapter to discuss the underlying causes of shortage under central planning. The reader is referred to the literature, for example, János Kornai, *The Economics of Shortage* (Amsterdam: North-Holland, 1980).

2. This is illustrated eloquently in the available microeconomic data, which show a significant lag in the share of services and infrastructure in employment, assets, and investment in all the former socialist countries in CEE, although ratios were on the rise by 1989 (see Bicanic and Skreb 1991; Major 1992).

3. The same was true of the tariff structures employed in the energy utilities (cf. Cave and Valentiny 1994; Major 1992).

4. For a detailed discussion of the systemic reasons for the lag in service-sector development in CEE, see Bicanic and Skreb (1991); Major (1992); Okolicsanyi (1992); Cave and Valentiny (1994); and Hunya (1995).

5. See, for example, Berend T. Iván, *A magyar gazdasági reform útja* (Budapest: Közgazdasági és Jogi Könyvkiadó, 1988); Nigel Swain, *The Rise and Fall of Feasible Socialism* (London: Verso, 1992); Roger A. Clarke, ed., *Hungary, The Second Decade of Economic Reform* (Harlow: Longman, 1989); Kornai, János, "The Hungarian Reform Process," *Journal of Economic Literature* (1986) 24(4).

6. Total fixed investment fell by nearly 25 percent during 1990–1993 (EIU, Economist Intelligence Unit Country Forecasts, Hungary, various issues).

7. By the second half of the 1990s, telecommunications services are expected to account for around 7 percent of GNP in the EU, according to European Commission forecasts (Telecommunications Survey, 1993). *The Economist* (1995, 6) reports that telecommunications profitability has accelerated almost continuously for the past decade; in 1994 the profits made by the world's ten largest telecommunications companies exceeded those of the twenty-five biggest commercial banks.

8. For a detailed discussion of the legal and institutional framework for privatization of the state sector in Hungary, see Canning and Hare, 1994.

9. This approach was not entirely new in Hungary, but had a precedent during the 1980s when the Hungarian Post issued debentures, holders of which were given priority in the telephone queue (*Heti világgazdaság,* October 10, 1992).

10. The two companies, along with the former monopoly Hungarian manufacturer BHG, won five-year concessions for the supply of digital exchanges and subexchanges. A review of the concession agreements at the end of 1995 may lead to the issue of a new tender, with the possibility of opening this segment of the market still further.

11. See Canning and Hare (1994) for details.

12. EU policy principles, providing for only gradual phasing out of member states' national telecommunications monopolies, were also cited as justification for this decision.

13. The Act on Concessions (1991) provided the basic legal framework for the granting of concessions, principally by public tender and subject to payment of a concession fee, to developers/operators of public infrastructure services including highways, road and rail transport services, telecommunications, and so on. Concessions are granted for a specified period and may by law be extended only once without issuing a new public tender, and then only for a maximum of half the original period.

14. The TF was established by the MTTW primarily to channel resources into tele-communications modernization and expansion in Hungary's least-developed regions. Its funds come from concession fees, together with some support from the central government budget.

15. Germany is Hungary's biggest trading partner, accounting for more than 25 percent of exports and imports. There were also (unsubstantiated) rumors, attributed mainly to STET—the highest, but unsuccessful, bidder—of diplomatic intervention in favor of the German company, and speculation that Deutsche Telekom was in some way being compensated for losing the GSM tender earlier in 1993 (Okolicsanyi 1994).

16. Analysts estimated the average market value of Western European telecommunications companies at the end of 1992 at around US$1,500 per main line, compared with US$4,000–7,000 in less developed Latin American and Asian countries. These figures reflect development potential rather than actual development level. In Hungary, the MagyarCom bid represented US$2,600 per main line purchased, reflecting, at least in part, Hungary's favorable geographical position and its potential as a regional hubbing center. (*Heti világgazdaság,* November 17, 1993, 105).

17. An article in the *Financial Times* (December 20, 1993) estimated that this could mean tax saving of as much as US$200 million to the company.

18. Data from *Figyelö*, Telecommunications Supplement, July 28, 1994, II. Regarding compensation policy and procedures, see Canning and Hare, 1994.

19. Magyar Hírlap, December 1, 1995, 11. This figure, translated into U.S. dollars at the rate of $1=HUF135 (November 1995), amounts to approximately US$815–829 million, and is thus substantially lower than the sum paid by MagyarCom for the original 30.2 percent stake in Matáv. While market access is no longer a key attraction in the second phase of the company's privatization, falling profits (despite increased revenues) may also be a factor contributing to depressed expectations regarding the sale price of the next tranche of shares: in 1993 Matáv's net revenues amounted to HUF 67,559 million, but gross profit was only HUF 1,606 million; in 1994 the figures were HUF 89,936 million and HUF 195 million respectively, and projections for 1995 profits (taking into account the losses incurred by Matáv in the property dispute with the regional concessionaries) are even lower (*Figyelö*, Telecommunications Supplement, August 24, 1995, 8).

20. Shares in Matáv (traded in Budapest's secondary markets) fell in value from 280 percent at the time of the initial privatization (end of 1993) to 160–180 percent in summer 1995.

21. Notably, they include Budapest, the capital, most of the other major towns and industrial centers of Hungary, and the area surrounding Lake Balaton. Many of the local municipalities of Budapest (originally comprising seven primary areas) did in fact vote to tender for a concession, but were thwarted by a ministry decision to keep the capital a unitary primary area, probably with a view to Matáv's privatization (Szalai and Weyer 1993, 115).

22. Average density in these twenty-three regions was 8.8 percent, compared with 18.6 percent in the regions automatically transferred to Matáv (Szalai 1994, 8.).

23. The case of Hungarian/Israeli-owned Digitel 2001 (Vác and Gödöllö regions) was reviewed in the wake of allegations that the concession award had been "rigged" by an official at the SHC in return for "material benefits." The concession was finally awarded in September 1995 to a reformed consortium, Digitel 2002, involving the Hungarian partners and a Dutch company.

24. The damage to Matáv, both in accounting terms and loss of market credibility, was serious enough to make the government decided to intervene and, in summer 1995, it was agreed that the losses should be borne in equal measure by the SHC, the TF, and Matáv, itself.

25. According to an OECD/ITU survey (cited in Budai 1995a) covering the period up to the end of 1993, Hungary's radio telephone service was the second worst in the region.

REFERENCES

Bicanic, Ivo, and Marko Skreb. 1991. "The Service Sector in East European Economies: What Role Can It Play in Future Development?" *Communist Economies and Economic Transformation* (2): 221–233.

Budai, János 1995 "Mobilverseny—Telefonákságok." *Figyelö* September 14, 1995, 15.

Canning, Anna, and Paul Hare. 1994. "The Privatization Process—Economic and Political Aspects of the Hungarian Approach." In *Privatisation in Central and Eastern Europe,* edited by Saul Estrin, London: Longman.

Cave, Martin, and Pál Valentiny. 1994. "Privatization and Regulation of Utilities in Economies in Transition." In *Privatisation in Central and Eastern Europe,* edited by S. Estrin, 69–82. London: Longman.

Hunya, Gábor. 1995. "Transport and Telecommunications Infrastructure in Transition." *Communist Economies and Economic Transformation* 7(3): 369–384.

Major, Iván. 1992. "Private and Public Infrastructure in Eastern Europe." *Oxford Review of Economic Policy* (4): 76–92.

Neumann, L. "Public Sector Adjustment through Privatization: The Case of Hungarian Telecommunications." International Labour Office, Geneva, Occasional Paper 21, March 1994.

Okolicsanyi, Károly. 1992. "Telecommunications in East Central Europe." RFE/RL *Research Report* 1(37): 55–60.

———. 1994. Hungarian Telephone's Landmark Privatization Deal. *RFE/RL Research Report* 3(6): 41–43.

Supplement: Telecommunications. *Heti Világgazdaság,* August 7, 1993, 43–56.

Survey of Telecommunications, *The Economist,* September 30, 1995, 6–40.

Szalai, Tamás. "Várjon a tárcahangra!" *Heti világgazdaság,* November 27, 1993, 104–107.

———. "Halló, ki hallgat?" *Heti világgazdaság,* March 12, 1994, 7–10.

Szalai, Tamás, and Béla Weyer. "Kézi kapcsolás." *Heti világgazdaság* October 9, 1993, 115–117.

Telecommunications Survey. *Business Central Europe,* May 1993, 35–48.

Telecommunications Survey. *Business Central Europe,* September 14, 1995, 46.

U.K. Government Overseas Trade Services. 1994. "Telecommunications in Hungary." Sector Report, Department of Trade and Industry, October.

COMPETITION RULES AND REGULATIONS IN TELECOMMUNICATIONS

10

The Case of Poland's Intent to Join the EU

Piotr Jasiński

TELECOMMUNICATIONS: COMPETITION VERSUS REGULATION

Since Bell invented the telephone in 1876, telecommunications has changed beyond recognition, but particularly in the last twenty or so years the speed of these changes has been accelerating. Telecommunication services available at present often have very little to do with sending a voice message along a copper wire between two telephones. On the other hand, although the border between telecommunications and media and information technologies is becoming ever more blurred, about three quarters of revenue from provision of telecommunication services is generated by voice telephony.

When we talk about telecommunications today, we usually mean three different lines of business:

- the public network and its provision
- terminal equipment connected to such a network
- telecommunication services

From the economic point of view, telecommunications has many characteristics that distinguish it not only from other types of economic activities, but also from other network industries (public utilities, sometimes also called natural monopolies). Telecommunications is a multiproduct industry, and its output, with few exceptions, is not storable (production and consumption are simultaneous). Demand is time-varying and stochastic. There exist considerable capacity constraints and sunk costs. In the telecommunications industry we also deal with externalities, both positive and negative; with elements of natural monopoly; and with a complex vertical structure (Mitchell and Vogelsang 1991).

Regardless of how we express the idea of "natural" monopoly, in the case of telecommunications there is no doubt that neither the production and supply of terminal equipment nor the provision of telecommunications services is naturally monopolistic. As far as networks are concerned, traffic on trunk and international lines is much heavier, and this means that once economies of scale in building capacity are exhausted, competition along such routes is likely to be efficient, provided of course that the integrity of the whole network is preserved. There remains, therefore, the problem of fixed-link local networks (local loop); in the case of such networks, if we consider their duplication wasteful, this will imply their naturally monopolistic character. There is, however, no reason why cable television networks, especially if they are already constructed, should not be used for provision of telecommunication services, including voice telephony. This is a matter of regulation, not of availability of appropriate technology. The speed with which new products are introduced to the telecommunications market also depends to a large extent on regulation.

The most important cause of "natural death of natural monopoly," as Naftel (1993) put it, is technological progress in telecommunications.[1] Recent years have witnessed the introduction of fiber optics on an ever larger scale. Cellular (mobile) telephony is undergoing rapid development, and its services are becoming more and more price competitive with respect to services provided on fixed networks. The same may become true for satellite communications. Instead of single public networks, networks of networks are being created, and, of equal importance from the point of view of competition, modern exchanges are electronic and programmable rather than electromagnetic. The latter development makes provision of telecommunication services ever more independent of network operation and ownership. On the other hand, new technological possibilities for the introduction of competition bring with themselves, apart from the necessity to protect competition, new challenges for regulators, particularly in such areas as technical standards, nondiscriminatory access to networks, interconnection, licensing, and, to a lesser extent, tariffs.

Technological progress in telecommunications has rapidly accelerated in the last twenty years, and the centralized, monolithic structure of telecommunications organizations proved to be a bottleneck in making it possible for users to enjoy and exploit all new possibilities. In this sense one can say that technological progress forced liberalization, which, as the example of the

United Kingdom shows clearly, really cannot be complete without privatization and without establishing independent regulatory agencies.

In telecommunications, the mutual relationship between competition (and its protection) and regulation is determined by many different factors. On the one hand, there are the specific economic characteristics of this industry and the tremendous technological progress in this area. On the other, one must not forget the inertia of the inherited structures and the balance of interests that they still represent. Not without importance are politico-economic and social aspects (Wellenius and Stern 1994). Telecommunications networks are for good reason called the "nervous systems" of modern societies, and their strategic importance is beyond doubt. It is also beyond question that some telecommunication services should be provided universally. And lastly, huge amounts of money are at stake. Only after having taken all of this into account, can one try to ask—and answer—the question about how much (and how protected) competition and how much and what kind of regulation should there be.

Yet reducing our problem exclusively to the issue of proportions (how much?) between competition and regulation, regardless of its importance, would certainly be wrong. From a dynamic perspective—in which we are most interested—the relationship between the two phenomena is much more complex and multidimensional, as related concepts show: liberalization (increasing the realm of economic freedom in the telecommunications industry, broadly understood), deregulation (relaxing restrictions to which firms are subject), reregulation (creating new regulatory structures and principles, corresponding to the existence and operation of many enterprises in this industry), not to mention "regulation for competition." The latter includes creating of a level playing field and facilitating new entry into the industry, where new entrants face, especially at the very beginning, a very powerful incumbent.

Deciding the "proportions" between competition and regulation is not likely to be a zero-sum game. Increasing the extent of competition and its intensification may require an initial expansion of the regulatory structures and of the scope of regulation. In other words, in such an industry as telecommunications, competition and regulation are inseparable, even if regulatory activities are limited, as in New Zealand,[2] to antitrust ones. Both economic theory and empirical evidence show that except in special circumstances competition is the most effective mechanism to ensure the efficient use of scarce resources, a broad range of choice for consumers, and innovation. Regulation, for its part, is supposed to remedy market failures, but one must not forget that government failure is also a very realistic possibility. Regulation may be also considered as a tool of public policy toward telecommunications, but the policy itself is by its very nature much more general.

There is no doubt that competition in telecommunications is possible, and even die-hard skeptics cannot say that we should still wait for the results of the experiments started in the early 1980s. The present dimension of the problem of competition rules and regulations in telecommunications is determined by the law actually in force in Poland in general and by the Competition Act of February 24, 1990, from which telecommunications is not exempted, and by the Communications Act of November 23, 1990, both with later amendments, in particular.[3] As we shall see, the extent to which competition is allowed in them is rather limited, the de facto extent of competition even smaller, and the regulatory structures underdeveloped and tainted with conflicts of interests. Nonetheless, competition, as far as it is legally allowed, should be protected, and particular attention should be given to all the opportunities that Telekomunikacja Polska S.A. (Polish Telecom) has to abuse its dominant, de facto monopolistic position. Help can be found, especially taking into account requirements of the Association Agreement, in legislation and decisions of the institutions of the EU, which are also interesting both in themselves and from the point of view of the effect that they have on developments around the world. The future of telecommunications in Poland is relatively open, but it will not start from scratch nor will it develop in a vacuum. The Antimonopoly and Communications Acts are being amended, and every step toward EU membership will pose new challenges in this area.

TELECOMMUNICATIONS IN THE EUROPEAN UNION

From the period of accelerated build-up of the telephone networks, Europe has inherited a fragmented nationally focused telecommunications industrial structure, with national markets largely closed to other member states, not to mention third world countries, and with national industry focused on national network requirements. What was even worse, the priority was given to provision of a very limited number of standard services and types of terminal equipment, mostly, let us repeat, under strict monopoly regimes and mainly on a national basis. The whole rapidly growing sector was in this way withdrawn from the operation of market forces and its self-regulating influence. At the same time it should be noted that the efforts of the Commission of the European Communities throughout the 1970s to open the telecommunications markets, in particular procurement and equipment markets, were unsuccessful up to the end of the decade—mainly because the prevailing opinion in the member states was that the existing structure would be sufficient to attain public service goals. In consequence, telecommunications was one of the three sectors excluded from the application of the 1976 EC directive on the opening of public procurement supply contracts (77/62/EEC).

All of this in turn raised important questions about various bottlenecks, as well as about the cost of "non-Europe." The immediate consequence of the lack of European integration was higher prices for telephone introduction than could otherwise have been achieved, and delayed and nonharmonized introduction of new services. But the longer term price of "non-Europe" was expected to be

much higher. Entering the technological revolution of the 1980s with a fragmented, nationally based structure, telecommunications administrations
(TAs) were unable to gain from the economies of scale, cost-efficiency, and
flexibility which only a pan-European market could offer.

The fundamental changes in basic costs and the newly emerging trend in
world telecommunications initially had little impact on the European industrial scene. It was only in 1984 and 1987 that the EC got its act together and
produced two Green Papers which were supposed to specify challenges and
propose ways of meeting them. Taking the necessary action was made easy
not only by the growing awareness of the importance of telecommunications
but also by certain characteristics of the ongoing changes. For example, the
importance of the "distance" cost factor has fallen compared with the "usage
time" or "connection time" cost factors. Additionally, the cost base of international, and in particular intercontinental traffic, has fallen substantially in
real terms. Last but not least, the cost to the user of terminal equipment has
been declining, and at the same time the level of sophistication has been increasing. In addition, the introduction of digital technology has made it possible for many functions that were previously available only inside the
network to be performed outside the network by increasingly sophisticated
equipment, including PABXs. Modern telecommunication network infrastructure is thus becoming more and more able to carry a broad range of services independent of the network infrastructure operator and provided by
operators outside the network (Noll 1991). Regulatory changes, therefore,
became necessary, and specifying competition rules in telecommunications
was certainly one of the most important tools that the commission could and
did use.

Various legal instruments, available under the Treaty of Rome, were used in
the process. Its provisions are of primary importance in this context because
they set out a comprehensive framework for the EC's telecommunications
policy, and therefore also for its competition policy in telecommunications.
An important role also has been played by case law developed by the European Court of Justice (ECJ) with regard to telecommunications and other sectors. The commission has stated that "it regards the Member States' postal and
telecommunications authorities as commercial undertakings since they supply goods and services for payment" which are subject to the application of
EC competitions law, an opinion confirmed by the ECJ (C-41/83).

LIBERALIZATION BY ISSUING NEW LAWS

The essence of changes in EU telecommunications can be expressed by
using the word "liberalization" (Cranston 1995). It was pursued in two ways.
First, it was introduced by issuing secondary legislation; that is, new laws
were issued concerning various aspects of telecommunications, in particular

provision of telecommunications services, network provision, and terminal equipment. Second, telecommunications was liberalized by applying existing laws, in particular the relevant articles of the Treaty of Rome, an example of which are the judgments of the ECJ.[4]

One of the first actions resulting from the Green Paper was the commission directive on competition in the markets of telecommunications terminal equipment (88/301/EEC). At the same time the council resolution of June 30, 1988, supported the commission proposal to create a telecommunications market by 1992. It invited the commission to pay special attention to the external effects (negotiations with third world countries) in its liberalization efforts.

In June 1990, the commission adopted a directive under Article 90 (3), designed to abolish the exclusive rights granted by the member states in the telecommunications services sector, with the exception of voice telephony (90/388/EEC). This came to be known as the Service Directive. The commission decided that this commission directive will take effect on the day on which the council adopts the so-called ONP Directive. ONP (Open Network Provision) lays down the ground rules for harmonization of the conditions of access to and use of public telecommunication networks, their interfaces, and tariffs. Another directive regarded the application of ONP to leased lines (92/44/EEC).

The final act of telecommunications services liberalization will consist in applying the ONP principles to voice telephony. According to the resolution adopted by the council on June 16, 1993, this will happen on January 1, 1998. A proposal for an appropriate directive was prepared by the commission in May 1993. It was approved in principle and formed the basis of a common position of agreement among member states (COM (92) 247, final), but in 1994 the European Parliament refused to pass it on procedural grounds. Therefore, the legal form of liberalization of this happening is not yet certain.[5]

Strictly connected with liberalization of voice telephony is liberalization of network provision, and it is these issues that the most recent developments regard. On November 17, 1994, the TC accepted the general principle that the provision of all telecommunications infrastructure should be liberalized by January 1, 1998, and on December 21, 1994, the commission adopted a draft Article 90 directive which, if implemented following consultation, would liberalize the use of cable television infrastructure for already liberalized service by January 1, 1996. The Green Paper on the liberalization of telecommunications infrastructure and cable television networks was published: Part I on October 25, 1994; Part II on January 25, 1995 (COM (94) 440, final and 682, final).

As far as ISDN is concerned, Recommendation 86/659/EEC regarded its introduction and contained a timetable. Matters regarding terminal equipment were regulated by Directive 86/361/EEC, amended by Directive 91/263/EEC, which introduced a single approval procedure for the interconnection of terminals to the network.

Directive 83/189/EEC regarded standardization. It laid down a procedure for the provision of information in the field of technical standards and regulations. Recommendation 84/549/EEC regarded the implementation of a common approach in the field of telecommunications, and Decision 87/95/EEC regarded standardization in the field of information technologies (IT) and telecommunications.

Directive 87/372/EEC regarded mobile communications. It reserved certain frequency bands for mobile communications. In 1991, the member states began installing a single standard for GSM. This is replacing the different incompatible systems in force in the EC. The council also adopted Directive 91/287/EEC and Recommendation 91/288/EEC to promote the introduction of DECT (Digital European Cordless Telecommunications) beginning in January 1992. Future development of mobile communications was outlined in the 1994 Green Paper that proposed five main changes:

- abolition of all remaining exclusive or special licensing rights in the sector
- removal of all restrictions on the provision of mobile services across the EU
- full freedom for mobile operators to develop their own infrastructure networks, whether by providing their own or sharing another company's infrastructure
- full freedom to offer combined services via both fixed and mobile networks, which implies the right of independent operators to bid for licenses on the fixed networks
- mutual recognition of standards and equipment type approval, coordination of licensing and award procedures, and the promulgation of pan-European mobile networks[6]

To define a European position on satellite communications, the commission has issued a Green Paper on the "Common Approach to Satellite Communications in the EC" (COM (90) 490). The commission has proposed the following:

- the full liberalization of the earth segment
- unrestricted access to space segment capacity
- harmonization and full commercial freedom for space segment providers

Council Directive 77/62/EEC, which coordinates procedures for public supply contractors was supplemented by a council Recommendation of December 12, 1984, directed at the first phase of opening up access to public telecommunications contracts allowing for the release of 10 percent of the annual value of public procurement contracts in telecommunications. Council Directive 90/531/EEC liberalized the procurement procedures of entities operating in the water, energy, and telecommunications sectors.

From all of this follows one simple conclusion, namely that any attempt to harmonize telecommunications legislation and competition legislation in the field of telecommunications is like trying to hit a moving target, and therefore requires some anticipation of future changes.

LIBERALIZATION THROUGH THE APPLICATION OF EXISTING LAWS

The second way of liberalizing telecommunications in the EU consisted of applying existing laws, and in particular articles of the Treaty of Rome. In this part of the chapter, the most relevant articles as well as the most important decisions and judgments will be summarized. We shall also present the *Guidelines on the Application of the Community Competition Rules in the Telecoms Sector,* which, although not binding, give a good idea of the EC's practice in matters regarding competition rules and regulation in telecommunications.

Although there are no articles of the treaty that apply specifically to telecommunications, the general rules of the treaty apply fully to the telecommunications sector, as was confirmed by the ECJ in 1985 (C-41/83). The most important articles in this context are Articles 59, 85, 86, and 90.

It is clear that throughout the EC established PTOs enjoy dominant positions within the meaning of Article 86. This dominance is largely the result of special and exclusive rights granted by governments in the past, but even where there has already been substantial liberalization (e.g., in the United Kingdom) market dominance persists.[7] As a consequence, competition in most parts of the EC is distorted; for example, access to national telecommunications markets for competing organizations is prevented, and this has an appreciable effect on trade between member states. In the absence of special treatment, therefore, most PTOs would find themselves in constant violation of Article 86.

The legal basis of policies that treat the telecommunications sector as "special" in some way or other derives from Article 90. Member State governments have assigned telecommunications operators the tasks of developing and providing universal networks and services. It can, therefore, be argued that with the introduction of competition some or all of the telecommunications operators would find themselves in positions where, through lack of finance, they would no longer be able to carry out their universal service obligations; and it is on this basis that restrictions on the freedom to provide telecommunications networks or services have been allowed in the past.

Although there seems to exist a general trade-off between universal service obligations and the development of competition in the telecommunications sector, technological advances and expanding markets have tilted the balance of net benefits significantly toward liberalization. As a consequence of these changes in the market, it has become increasingly difficult to justify restrictions of competition on public interest grounds. And maintenance or introduction of any exclusive or special rights that cannot be proven to be in the general public interest are a breach of Article 90 (1) in conjunction with Article 59, or of Article 90 (1) in conjunction with Article 86.

In September 1992, the commission published a communication setting out *Guidelines on the Application of the Community Competition Rules in the Telecoms Sector*, with the aim of clarifying the position to market participants on the basis of previous experience from commission investigations and from ECJ judgements. The guidelines themselves are not legally binding; they only provide an indication of how the authorities might react to a particular situation.

The following are some of the main points of the guidelines:

1. Articles 85 and 86 of the EEC Treaty apply to all companies in the telecommunications sector, whether public or private. In addition, Article 90 (1) of the EEC Treaty prevents governments from forcing such companies to infringe upon the rules contained in Articles 85 and 86. If anticompetitive activities are undertaken voluntarily by a company, the Commission will apply Articles 85 and 86 to prevent such activities. If the anticompetitive activities are imposed by the state authorities, the commission will prevent such an imposition on the basis of Article 90 (1) using its powers under Article 90 (3).

2. In the context of the use of Article 90, the commission claims the right, subject only to the control of the ECJ, to determine the application of the exception clause in Article 90 (2) whereby member states can exempt companies entrusted with the operation of services of general economic interest from the normal rules of competition if it is necessary to do so in order to allow such companies to fulfill their function effectively.

3. In order to assess effects on competition for the purposes of Articles 85 and 86, it is necessary to define the relevant product and geographical market. The guidelines set out some of the principles for determining the relevant market in telecommunications, stressing that changes in technology are likely to render the definition "dynamic and variable."

4. Attention is drawn to cases where EC telecommunications policy seeks to encourage coordinated introduction of particular products and services, such as in the measures for the provision of open networks. It is implied that companies may cooperate to the extent necessary to achieve the aim of introducing new products and services, even if this results in restricting competition. However, any such restrictions must be the minimum necessary in order to achieve the objective, and either they first must be cleared by the commission before implementation or they must be covered by one of the "block-exemption" regulations applying Article 85 (3) of the treaty.

5. Agreements concerning prices will be dealt with especially vigorously. Other generally unacceptable clauses in agreements are those that try to prevent new market entrants, that seek to prevent access to networks, that price such access at unreasonable levels, or that strengthen existing dominant positions.

6. With respect to possible abuses of a dominant position within the meaning of Article 86, the commission is particularly concerned to prevent telecommunications companies with monopoly or protected rights in certain markets from using those positions to compete unfairly in other unprotected and hitherto open markets (i.e., to prevent extensions of market power from one activity to another). Cost transparency is necessary to ensure that unacceptable cross-subsidization is not taking place between protected and open markets. Article 86 can also be applied to companies with a dominant purchasing position (for telecommunications equipment or services) if that position is being abused.

7. It is stressed that the community treaty applies fully to the satellite domain and that restrictions on the ability of third parties to compete would normally render such agreements illegal. If access to distribution of space segment communications facilities is restricted together with direct access to uplink facilities, the commission is likely to consider the overall restriction on competition as unacceptable.

8. International Conventions, such as those emanating from the CCITT or the WATTC, do not necessarily conform with EC rules and should not be followed by companies or member state governments until their compatibility with EC law has been established.

Among the most important decisions in the telecommunications sector are the following:

• British Telecom: The judgment clearly confirmed the commission's view that the competition rules of the treaty apply to TAs. The ruling could therefore be interpreted as a clear signal by the ECJ to allow more competition in this market. It also made clear that the ECJ would favor a narrow interpretation of monopoly rights and would strongly disfavor the extension of a service monopoly as new technologies arise. It is precisely in this direction that subsequent developments have been going.

• Prerogatives of the commission: The judgment in Case 202/88 (*The French Republic* v *Commission*) upheld the commission's right to adopt the directive and its right to adopt important internal market legislation on public service monopolies without formal approval from the EC member states. Similarly, in cases 271/, 281/, 289/ 90 (*Kingdom of Spain, Kingdom of Belgium and Italian Republic* v *Commission of the European Communities*), in a November 1992 ruling, the ECJ once more upheld the validity of the Services Directive, and thus the commission's powers to use Article 90 (3) to legislate on competition matters.

• CEPT and leased circuits: In March 1990, the EC Commission imposed an obligation on the European post and telecommunications authorities to end high surcharges imposed when leasing out telecommunications circuits to private operators.

• Telecom Eireann-Motorola Ireland Ltd: The commission concluded that although the agreement in question contravened Article 85 (1) of the treaty banning anticompetitive agreements and concerted practices, it offered compensating benefits to users by introducing a new paging service that was previously unavailable in Ireland.

• Marketing of terminal equipment: The ECJ ruled that Articles 3(f), 90, and 86 of the EEC Treaty together prevent a member state from giving power to the operator of its public telecommunications network to specify standards for telephone sets when that operator itself competes on the markets for such sets. The ECJ also concluded that Article 30 of the treaty prevents a public telecommunications operator from being given powers to approve telephone sets supplied by other organizations and intended to be connected to the public network if its decisions are not subject to judicial review. The ECJ's decision supported the commission's general view that member states' telecommunications regulatory bodies should be independent from their telecommunications operators.

TELECOMMUNICATIONS IN POLAND

The process of systemic transformation, started in Poland in the summer of 1989, found telecommunications there in a very bad state. As far as penetration rates are concerned, among European countries only Albania had a lower rate than Poland. A similar picture is given by rankings of the share of telecommunications in the GDP and of revenues per main line. An important aspect of the problem is also the quality of service. Not long ago only 20 percent of local telephone calls and 28 percent of long-distance ones were successful on the first dialing. The main cause of this unfortunate state of affairs was the condition of infrastructure.

Since 1989, efforts have been undertaken to improve the state of telecommunications in Poland. The number of lines per 100 inhabitants is now slightly less than fifteen; new digital exchanges are being installed (an intercity digital overlay network containing thirty-seven exchanges has been completed); and optical fiber lines are being constructed. The first cellular telephony company, Centertel, started operating. Unfortunately, it constructed an analog network, the so-called NMP 450, but two licenses for digital GSM networks are to be issued in 1995, and one for DCS 1800 a year later.[8] The first licensed local networks also have been put into operation, although all of them are relatively small (inter alia, Laka, Tyczyn, Swidnik); larger players are, however, preparing their entry (Telekom Pila, Telekom Silesia), including Polish firms like Optimus. Data networks and satellite connections are being developed, and new services are being introduced, such as a national paging system (Stachów 1994, Law 1995).

All in all, it is estimated that telecommunications in Poland lags behind its Western counterparts by about twenty years. Telekomunikacja Polska S.A. has a negative reputation among its customers, and foreign investors consider the state of Polish telecommunications as one of the main obstacles to developing their economic activities in Poland. Telecommunications as a consumer good is absent in practice. On the one hand, there follow from this huge investment requirements. On the other hand, one can safely expect that the telecommunications market will grow very quickly; a technological backwardness creates the possibility of leapfrogging in respect to both being able to introduce the most modern technologies and in respect to restrictions imposed on the market structure.

The Communications Act of 1990, amended in October 1991, and most recently in May 1995, is a step in the right direction, but it has left many things still unclear and unregulated. The most important novelty of the act, apart from the organizational changes, consisted in limiting state monopoly to international traffic. Article 16 (1) says that no permit (license) can be given for "the provision of international telecommunications services to the public. A similar prohibition holds in relation to interurban telecommunications lines, or networks and services providing interurban telecommunications . . . if the applicant is a foreign entity or if more than 49 percent of the shares in the Polish company are held by a foreign entity" (Article 16 [3]). No permit for interurban telecommunications has been issued yet, and both prohibitions will have, because of widespread cross-subsidies, far reaching consequences for the development of competition in Polish telecommunications.

According to the act "activities in the telecommunications field" can be performed by one of the following:

• Telekomunikacja Polska S.A.
• the administrative departments of the Ministry of Defense, Ministry of Internal Affairs, and Ministry of Foreign Affairs (for their own purposes only)
• entities which have been issued a telecommunications permit (the Permit)(Article 6)

The act provides that permits are granted for both "the installation and use of telecommunications facilities, lines, and networks; and for the provision of services over such facilities, lines, and networks" (Article 12).

Telekomunikacja Polska S.A. does not require a permit, but its activities, rights, and obligations are governed by the provisions of the Communications Act and the provisions of its incorporation documents. Since permits are issued by the Minister of Communications who represents the only shareholder (the Treasury, i.e., Minister of Communications, exercises the ownership rights with respect to Telekomunikacja Polska S.A.), and since entities asking for permits will not only complement services provided by Telekomunikacja Polska S.A. but also also want to compete with it, the possibility of a conflict of interest is all too evident, again with all too obvious negative consequences for the development of competition in this area. Will the ministry really be interested in promoting competition, or will it prefer financial benefits from monopolizing the most profitable services? Such an alternative may appear oversimplified, but the problem is a real one.

A similar conflict of interest may appear in the process of type approval (approval certificates are again issued by the Minister of Communications) and price setting ("The Minister of Communications may introduce maximum charges for telecommunications services provided to the public" [Article 39 {3}]). The amendments, currently debated, create a theoretical chance to eliminate at least some of the aforementioned shortcomings.

From the point of view of competition and regulation, of great importance are also the provisions of Article 38, which says that, on the one hand, "the operator of the public telecommunications network cannot refuse connecting to its network another telecommunications network, and on the other that conditions of and charges for interconnections . . . are decided by a contract between the owners of the two networks." Similar contracts are supposed to determine "settlement principles for services, the provision of which requires cooperation of networks and equipments belonging to different telecommunications networks" (Article 39). In both cases, the advantage enjoyed by Telekomunikacja Polska S.A. over new entrants is enormous, and the absence of an independent regulator who would have the right to adjudicate conflicts, as happened in the United Kingdom in the dispute between BT and Mercury (the so-called Interconnection Determination, issued by the Director General of Telecommunications in 1985), creates major obstacles on the road of developing competition.

As we have already mentioned, Telekomunikacja Polska S.A. has a negative reputation among its customers. Prices long ago reached "world levels," especially prices for international connections (and both GDP per capita and labor costs are much lower in Poland!), and subsequent price increases were not supported by any convincing cost calculations. (The efforts of the Antimonopoly Office to get more information failed, and the controversies, repeated every year, are solved in the darkness of ignorance.) Consumers' interests are frequently violated because of low quality of services and ineffective complaints procedures. Itemized billing is still unavailable, and therefore complaints about overcharging are in practice almost impossible to check. The way in which Telekomunikacja Polska S.A. deals with complaints (according to the regulation it itself issued; see Article 36 of the Communications Act) and extra charging for connections (prohibited later on by the Antimonopoly Office) are nothing else but imposing burdensome contract conditions. The number of consumer complaints is still very high, but it is consumers on whom, despite the very high rate of return earned by Telekomunikacja Polska S.A. (about 70% in 1993), the costs of new investment are pushed immediately: the necessity of new investment is supposed to justify price increases.

Telekomunikacja Polska S.A. also is often accused of wastefulness and suffocating competition. The latter has a threefold aspect. First, the tariff structure, despite the Antimonopoly Office's efforts to enforce its rebalancing, still discourages investors from entering those segments of the telecommunications market where getting the permit is relatively easy. Second, in its dealing with small rural operators, as well as all others for that matter, Telekomunikacja Polska S.A. prolongs the negotiation process in order to use this time to connect a few subscribers in the given area, in this way depriving the whole initiative of its financial viability. Third, and in the long run most important, the problem of interconnection has no definitive solution. On February 18, 1994 the ministry issued a document called *Settlement Principles between Telecommunications Operators*. Its legal status is, however, uncertain, because it was issued by the minister in his capacity as owner rather than as regulator. What is more, this document is still rather provisional, and does not provide sufficient guarantees for investors, for whom stability of rules and protection against arbitrariness of actions of Telekomunikacja Polska S.A., not to mention any abuse of its dominant position, is of foremost importance.

All of this also explains why, despite the fact that there have been more than seventy permits issued, so few operators actually started providing services.

It seems that the main causes of this state of affairs are weaknesses of the control (regulatory) mechanisms of Telekomunikacja Polska S.A. On the one hand, various aspects of the Polish telecommunications are regulated by different institutions (the Ministry of Communications, the State Telecommunications Inspectorate, the National Radiocommunications Agency), but on the other hand, most activities of economic regulation are still exercised by the Antimonopoly Office, which in practice, despite acute shortages of personnel, has to deal with issues ranging from consumer complaints to the level and structure of prices. Even though in principle it is possible to turn an appropriately resourced department of the Antimonopoly Office into a telecommunications regulatory agency (just as in the United Kingdom, before OFTEL was established, a similar role was considered for the Office of Fair Trading), it may be more desirable to create an independent regulator, as is envisaged by the new Energy Act currently being prepared in Poland. Such an institution would allow harmonizing activities in the field of telecommunications and increase regulatory expertise, which is particularly important in a situation in which the regulated often enjoys informational advantage over the regulator anyway.

THE FUTURE OF TELECOMMUNICATIONS IN POLAND

I shall end by formulating a few more general suggestions regarding the future telecommunications policy in Poland. Although they do not follow directly from the harmonization requirements (see the last section of this chapter), their implementation may well be very important for developing competitive telecommunications in Poland.

The dynamic development of telecommunications in countries that entered the path of liberalization clearly confirms that their decisions were right. In these countries, diversity and quality of services is increasing, prices are declining, and whole economies benefit. Even though developing effective competition usually takes some time, each and every step in this direction requires a review of regulatory policy.

Generally speaking, there should be as much competition and as little regulation as possible. But symbiosis between government circles and industry is able to survive even the most far-reaching systemic transformation, and this way of formulating the problem can be easily exploited by politicians, who can always find economists and lawyers prepared to justify their interests and prejudices. As far as proportions are concerned, and the exact determination thereof, it would be better after taking account of differences between different sectors of telecommunications to err in favor of liberalization than to end up with an overregulated and insufficiently open market, because in such a case nobody will want to enter it. And an important determinant of the success of both kinds of actions is privatization, and preferably privatization accompanied by procompetitive restructuring. In this way, one also will be able to learn something from the mistakes of pioneers of liberalization.

Do the facts that in Poland both economic and political systems are undergoing a process of systemic transformation; that Polish telecommunications is lagging about twenty years behind its most developed counterparts; and that Poland wants to join the EU modify the previous conclusions, very general as they are? How should principles of competition and regulation, as well as their mutual relationship, look in the Polish telecommunications in the mid-1990s?

If the main objective of changes in the Polish telecommunications is to be, on the one hand, catching up with more developed countries, and, on the other, creating an infrastructure for the twenty-first century, without which infrastructure no steady economic growth or integration with the world economy is possible, then changes should go in two directions. Briefly speaking, one should decisively liberalize, and at the same time the regulatory structures should become formalized and independent. As far as the extent of liberalization is concerned, there is no reason to limit it only and exclusively to the minimum required by the laws of the EU, or, following the example of some member states, to seek the possibility of postponing their implementation, which would be even worse. The EU is restricted both by its decisionmaking processes and the interest group structure of each and every member state. Poland, instead, should do everything to make the best possible use of its backwardness. It should rather try to jump over the technological gap than to try to close it gradually.

The gains from developed and modern telecommunications are potentially enormous. Better flow of information and access to it increases the degree of competition in an economy as a whole. In individual firms it can help to raise economic efficiency and, therefore, the firms' competitiveness, both domestically and internationally. Foreign trade becomes easier, which may result in its growth; and for a country such as Poland international traffic in telecommunications services will certainly improve the balance of payments. A country having at least decent telecommunications will have an advantage in the eyes of foreign investors, not to mention the possibility of using telecommunications to inform them about investment opportunities (databases, etc.). Developing telecommunications as a consumer good also brings with it huge possibilities (and demands from telecommunications policy). Growth of the telecommunications industry will create new jobs while at the same time forcing people taking them up to improve their skills. Together with still lower labor costs, this could create one more instance of comparative advantage in the international division of labor.

Potential gains from developing telecommunications and the extent of Poland's backwardness in this area determine the coordinates within which one decides telecommunications policy in general and competition policy in telecommunications in particular. Will liberalization be a panacea for Polish problems? On the one hand are apparently convincing arguments about the necessity to concentrate resources, which are insufficient anyway, and about the guarantees for foreign investors and banks. Too narrowly understood is the strategic importance of telecommunications, which also seems to support state monopoly, a de facto monopoly in some areas (long-distance telecommunications) and de jure in others (international traffic). On the other hand, it is well known that it is not objective needs but new entry into the industry that really stimulates its expansion and modernization. What is more, fast and far-reaching liberalization certainly is not a zero-sum game. Users doubtless will gain, and nobody will provide services on a charity basis. From the point of view of Telekomunikacja Polska S.A., fast growth of the market itself guarantees that a falling share will not mean any fall in revenue or profits. The adjustment process to the new situation will be painful, but delay is not going to reduce the pain, which sooner or later has to be inflicted. It also makes no sense to decide for investors whether entry is profitable or not. Discretion in issuing permits may be impossible to eliminate completely, but it is important to make it clear to what extent the requests are investigated and according to which criteria the permits are issued. It should be possible to get permits for all kinds of services. Although the EC legislation expresses no preference for any form of ownership, privatization of Telekomunikacja Polska S.A. (at best more than 49% of shares, the sale of which the Communications Act envisages) and establishment of an independent regulatory agency (regulating, among other things, for competition) will remove the existing conflicts of interests and ensure a better balance of consumers' and producers' interests in telecommunications.

CONCLUSIONS *DE LEGE FERENDA*

In order to harmonize the Antimonopoly Act with the legislation of the EU it was necessary to introduce changes or clarifications regarding the following issues:

- prohibition of agreements restricting competition
- prohibition of abusing a dominant position
- control of mergers of economic entities

The amendments to the act enacted in 1995 fulfilled these requirements in principle, in particular with respect to mergers. However, neither the act nor its amendments to it contain anything specific regarding telecommunications, either as such, as a statutory monopoly, or as a de facto monopoly. What is more, the whole harmonization process regarding the type of competition rules and how to apply them to telecommunications goes far beyond antitrust legislation.

From the point of view of the Polish legislators whose task is to harmonize Polish law with that of the EU, clearly the most important are the council and commission directives. They are binding on member states as to the aim to be reached, but leave member states the choice of form and methods for attaining, within the national legal system, the objectives laid down at community level. In a predetermined period of time, directives' provisions must become included in national laws, but directives are no substitute for national laws, nor can they become national laws in the form in which they were issued. In other words, one is interested not in ratification of directives, but in a separate legislative process.

From the diverse nature of the requirements contained in various directives follows (even though not always unequivocally) a diverse array of means through which they are going to be fulfilled. Only some of them imply the necessity of changing the law. The importance of individual provisions is not equal either, which is well illustrated by the Annex to the White Paper on preparation of the associated countries of CEE for integration into the internal market of the EU of May 1995 (COM (95) 163, final). The 1995 White Paper divides the harmonization measures into two stages. In the case of telecommunications, Stage I measures include the following:

1. Equipment
   * Commission Directive 88/301/EEC on competition in the markets for telecommunications terminal equipments
   * Council Directive 86/361/EEC on the initial stage of the mutual recognition of type approval for telecommunications terminal equipment
   * Council Directive 91/263/EEC on the approximation of the laws of the member states concerning telecommunications terminal equipment, including mutual recognition of their conformity

2. Frequency allocation and numbering
   * Council Directive 87/372/EEC on the frequency bands to be reserved for the coordinated introduction of public pan-European cellular digital land-based mobile communications in the EC
   * Council Directive 90/544/EEC on the frequency bands designated for the coordinated introduction of pan-European land-based public radio paging in the EC
   * Council Directive 91/287/EEC on the frequency band to be designated for the coordinated introduction of DECT into the EC
   * Council Decision 91/396/EEC on the introduction of a single European emergency call number
   * Council Decision 92/264/EEC on the introduction of a standard international telephone access code in the EC

3. Competition policy
   * Commission Directive 90/388/EEC on competition in the markets for telecommunications services

- Council Directive 90/387/EEC on the establishment of the internal market for tele-communications services through the implementation of open network provision
- Council Directive 92/44/EEC on the application of open network provision to leased lines

Stage II measures are described in the document in the following way:

As for the legislation already adopted, the Directive 94/46/EC on the liberalisation of the markets for satellite terminals and services should be part of the stage II measures (Category I), because the relevant technical regulations have not been adopted yet in the European Union.

The second category of stage II concerns draft legislation in the field of infrastructure, ONP, mutual recognition of licences for satellite services and data protection, which is likely to be adopted within the next two years (Annex, 263).

Taking into account that we are especially interested in the competition aspect of telecommunications reforms and restructuring, the following issues in particular should attract our attention:

- de jure monopoly of Telekomunikacja Polska S.A. in international traffic
- de facto monopoly of Telekomunikacja Polska S.A. in long-distance traffic and additional conditions with respect to ownership (limitations of the foreign partner(s)'s stake) when issuing such permits
- conflict of interests between the Minister of Communications as the regulator and as the authority exercising ownership rights with respect to the dominant incumbent
- conflict of interests that may appear when the authority exercising ownership rights with respect to the dominant incumbent (i.e., the Minister of Communications) issuing type approval certificates for telecommunications equipment
- the requirement that at least 50 percent of the value of the equipment installed in Poland be produced domestically

The issue of the extent of monopoly rights seems to require that a distinction be made between voice telephony and other telecommunications services (value-added services, data transmission, etc.). Provision of the latter has been totally liberalized in the EU, and, therefore, the monopoly in international traffic in these services would have no justification. What is more, there is no doubt that voice telephony, both domestic and international (at least among the member states of the EU) will be liberalized before Poland joins the EU, which should be accounted for in the new Polish telecommunications laws.

The issue of network provision is more complex. In principle, it is possible to build competitive (local) networks in Poland, even though those already operating are complementary rather than competitive with respect to the network belonging to Telekomunikacja Polska S.A. There do not seem to be any legal problems with cable television companies entering this market, although the fact that Telekomunikacja Polska S.A. is a significant shareholder in Polska Telewizja Kablowa S.A. certainly does not help develop this kind of competition. Perhaps such ownership should be prohibited, at least for an initial period, particularly since Telekomunikacja Polska S.A. has many more pressing priorities. In the situation of excessive fragmentation of the Polish cable television industry, this is the only realistic possibility to counteract abuse of the dominant position by Telekomunikacja Polska S.A. Such a prohibition does not follow from the laws of the EU, even though, for example, in the United Kingdom BT is prohibited from providing entertainment services over its telephone network. Network provision will be liberalized at the same time as provision of voice telephony services, even earlier at existing networks.

However, the very essence of the problem of competitive network provision lies elsewhere, namely, in the way in which permits are issued and in the principles governing their issuance, and, ultimately, in the regulatory structure of Polish telecommunications. The law of the EU explicitly imposes the duty to separate operation from regulation. Taking telecommunications out of the ministry structure, separating it from Poczta Polska, and transforming it into a joint stock company were certainly steps in the right direction, but much still remains to be done in order to remove various conflicts of interests, mentioned earlier, in the activities of the minister. The nature of these conflicts is structural, but years-long links between the ministry and the structures that eventually have taken the form of Telekomunikacja Polska S.A. make the actual situation of entities wanting to enter the market even more difficult.

In order to fulfill the requirements of the EU, an independent regulatory agency for telecommunications should be created, and among its tasks should be

- issuing permits (Telekomunikacja Polska S.A. should also operate on the basis of such a permit)
- price and quality control, for a transitory and possibly quite short period
- adjudicating conflicts between operators, especially conflicts regarding principles of interconnection and settlement agreements
- type approval of telecommunications equipment

When such a body is created, its mutual relationships with the Antimonopoly Office should be clarified.

Finally, there remains the problem regarding the borderline between telecommunications and public procurement, namely the issue of supplying terminal equipment. In this area one first will have to introduce—and the earlier, the better—European standards gradually; and, secondly, any limitations regarding the value of equipment produced domestically will have to be dropped.

NOTES

1. For a not too technical discussion of telecommunication technology, see Noll (1991).

2. For a brief summary of the unique New Zealand experience, see Donaldson (1994).

3. For a commentary on the Polish antitrust law, see Gronowski (1994) and Skoczny (1995), and for an in-depth analysis of cases, Skoczny (1994).

4. The most complete overview can be found in Mosteshar (1993), but one has to remember that the situation changes continuously; see, for example, *Telecoms Markets*, various issues.

5. Operators from countries outside the EU will not be allowed to participate fully in the newly liberalized market *unless there was comparable access to the countries' markets*.

6. Of particular importance is the right to self-provide infrastructure, as it is estimated that cellular network operators hand over between 15 and 25 percent of their subscriber revenues to fixed network operators as payment for leased lines. The right to directly interconnect operators' networks in different countries would also result in significant saving for network operators, as they would no longer have to pay the high international charges levied by a fixed-network operator (Cranston 1995).

7. According to *The UK Telecommunications Industry: Market Information* (published by OFTEL in February 1995), although the first competitor was given a license in 1982 and the 1991 Duopoly Review further removed barriers to competition, BT, in terms of PSTN retail call minutes, still controls 91.2 percent of the market. Other criteria give similar results.

8. Contestants will have to be 51 percent Polish, which is a serious limitation and as such would be contrary to the EU law.

REFERENCES

Cranston, Richard. 1995. *Liberalising Telecommunications in Western Europe*. A Financial Times Management Report, Financial Times Telecoms and Media Publishing, London.

Donaldson, Hunter. 1994. "Telecommunications Liberalisation and Privatisation: The New Zealand Experience." In *Implementing Reforms in the Telecommunications Sector. Lessons from Experience,* edited by Bjorn Wellenius and Peter A. Stern, 253–260. Washington, D.C.: World Bank Regional and Sectoral Studies, The World Bank.

Gronowski, Stanislaw. 1994. *Ustawa o przeciwdzia laniu praktykom monopolistycznym*. Warszawa: Wydawnictwo Zrzeszenia Prawników Polskich.

Law, Carl Edgar. 1995. *Telecommunications in Eastern Europe and the CIS: Market and Prospects to 2000*. London: Financial Times Telecommunications and Media Publishing.

Mitchell, Bridger M., and Ingo Vogelsang. 1991. *Telecommunications Pricing. Theory and Practice*. Cambridge: Cambridge University Press.

Mosteshar, Sa'id. 1993. *European Community Telecommunications Regulation*. London: Graham and Trotman.

Naftel, James Mark. 1993. "The Natural Death of a Natural Monopoly: Competition in EC Telecommunications after the Telecommunications Terminals Judgement." *European Competition Law Review* 3: 105–113.

Noll, A. Michael. 1991. *Introduction to Telephones & Telephone Systems*, 2nd ed. Boston, London: Artech House.

Skoczny, Tadeusz. 1994. *Przeciwdzialanie praktykom monopolistycznym w swietle orzecznictwa*. Warszawa: Dom Wydawniczy ELIPSA. (English translation: *Polish Antimonopoly Case Law*. Warszawa: Dom Wydawniczy ELIPSA. 1995).

Skoczny, Tadeusz. 1995. *Prawo konkurencji*. Warszawa: C. H. Beck.

Stachow, Leszek. 1994. *Regulatory Oversight of Polish Telecommunications*, mimeo.

Wellenius, Bjorn, and Peter A. Stern, eds. 1994. *Implementing Reforms in the Telecommunications Sector. Lessons from Experience*. Washington D.C.: World Bank Regional and Sectoral Studies, The World Bank.

PRIVATIZATION, MARKET LIBERALIZATION, AND REGULATORY REFORM IN THE MEXICAN TELECOMMUNICATIONS SYSTEM

11

Lilia Pérez Chavolla and Rohan Samarajiva

Telecommunication networks are seen today as crucial elements of infrastructure which enable countries and regions to participate in global economic processes. In addition, governments emphasize the value of telecommunications for development of the domestic economy and national integration. Pressure to improve the functioning of these traditionally inefficient systems has come from domestic and foreign business enterprises, the middle class, and international agencies such as the World Bank.

Historically, most countries, with the exceptions of the United States, Canada, and a few others, have had government-owned and -controlled telecommunications monopolies because they were considered to be "natural monopolies," strategic elements of the national economic infrastructure vital to national security. The national security argument also provided justification for the exclusion, or at least the limitation, of foreign investment in national telecommunications systems. State monopoly arrangements, however, have been questioned because of chronic problems in meeting demand and improving quality of service. A further challenge has been posed by potential competitors eager to provide services that the monopoly could not or would not provide. These pressures, together with movement toward a global economy and the recognition of the pivotal role of telecommunications, have compelled many governments to reform their telecommunications systems. Institutional reform has been accomplished through initiatives that allowed varying degrees of competition in previously monopolized telecommunications sectors, the establishment of regulatory agencies separate from the Public Telecommunication Organizations (PTOs), corporatization, and, in some cases, the privatization of government-owned and -controlled PTOs.

In Mexico, the most prominent institutional reform took the form of a massive privatization that included relaxation of foreign investment restrictions, allowing up to 100 percent foreign ownership in enhanced telecommunications services, and up to 49 percent foreign investment and partnership in the provision of basic telephone services, provided that Mexican citizens own the remaining 51 percent (Ley de Inversión Extranjera 1994, chapter 3, article 7). Changes in the form of regulation, including a timetable for opening different market segments to competition and the setting of performance targets and their enforcement, have received less attention but are of significance.

In this chapter, we describe the institutional reform of Mexico's public telephone network, including the privatization of Teléfonos de México (Telmex) and the Mexican government's efforts to exercise control through means other than direct ownership. We also outline the future challenges that the government will face in establishing a competitive environment that supports the development of the Mexican telecommunications system. The lessons that may be drawn from Mexico's experience are discussed as well.

INSTITUTIONAL REFORM

The historical development of the Mexican wire-line telecommunications network provides an interesting background for the recent institutional reform. Mexico's network has passed through a range of ownership arrangements since the introduction of telephony in 1878. It was foreign-owned until 1950, when the government began to Mexicanize the company. In 1972, the government acquired majority ownership of Telmex, control that remained in its hands until 1990, when controlling ownership passed to a "trust" of Mexican and foreign investors.

The decision to allow foreign ownership in this strategic sector was part of an about-face in policy regarding foreign investment. During the 1970s, under President Luis Echeverría Alvarez, Mexico was a leader among developing countries promoting the New International Economic Order (NIEO) platform, which placed great weight on national ownership. By contrast, in the 1980s, during the De la Madrid and Salinas administrations, Mexico led the way in relaxing foreign direct investment restrictions, including those affecting telecommunications. Mexico has even taken the lead within the North American region with respect to telecommunications. While Canada and the

United States have limited foreign investment to 20 and 25 percent (in indirect investment in a parent or holding company), respectively, Mexico has set the limit at 49 percent for basic telephone services and has no restrictions on enhanced services.

President Salinas's rhetoric suggests that he saw modernization of the infrastructure and integration into the global economy as essential to the preservation and strengthening of Mexico's national sovereignty. This is evident in the Salinas administration's National Development Plan, which stated that

[The world] transformations affect us directly. We cannot evade their impact. To suppose that would be like inviting one to impose the change on us, to suffer its negative effects and to lose the opportunity to take advantage of its potential benefits. Let us not fool ourselves, in today's world the challenge to the sovereignty of nations is formidable (Salinas, 1989 32 [author's translation from Spanish]).

On one hand, Salinas justified the privatization of Telmex on grounds of inefficiencies and slow growth caused by lack of resources (Salinas 1990, 2–3). The modernization of Telmex was said to require an investment of more than US$10 billion, only 70 percent of which, according to Caso Lombardo, then Secretary of Communications, could be raised from internal investment, thus requiring foreign private investment to fulfill the modernization goal (SCT, 1991, 19). On the other hand, Telmex's privatization was announced as a part of President Salinas's modernization strategy (Teléfonos de México 1991). As Salinas stated during his presidential campaign, "telecommunications [would] become the cornerstone of [the] program to modernize Mexico's economy" (cited in Székely 1989, 81).

Salinas announced the decision to privatize Telmex on September 18, 1989, at the National Convention of the Telephone Workers' Union (STRM). He stated that the privatization would (1) guarantee government oversight of telecommunications; (2) improve quality of service; (3) guarantee employees' rights and give them equity participation in the company; (4) expand the telephone system; (5) engage in research and development to strengthen Mexican sovereignty; and (6) keep Telmex under Mexican majority control (Salinas 1990, 3–4). In order to prepare Telmex for privatization, the Ministry of Finance pushed aside the Telecommunications Ministry, which traditionally exercised oversight over Telmex by naming Pedro Aspe (a close Salinas ally) as chairman of the Telmex board, replacing the secretary of communications in October 1989 (Business International Corporation 1990, 44).

The Reglamento de Telecomunicaciones (Telecommunications Regulation) was proclaimed in October 1990, and Telmex's Concession Title (the legal document specifying the terms and conditions of the company's monopoly status) was modified in December of that year. The Reglamento, issued under the Communication Law of 1989, allowed the government to (a) regulate new technologies not specified in the Communication Law, (b) maintain oversight of the telecommunications sector by clarifying the regulatory capabilities of the Secretariat of Communications, and (c) retain exclusive ownership of telegraph and satellite systems (however, in 1995, the Zedillo administration announced its intention to privatize the satellite system). The Reglamento also established a regulatory framework for all telecommunications businesses in Mexico, defining the rules for the establishment, maintenance, and operation of telecommunication networks, and for the provision of services; specifying the services requiring licenses or permits; and establishing rules for tariff-setting and sanctions (SCT 1990).

The Concession Title affects the entire telecommunications sector because of Telmex's dominant position. The SCT stated that the Concession Title was being modified to ensure "technological development, to ensure that Telmex fulfills its commitments of expansion, quality, and pricing for its services, as well as to promote equal competition with other telecommunication enterprises, so that it favors improvements in the services demanded by the subscribers" (SCT December 10, 1990, 15). The modified Concession Title retained the administration and control of the company for Mexican citizens and allowed minority participation by foreign enterprises, provided they renounce the right to request any diplomatic intervention from their countries of origin (this is a reiteration of a constitutional provision known as the Calvo Clause). According to the new Concession Title, Telmex would enjoy a monopoly over basic local telephone service until 2026 and over long-distance services through 1996. Rural radiotelephony services also were included as part of the basic-services monopoly of Telmex. The Concession Title allows Telmex to compete in the provision of cellular and radiocommunication services, but it also requires Telmex to allow interconnection by competitors and prohibits the provision of television broadcasting services to the public. However, in June 1995, the Federal Competition Commission authorized Telmex to buy a 49 percent interest in Televisa's cable network, Cablevision, and, thus, to engage in the supply of cable services, subject to allowing other cable companies to use its lines.

The Concession Title establishes specific performance criteria and deadlines (see Table 11.1). The government reserved the right to advance the introduction of competition if the specified expansion and efficiency goals were not met and established penalties for noncompliance. In this way, the government indicated its interest in influencing Telmex's performance even after privatization. According to Caso Lombardo, then secretary of communications, the modified Concession Title was "the result of the balancing of expansion and quality goals and incentives and guarantees for investment" (SCT 1991, 16).

Two financial measures that paved the way to privatization deserve attention. First, Telmex changed its pricing structure to ostensibly eliminate cross-subsidies and distortions. Second, Telmex modified its capital structure. In

Table 11.1
Expansion and Quality Goals of the Concession Title

EXPANSION GOALS	QUALITY GOALS
Expansion of public network by 12 percent per annum for the first 5 years	Decrease in percentage of faulty lines from 1.5 to 0.5 by 1994
Increase of public telephones to a minimum of 100,000 by 1994. Increase to 2 public telephones per 1,000 inhabitants by 1994, and to 5 telephones per 1,000 by 1998	Decrease in number of faulty lines for a period of more than 3 days from 1 per 200 to 1 per 1,000
Supply of rural telephone service to 10,000 steelements above 500 inhabitants by 1994	99 percent of lines repaired in less than 3 days by 1991
Commercial service growth at an annual 15 percent rate and residential service at a 10 percent rate	Increase in the percentage of calls answered by an operator within less than 10 seconds of the first ring to 90 percent by 1991 and 91 percent by 1992
Commitment to introduce technological advancements to diversify services, improve quality, and reduce costs	50 percent of faulty lines repaired on the same day by 1990
Commitment to satisfy any application for basic telephone serviece in cities with automatic switching and more than 5,000 inhabitants, within no more than six months by 1995, and within no more than a month by 2000	Implementation of verifiable, quantifiable, and internationally comparable quality control and efficiency indicators
Digitalization of 8,500 kilometers of the microwave network. By 1994 at least 50 percent of the local exchange and 65 percent of long distance exchanges should become digital	Engagement in industrial and technological research to increase Telmex's and Mexico's competitiveness in telecommunications and foster Mexico's self-sufficiency in these services
Installation of 3,000 kilometers of fiber optic cable and of a network of 14 stations for satellite communication	Commitment to train Telmex's personnel to support the company's modernization process

Sources: F. Caso Lombardo (1990) "Desincorporación de Teléfonos de México (Teléfonos de México divestiture)," *Restaurador 22 de abril* 10(25): 11–14; SCT, "Modificación al Título de Concesión de Teléfonos de México (Modification to the Concession Title of Teléfonos de México)," *Diario Oficial de la Federación,* December 10, 1990, 22–26; SCT, *La reforma del Estado y la desincorporación de Teléfonos de México: Comparecencia del C. Secretario de Comunicaciones y Transportes ante comisiones de la Cámara de Diputados (The State Reform and the Divestiture of Teléfonos de México: Speech of the Secretary of Communication and Transportation to Commissions of the Congress)* (Mexico City: SCT, 1991), 18–20; Teléfonos de México, *Información sobre Teléfonos de México, S.A. de C.V.* (Information about Teléfonos de México S.A. de C.V.), unpublished manuscript (Mexico: Subdirección General de Comunicación y Relaciones Públicas, 1993).

early 1990, prior to privatization, international long-distance rates were cut by 40 percent, local long-distance rates were raised by as much as 100 percent, and local calls above a specified monthly maximum became subject to charge (Mexico Service June 20, 1990, 6). Local rates increased by 620 percent. The result was a 126.54 percent profit increase for Telmex in 1990 (Petrazzini 1993, 194). In December 1990, shortly before the transfer of control, the government authorized another rate increase, which brought prices in Mexico up to U.S. levels (Ramamurti 1994, 6). In this way, Telmex was made more attractive to prospective foreign and domestic buyers. At the same time, the government eliminated the telephone sales tax. Telmex now has to pay 29 percent of its net profits in taxes; this payment, however, can be avoided by reinvestment. According to a World Bank report, this price and tax reform increased the current value of Telmex by US$15 billion (Ramamurti 1994, 7).

On June 15, 1990, Telmex's shareholders agreed to modify the company's equity structure to reduce the amount of shares necessary for effective control. At the beginning of 1990, the government owned 56 percent of Telmex's total equity, representing the totality of Telmex's AA shares, while the remaining 44 percent, in the form of A shares, was owned by domestic and foreign private investors. Five percent of the government's AA shares was converted to A shares, so that by June 1990 AA shares constituted 51 percent of the total and A shares 49 percent. Telmex's capital was increased by means of a stock dividend, whereby a new type of shares, called "L" shares, with limited voting capabilities was created. The L shareholders can vote only on the following three matters: changes in the company's line of business, merger with another company, and withdrawal of the company from the Mexican stock exchange. The last two items are particularly interesting, in that they provide a barrier to the acquisition of Telmex by an outside company or a private leveraged buyout (Galal et al. 1994, 455). For each A or AA share, 1.5 L shares were created. In this way, the 51 percent of AA shares held by the government was changed to 20.4 percent of the new total equity. The AA shares, representing the government's controlling interest, were then made available for purchase solely by Mexicans or by trusts with at least 51 percent Mexican ownership (Ramamurti 1993, 59). Because of the complicated new equity structure, Mexican members of a trust were required to buy only 10.4 percent of Telmex to gain 51 percent majority control over the AA voting shares of the company (see Figures 11.1 and 11.2).

Foreigners were not allowed to own more than 49 percent of AA shares, and no individual foreign investor could hold more than a 10 percent interest in Telmex's controlling shares, either directly or indirectly. In addition, foreign and domestic AA shareholders had to vote together. To attract foreign investors, the government eliminated income tax on dividends and capital gains and restrictions on the repatriation of profits and capital (Ramamurti 1993, 59). A ruling of the National Commission of Foreign Investment allowed L and A shares to

Figure 11.1
Telmex's Ownership Distribution

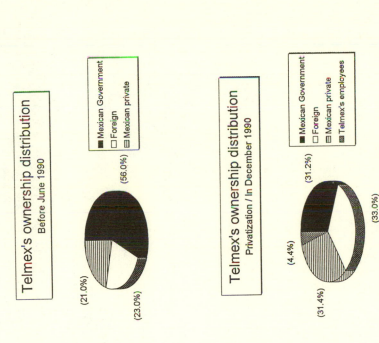

Telmex's ownership distribution
Before June 1990

(21.0%)

(23.0%)   (56.0%)

Legend: ■ Mexican Government   □ Foreign   ▦ Mexican private

Telmex's ownership distribution
Privatization / In December 1990

(4.4%)   (31.2%)

(31.4%)   (33.0%)

Legend: ■ Mexican Government   □ Foreign   ▤ Mexican private   ▦ Telmex's employees

Telmex's ownership distribution

	Share	%	Subtotal
PRE-PRIVATIZATION Before June 1990			
Mexican Government	AA	56	55
Foreign	A	23	23
Mexican private	A	21	21
Total		**100**	**100**
PRIVATIZATION In December 1990 (After a 150% increase of capital)			
Mexican Government	A	0.24	31.2
	L	30.96	
Foreign	AA	10.00	33.0
	A	9.20	
	L	13.80	
Mexican private	AA	10.40	31.4
	A	8.40	
	L	12.60	
Telmex's employees	A	1.76	4.4
Union employees	L	1.24	
Other employees' trust	L	1.40	
Total		**100**	**100**

Sources: Teléfonos de México, Oferta pública secundaria de 100 millones de acciones serie "L" de Teléfonos de México S.A. de C.V. (Secondary public offer of 100 million "L" shares of Teléfonos de México S.A. de C.V.) (Mexico City: Comisión Nacional de Valores, 1991), 210–211; Teléfonos de México, *Programa de inversiones 1994 (1994 Investment Program)* (Mexico City: Subdirección General de Comunicación y Relaciones Públicas, 1995).

Figure 11.2
Telmex's Capital Distribution

Telmex's capital distribution

	AA	A	L	Total
Before June 1990	56	44	0	100
In December 1990	20.4	19.6	60	100

Telmex's capital distribution in December 1990

Group	AA	A	L	Total
Grupo Carso	10.4	0	0	10.4
SBC International Holdings	5	0	0	5
France Cables et Radio	5	0	0	5
Mexican government	0	0.24	30.96	31.2
Foreign investors	0	9.2	13.8	23
National investors	0	8.4	12.6	21
Telmex's Union/other empl.	0	1.76	2.64	4.4
Total	20.4	19.6	60	100

*With option to buy 5% of L shares

Telmex's capital distribution in April 1995

Group	Type of shares	Percentage
Carso, SBC, France Cables et Radio	AA	20.4
SBC International Holdings	L	5
Mexican Government		0
Telmex's Union employees	A, L	0.3
Other employees' trust	L	0.3
National and foreign investors	L	74
Total		100

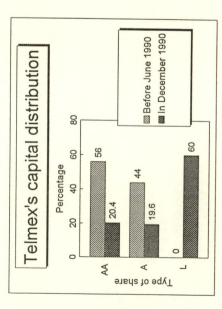

Telmex's capital distribution

Sources: Teléfonos de México, *Oferta pública secundaria de 100 millones de acciones serie "L" de Teléfonos de México S.A. de C.V.* (Secondary public offer of 100 million "L" shares of Teléfonos de México S.A. de C.V.) (Mexico City: Comisión Nacional de Valores, 1991), 210–211; Teléfonos de México, *Programa de inversiones 1994* (*1994 Investment Program*) (Mexico City: Subdirección General de Comunicación y Relaciones Públicas, 1995).

be excluded from the 49 percent limit of foreign investment (Teléfonos de Mexico, 1991, 53). Telmex's employees were granted 4.4 percent of the company's shares.

On December 13, 1990, Telmex was sold to a trust comprising Grupo Carso (a mining, manufacturing, and tobacco conglomerate headed by Carlos Slim Helú) and two foreign telephone companies, SBC International Holdings (a subsidiary of the U.S. regional telephone holding company, Southwestern Bell, providing telephone service in Arkansas, Kansas, Missouri, Oklahoma, and Texas and engaged in a range of related and unrelated businesses) and France Cables et Radio (a subsidiary of France Telecom Inc., the government-owned monopoly). The trust won the auction with an offer of US$1,757.6 million, outbidding a consortium made up of Acciones y Valores (a Mexico City investment house), GTE Corp. (based in Stamford, Connecticut), and Telefónica de Espana S.A. of Spain, which offered US$1,687.2 million. The consortium paid US$609.8 million above the December 1988 market value of Telmex (Kim 1992, 139).

Different members of the winning trust were responsible for different strategic activities in Telmex. SBC would assist Telmex with network maintenance, customer service, billing, Yellow Pages, and office procedures. France Telecom would provide its expertise in network planning, as well as in the installation of long-distance and credit card phones. Grupo Carso was in charge of general administration and of government and labor relations (Luxner 1992). The Concession Title required that Telmex's administrative control and management remain in the hands of Mexican shareholders.

In June 1991, 16.5 percent of the government's L shares were placed in national and international markets. The sale yielded US$2.27 billion. In May 1992, the government sold another 500 million L shares (4.7 percent of the total) in a public offering and earned US$1.35 billion (Petrazzini 1993, 201–202). Upon completion of these sales, the government held only 4.8 percent of Telmex. By April 1995, the government and Telmex's employees had reduced their holdings to 0.0 and 0.6 percent, respectively. On January 1, 2001, each L share may be exchanged at the option of the holder thereof for one AA share, provided that the holder or purchaser is a Mexican or a trust with a majority of Mexican participation, among other restrictions (Teléfonos de México, 1991, 53).

The Telmex privatization served multiple purposes. Based on interviews with key actors, Ramamurti (1994, 3) states that the Telmex privatization was intended to serve as a signal of the shift in government policy toward foreign investment and of the attractiveness of Mexican investments. It was to exemplify the Salinas administration's transformation of Mexico from an inward-looking, state-dominated, protected economy to an outward-looking, privatized, open economy that would take advantage of its proximity to a large, rich neighbor. Ramamurti attributes the selection of Telmex as one of the first state enterprises to be made available for foreign investment to three factors. First, Telmex was a big, profitable company, with enormous growth potential. Second, the privatization could be effected quickly, because telephone services were not constitutionally reserved to the government or to Mexicans, as was the case with the oil industry. Third, Salinas' participation in Telmex's board of directors during the De la Madrid administration gave him first-hand knowledge of the company.

The 1994 Foreign Investment Law formalized the liberalization of value-added services while keeping satellite communications as an activity reserved for government and limiting foreign investment in basic telephone services to 49 percent. Under the NAFTA and the new Foreign Investment Law, the establishment, acquisition, expansion, administration, management, or operation of a foreign-owned firm in any of the three countries cannot be subject to performance criteria such as national content and level of export, other than those intended to fulfill health, security, or environmental requirements. It must be noted that the performance criteria written into the Telmex Concession Title derive from its monopoly, and not from the fact of foreign ownership.

The Concession Title and its criteria provided a clearer regulatory basis that allowed the new owners to know in advance what was expected from them in the short and medium term. By 1994, three years after privatization, Telmex had fulfilled and in some cases surpassed several of the goals in the Concession Title, particularly those related to network expansion and rural telephony (see Table 11. 2). One goal that was not met was quality of service. During the first three years of private operation, Telmex reorganized installation and repair operations, opened 36 new maintenance centers for a total of 186, and reduced the wait for connections and the time required to repair faulty lines. It expanded operator–information services and introduced automatic systems in 288 customer service offices. Nevertheless, service disruptions continued, because of the obsolescence of a great portion of the company's outside plant. Targets for calls answered by an operator in less than ten seconds were not met in 1991 and 1992, and neither was the target for reducing faulty lines. As a result, Telmex had to pay rebates to some customers in 1992 (SEC Online 1993, 11). Complaints by customers have risen because of higher expectations under a privatized Telmex (Ramamurti 1994).

The privatized Telmex has improved financial performance by improving asset deployment and changing inventory-management and purchasing procedures. For example, Telmex has benefited from diversifying suppliers and forcing them to reduce prices. In 1994, AT&T was the third biggest Telmex supplier, after Ericsson de Mexico and Alcatel de Mexico, and the primary supplier of fiber-optic cable (MacDonald 1994, 66). Productivity has been increased by reducing the number of employees per telephone line, even though Telmex's Concession Title does not require it. The number of employees per 1,000 lines decreased from 9.6 in 1990 to 6.6 in 1993 (Teléfonos de México 1994).

Table 11.2
Telmex's Performance (1991–1994)

Performance Goal	December 1990	December 1993	December 1994	Increase 1993-1994 (%)
Lines in service	5,189,802	7,621,000	8,582,000	12.61
Rural communities served	10,221	18,236	20,732	13.69
Public phone booths in service	83,110	177,110	205,110	15.81
Percentage of digitalization achieved	29	68.42	80.37	17.47
Kilometers of fiber optic cable for long-distance installed	0	8,701	18,301	110.33
Integrated digital network exchanges installed	83,000	218,635	280,007	28.07
Digital traffic centers in Mexico	0	39	Concluded	
Kilometers of submarine fiber optic cable (Columbus II)			12,200	

Source: Teléfonos de México, *Programa de inversiones 1994 (1994 Investment Program)* (Mexico City: Subdirección General de Comunicación y Relaciones Públicas, 1995).

In contrast to the highly specific expansion, productivity, and quality goals, the Concession Title's mandate to engage in research and foster Mexico's self-sufficiency in telecommunications includes no measures or deadlines. This may be interpreted as an element of nationalist rhetoric addressing the concerns of groups within Mexico still attached to the objectives of national self-sufficiency so popular in the 1970s. The complex rules regarding percentages of foreign ownership and voting rules have preserved Mexican control over controlling shares; however, the SCT has no direct control over the nationality of the owners of shares traded in the New York and Mexican stock exchanges. As shown in Figure 11.2, the amount of L shares freely exchanged in these stock exchanges represents 74 percent of Telmex's capital. The lack of specific enforcement mechanisms suggests that the foreign ownership rules were crafted as part of the nationalist rhetoric and not as truly central elements of policy.

FUTURE CHALLENGES

Telmex faces two main challenges: the economic crisis triggered by the peso devaluation on December 20, 1994; and accelerated introduction of competition. The devaluation has had mixed effects on Telmex. On the one hand, Telmex lost about US$760 million (4.4 billion new pesos at the January 1995 conversion rate), solely because of the change in foreign exchange rates;

1995 conversion rate), solely because of the change in foreign exchange rates; its foreign currency debt, which at the end of 1994 reached US$2.05 billion, has been boosted; the company's stock price dropped by more than 30 percent by February 1995 (Collier 1995), and its growth will be slowed by reductions in investment from a level of US$2.1 billion in 1994 to US$1.3 billion in 1995 (Langfield 1995). On the other hand, the revenue for long-distance calls will increase Telmex's income. The company gets about 25 percent of its revenue from such calls, which now will be paid in stronger dollars ("Investors Ponder" 1995). As for the decrease in investment, Telmex explained in a report to the Mexican Stock Exchange that "it is not necessary to continue investing in order to meet the requirements of the concession. Investment will hence be directed mainly by economic and market considerations . . . [with] more investment in systems and necessary support for the introduction of new services" (Langfield 1995).

The economic crisis also affected the terms of competition. President Ernesto Zedillo's emergency economic plan includes a proposal to immediately open competition in local phone services and allows auctioning of the radio spectrum and the privatization of the state-owned satellite system ("President Ernesto Zedillo" 1995). Regulations for long-distance competition have been delayed, apparently to give the Communication Ministry time to adjust to the changed political and economic circumstances, including the transition from the Salinas administration to that of Zedillo and the peso crisis. According to Robert Hulme, an analyst for the Mexican finance group Grupo Financiero Serfin, "the new regulations will show how much competition the government really wants to have . . . Many people take it as a test case . . . a face-off between free trade and political power" (Collier 1995).

The regulations are expected to specify the number of competitors, entry fees, parameters for interconnection fees, and conditions for providing long-distance services. In July 1994, the SCT announced an outline for long-distance regulation, wherein Telmex is required to interconnect new entrants to its local networks in 60 of the country's largest cities (50 more than what was announced in 1993) by August 1996, and in 200 cities by 1999 ("Mexico Finalises" 1995). The SCT also stated that interconnection fees would be cost-based and negotiated between Telmex, SCT, and the new operators. Telmex wants new entrants to provide mandatory local service. According to Slim Helú, competitors should not be allowed to target only the big cities and "skim the cream" (Torres 1994).

Even without the regulations, the playing field for competition already is being prepared. Several foreign telephone and manufacturing companies are establishing strategic alliances and joint ventures with Mexican partners for the provision of long-distance services or for providing value-added services in the near future (see Table 11.3). Contrary to expectations, AT&T allied itself with Grupo Alfa, instead of Telmex, in November 1994. It should be noted that

Table 11.3
Mexican–Foreign Joint Ventures Positioned to Compete with Telmex (as of December 1994)

Date	National Group	International Partner	Services to be provided
Feb. 1992	Protexa (cellular licensee for Mexican border region)	Motorola	NA
Oct. 1993	Iusacell	Bell Atlantic (42 percent interest in Iusacell)	Value-added services, and fixed wireless services
1994	Grupo Domos (conglomerate with interests in tobacco and industry)	Bell South	Value-added services, pending long-distance deal
Jan. 1994	GF Banamex-Accival (Banacci)(banking and financial services) (55 percent in joint venture)	MCI (45 percent in joint venture)	Value-added and long-distance services to high-volume businesses, construction of a fiber optic network between Mexico City, Guadalajara and Monterrey, with a planned investment of US $650 million
June 1994	Protexa	Motorola	Long-distance service and cellular service in border region
June 1994	Grupo Pulsar (with interest industry, finance and textiles)	Ionica (Great Britain)	Wireless and local services. No interest in long-distance services stated
July 1994	Iusacell	Sprint	Local and residential services joining venture (negotiations terminated)
Sept. 1994	GF Bancomer/ Valores Insutriales (VISA) (financial and banking)	GTE Telephone Operations	Telephone services for high-volume businesses
Nov. 1994	Grupo Industrial Alfa (with interests in steel, food and petrochemicals, and strategic alliances with 15 TNCs) 51 percent interest	AT&T (49 percent interest)	Joint venture for the provision of long-distance services for business and residential sectors.

Sources: Bardacke, "Tough Times for Telmex as Mexico Prepares to Open Market," *Financial Times*, November 17, 1994, 28; "Telmex Looks to North as Competitor Moves in Mexican Firm," *Dallas Morning News,* November 12, 1994, 1F; "Mexico Finalises Competition Plans, as U.S. Entrants Line Up, *FinTech Telecom Markets,* January 19, 1995.

his financial group, Grupo Financiero Inbursa, Slim Helú has held 15 percent of Alfa's stock in recent years (Bardacke 1994). A month after the announcement of AT&T and Alfa's alliance, Telmex announced its alliance with Sprint.

According to analysts of Baring Securities, the Mexican long-distance market is expected to produce revenues of US$20 billion by the end of the 1990s. Competitors are expected to gain as much as 20 percent of the market in the first year alone. The impact on Telmex will be softened by the growth of the long-distance market, expected to be at least 12 percent annually (Bardacke 1994). In addition, Telmex will have new sources of income from interconnection charges and through a gateway agreement between Mexico and the United States governing the distributions of calls among carriers. This agreement, effective in 1997, provides that incoming traffic between Mexico and the United States will be distributed in the same proportion as outgoing traffic ("Mexico Finalises" 1995; Bardacke 1994, 28). The new environment may force a redefinition of the government–Telmex relationship. In November 1994, Slim Helú told the *Wall Street Journal* that Telmex "would take distinct actions, formal actions" if the terms of the Title Concession are violated (Torres 1994).

LESSONS FROM MEXICO

Changes in the global political economy and government policy on how Mexico should respond to those changes led to a still ongoing process of institutional reform of the Mexican telecommunications system. The government sought to increase investment in telecommunication while also communicating a larger message of openness to foreign investors in all sectors. The reforms replaced direct government control in the telecommunications sector with a regulatory regime based on performance and gradual loss of monopoly status for the dominant carrier, and greater freedom of action for domestic and foreign suppliers of enhanced telecommunications services.

The Concession Title allowed the government to achieve social goals such as an increase in the number of rural communities served, higher public-telephone density, and improvements in quality of service. In addition to being desirable in and of themselves, these aspects of the Concession Title provided legitimation for the entire exercise. While the Concession Title did impose some obligations on Telmex's new owners, it also gave the company time to grow and become competitive at international levels, protected from the pressure of competition. Related government actions allowed them to enjoy the benefits of price increases without the accompanying opprobrium. In addition, they were assured of a stable regulatory environment, at least at the start.

The performance of Telmex over the past four years indicates arguably good results in expansion and modernization that not only met but surpassed the standards set in the Concession Title. The fulfillment of these criteria required the coexistence of regulation and profit-maximization goals in order for Telmex to become competitive and efficient. As mentioned above, regulation protected Telmex from competition in exchange for the fulfillment of social goals. Profit-maximization and the need to become a strong competitor in the liberalized long-distance market encouraged Telmex to go beyond the expansion and modernization requirements of the Concession Title, standards that the company might have met anyway. Meeting the Concession Title's standards might also have political and social benefits for Telmex. On one side, it would improve the former bad image of the company in the eyes of its current and future clients. On the other side, it would allow the company to maintain a smooth relationship with the regulatory body, increasing its influence and, thus, the standing of Telmex before the government.

The Mexican experience, at least in the first four years after the Telmex privatization, suggests that governments in developing countries can utilize mechanisms other than direct ownership to achieve social objectives related to telecommunications. It also shows how governments can attract significant foreign investment and expertise to the telecommunications sector while addressing concerns about foreign ownership. The Mexican solution has come under some strain as a result of the political and economic crises of 1994–1995. The real test will be the resilience of the regulatory regime under the pressures of competition and political change in Mexico.

REFERENCES

Bardacke, T. "Tough Times for Telmex as Mexico Prepares to Open Market." *Financial Times*, November 17, 1994, 28.

Business International Corporation. 1990. *Privatization in Latin America: New Competitive Opportunities and Challenges.* New York: Business International Corporation.

Caso Lombardo, F. 1990. "Desincorporación de Teléfonos de México" (Teléfonos de México divestiture). *Restaurador 22 de Abril* 10 (25): 11–14.

Collier, R. "Telmex Monopoly Is Hard to Break. Mexico Beckons U.S. Firms. *San Francisco Chronicle*, February 7, 1995, D14.

Galal, A., L. Jones, P. Tandon, and I. Vogelsang. 1994. *Welfare Consequences of Selling Public Enterprises: A World Bank Book.* New York: Oxford University Press.

"Investors Ponder Future of Mexico's Telmex." *Telecommunications Alert*, February 13, 1995. (Machine-readable data file). United Communications Group (Producer). Lexis-Nexis (Distributor).

Kim, W. H. "The Mexican Regime's Political Strategy in Implementing Economic Reform in Comparative Perspective: A Case Study of the Privatization of the Telephone Industry." (Ph.D. diss., University of Texas, Austin, 1992. Abstract in *Dissertation Abstract International* 53/12, 4472.

Langfield, M. "Mexico Phone Giant Sees Huge Forces Loss in 1994." *The Reuter Business Report,* January 24, 1995. (Machine-readable data file). Reuters (Producer). Lexis-Nexis (Distributor).

Ley de Inversión Extranjera 1994 (1994 Foreign Investment Law). Mexico: Ediciones Fiscales ISEF, S.A.

Luxner, L. 1992. "Mexico Reaches for New Telecom Heights." *Telephony Global* 22 (5): 22–28.

MacDonald, C. 1994. "AT&T Integrates Mexico into Global Communications: The World at Your Fingertips." *Business Mexico* (special edition) 6 (1/2): 66–67.

"Mexico Finalises Competition Plans, as U.S. Entrants Line Up. *FinTech Telecom Markets*, January 19, 1995.

Mexico Service. "Telmex Sale." *Mexico Service*, June 20, 1990. [Machine-readable data file]. IBC USA Publications Inc. (Producer). Lexis-Nexis (Distributor).

Petrazzini, B. A. 1993. "The Political Economy of Telecommunication Reform in Developing Countries: Privatization and Liberalization in Comparative Perspective." Ph.D. diss., University of California, San Diego, 1993. Abstract in *Dissertation Abstract International* 54/12, 4293.

"President Ernesto Zedillo Announces Terms of Emergency Economic Plans Agreed by All Sectors of the Mexican Economy." *PR Newswire*, January 3, 1995. (Machine-readable data file). PR Newswire Association. (Producer). Lexis-Nexis (Distributor).

Ramamurti, R. 1993. "Teléfonos de México: The Privatization Decision." *Case Research Journal* 13 (2): 43–67.

———. 1994. "Telephone Privatization in a Large Country: Mexico." *The North-South Agenda*, Paper No. 9. Coral Gables, Fla.: North–South Center, University of Miami.

Salinas de Gortari, C. 1989. "Presentación del Plan Nacional de Desarrollo 1989–1994 (Presentation of the National Development Plan 1989–1994)." In *Presidencia de la República*. Mexico City.

———. 1990. "Atender a los reclamos sociales, base para la reforma del Estado (To meet social demands, base for the State's reform)." *Restaurador 22 de Abril* 10 (25): 2–4.

SEC Online. *Teléfonos de Mexico's Annual Report*, December 31. Form 20-F. Washington, D.C.: Securities and Exchange Commission.

Secretaría de Comunicaciones y Transportes (SCT). 1990. *Reglamento de Telecomunicaciones* (*Telecommunications Regulation*). Mexico City: SCT.

———. "Modificación al Titulo de Concesión de Teléfonos de México (Modification to the Concession Title of Teléfonos de México)." *Diario Oficial de la Federación*, December 10, 1990, 12–38.

———. 1991. *La reforma del Estado y la desincorporación de Teléfonos de México: Comparecencia del C. Secretario de Comunicaciones y Transportes ante comisiones de la Cámara de Diputados* [*The State Reform and the Divestiture of Teléfonos de México: Speech of the Secretary of Communication and Transportation to Commissions of the Congress*]. Mexico City: SCT.

Székely, G. 1989. "Mexico's Challenge: Developing a New International Economic Strategy." In *Changing Networks: Mexico's Telecommunications Options,* edited by P. F. Cowhey, J. D. Aronson, and G. Székely, 81–90. San Diego: Center for U.S.–Mexican Studies of University of California, San Diego.

Teléfonos de México. 1991. *Oferta pública secundaria de 100 millones de acciones serie "L" de Teléfonos de México S.A. de C.V.* (Secondary public offer of 100 million "L" shares of Teléfonos de México S.A. de C.V.). Mexico City: Comisión Nacional de Valores.

————. 1994. *Annual Report to Shareholders 1993*. Mexico: Subdirección General de Comunicación y Relaciones Públicas.

Torres, C. "Mexico's Slim Helú Makes Big Bet on Telmex." *Wall Street Journal*, November 23, 1994, C1, 2.

THE HISTORY OF PRIVATIZATION AND LIBERALIZATION IN BRAZILIAN TELECOMMUNICATIONS

12

Joseph Straubhaar and Christine Horak

This chapter focuses on the development of the telecommunications sector in Brazil. Brazil is an ideal site for such research because of its often disparate levels of economic and social development and because of the attention given to communications policies by the Brazilian state over the past thirty years. In global terms, Brazil has the eighth largest GDP. It has a highly developed industrial sector, an advanced media and communication system, and a rapidly expanding use of and demand for information technology. At the same time, Brazil ranks among the poorest nations of the world in terms of many socioeconomic indicators, and even in the relatively well developed telecommunications sector, with the fifteenth largest telephone network in the world, there is an estimated current deficit of ten million business and residential telephone lines (ITA 1989; Ruido na Linha 1993).

Although currently ruled by a democratic regime, an important phase in the development of Brazil's telecommunications system occurred under the politically authoritarian and economically centralized rule of the military from 1964 through the early 1980s. The military's desire to consolidate power and promote rapid industrialization intensified the state's role in directing telecommunications policy and promoting the development of the sector. These policies are reflected in the current organization of the telecommunications system, and they shape future developments as well. This examination of the development of telecommunications policy also can provide insights into the Brazilian government's current strategies toward new information technologies.

While Brazil's informatics policies of the 1980s have been cited as a model in terms of promoting a sovereign national communications policy (Gonzalez-Manet 1987, 1992), the telecommunications sector has been explored less completely than other facets of information policy. These include the particularities of information policy (Rosenberg 1982), value conflicts inherent in the development of computing in developed and developing country settings (Kling 1983), and the economic and political organization of the computer industry (Evans 1986; Adler 1986; Straubhaar and Senger 1990; Katz 1981; Westman 1985).

Descriptions of the Brazilian telecommunications policy are often presented by representatives of the state-owned telecommunications system or national industry (Del Fioz and Ferraz 1985) or by Brazilian government agencies serving as contributors to research efforts conducted by international agencies (UNCTC 1984). The most comprehensive examination on the subject focuses on the link between technology policy and industrial development in the telecommunications sector (Hobday 1990). Communications researchers also have included the state-directed development of the Brazilian telecommunications sector into their discussions of culture and information policy (Fadul 1989; Fadul and Straubhaar 1995), the authoritarian state and the formation of Brazil's national cultural identity (Ortiz 1985), and more general overviews of the development of communication policy in Brazil (Ramos 1993; Gonzalez-Manet 1987). This literature provides a framework for understanding the development of communications policy within Brazil by pointing to the general determinants of such policy. For example, Fadul (1989, 16) views the desire to achieve modernization and preserve "national security" (i.e., self-maintenance of the authoritarian regime) as the two primary influences on the military's decision making vis-à-vis the communications sector. According to Fadul, "rapid and efficient communication could help construct the military's notion of a nation. The integration of Brazil through communications was a goal clearly reached by various military governments." For Ortiz (1985), the military's desire to establish a centralized national system of telecommunications responded to an authoritarian ideology in search of so-called "national integration," which essentially consisted of a homogenization of national culture directed by the military using the national telecommunications system as its base. This integration had a political end— consolidating loyalty of geographically dispersed Brazilians to the Brazilian state and Brazilian culture. For example, one of the most politically significant uses of the telecommunications infrastructure was to permit the coverage of the entire Brazilian territory by television, particularly TV Globo, which several scholars see as contributing greatly to the cultural consolidation of Brazil (Kottak 1990; Straubhaar 1991). Telecommunications integration also had economic ends, in part through the promotion of consumer culture via television distribution (Salles 1977) and in part through the facilitation of national level firm expansion, facilitated by various forms of telecommunication. Finally, Ramos (1993) urges us to recognize the innate links between the authoritarian state and its communications policies by arguing that national communications policies explicitly anticipate direct or indirect state intervention through state-owned broadcasting, regulations, and the diverse norms that allow for the entry of private interests.

Katz (1988, 37) further examines the link between the state and communications policy put forth by these Brazilian scholars by arguing that the development of new information technologies is shaped largely by political forces. According to Katz, "while correlations exist between economic development and the diffusion of information technologies, some of the relationships between the economic system are mediated by the political system. In fact, in some cases, diffusion of information technologies can be entirely the result of needs emerging from the political system having little or nothing to do with market mechanisms."

The large body of literature focusing on how investment in telecommunications may increase levels of economic development also can be used to inform and examine the telecommunications policy in a country like Brazil (Wellenius 1984; Saunders, Warford, and Wellenius 1983; Hudson 1984; Jussawalla and Cheah 1987; Jequier 1984). The Brazilian military in the 1960s anticipated the essential conclusions of this wave of research, as did South Korea, Hong Kong, and other countries, which invested massively in telecommunications in the 1960s and 1970s. But overall, the view that political systems shape the national communications environment drives our analysis. In Brazil, a "national" policy must be read as a state policy, and the actions of the state and its primary allies and agents (private capital, both national and transnational) must be examined. In the case of the telecommunications sector, we hope to accomplish this by studying national planning documents; we present the often contradictory policy discourse of the Brazilian state vis-à-vis the telecommunications sector during the periods of military rule (1964–1984) and later democratic rule (1984–present). During these two periods, we examine how official discourse was modified.

By tracing the actual development of the telecommunications equipment sector, especially the manner in which private national capital allied itself with multinational capital despite the military regime's official rhetoric and policy directives which emphasized the nationalization of the sector, we document the contradictions between the rhetoric of telecommunications planning and actual events in the sector. Eventually, the resulting oligopoly of manufacturers, dominated by three foreign firms—Alcatel, Siemens, and NEC— began to be seen as a barrier to further progress. Prices were sufficiently higher than world market prices for switches and other equipment, so that local users began to be dissatisfied, particularly as companies beyond the Telebras monopoly began to need to acquire equipment. A further complication arose with alliances formed between companies like NEC and politically powerful local firms like TV Globo. Such alliances were seen as having both too much economic power and too much political power. The urge to break up such power concentrations also contributed to movements toward opening the market.

Finally, we link the perceived failure to maintain national control over the most lucrative parts of the telecommunications sector to the debate regarding the formulation of Brazilian informatics policy, which established rigid barriers to foreign equipment and technology. Although scholars such as Fadul (1989) felt that progress had been made by the joint venture strategy within telecommunications manufacturing, an alliance of would-be manufacturers, activist planning officials, the military, and the nationalist left clearly wanted to go further in the informatics sector toward reserving the market for Brazilian manufacturers alone, without foreign alliances (Adler 1986).

The Informatics Law that resulted from the campaign to reserve the personal computer manufacturing sector for Brazilian firms resulted in domestic prices that frequently reached four times world price levels and produced equipment with fairly serious quality control problems. A public debate ensued, driven partially by U.S. pressure to open the market and reduce piracy of software and hardware, but principally by both domestic and foreign business users of computers. This resulted in opening the software market in 1992, and then opening hardware manufacturing to foreign investors in 1994. Imports of computers were gradually liberalized, but the effective tariff remained at more than 50 percent.

A similar, continuing problem with prices and services by telecommunications manufacturers, Telebras, and state-level telecommunications monopolies also resulted in serious pressures for liberalization from several sectors, particularly business users but also foreign and domestic firms that wished to enter the markets for specific telecommunications services. This debate was somewhat less public and political, except that it eventually was caught up in a larger debate about privatization of government monopolies. In this debate, the foreign/domestic problem was overshadowed by union concerns about jobs versus efficiency and price concerns by users. This process moved more slowly toward gradual liberalization of competition in areas like cellular telephony, in which the old pattern of foreign and domestic consortia was maintained and perhaps even strengthened.

DEVELOPMENT PLANNING IN THE BRAZILIAN
TELECOMMUNICATIONS SECTOR

This examination of the telecommunications sector in Brazil is based largely on how the objectives and policies for the sector have been presented in national development plans. We have recorded how Brazil's official development planning documents incorporate telecommunications policies (the stated objectives of the sector) into overall national development efforts. We also have examined how these objectives have changed over time and have traced the extent to which these objectives have or have not been obtained in terms of actual developments in the telecommunications sector.

The choice of national planning documents as a base for analysis is not a frequently employed method for studying the development of telecommunications in LDCs. When national planning objectives are incorporated in studies of the telecommunications sector, they are often summarily cited, but rarely are they carefully examined and deconstructed (O'Sullivan-Ryan 1983). However, such documents are extensively used in most developing countries and have an important influence on the allocation of national resources. International financing generally is forthcoming only after incorporation and approval of sectoral plans into national planning documents (Gellerman 1977). In the developing world, telecommunications entities are usually owned or managed by the government and, therefore, are subject to close supervision by national planning departments. In Brazil, the development of national planning documents, especially after the 1963 coup d'état, was extremely centralized at the presidential level and tended to reflect the priorities of the military regime (Daland 1967).

Within the Brazilian telecommunications sector, such strategic national planning is the first step in a three-part planning process. It is followed by operational planning by the state-owned telecommunications provider (Telebras) and the approximately twenty local subsidiaries. According to former Telebras executives (Del Fioz and Ferraz 1985), strategic planning within the telecommunications sector is "based on directives given by the Ministry of Communications, the major shareholder in Telebras, and takes into account typical situational analysis—social, political, economic and cultural aspects, strengths and weakness of the organization—leading to the definition of global strategic objectives." Telecommunications research and investment stem in large part from the directives specified in national-level economic planning documents. To be fair, we should note that because this step of the planning process is based largely on documents which cover a long-range period (more than five years) many specific goals and objectives are frequently modified and updated. Without incorporating the operational planning phase into our analysis, during which actual funding commitments are made by the federal government, we cannot fully evaluate the extent to which strategic planning objectives were fully incorporated by the sector. However, an in-depth reading of strategic planning documents can allow us to critically examine the claims of telecommunications industry representatives who state that "policies that have emerged from the planning process were implemented and provided good economic results and satisfaction to customers" (Del Fioz and Ferraz, 1985, 229). Our analysis would hope to revise such conclusions by asking who benefited from the "good economic results," and which customers benefited most from the development of the national telecommunications system in Brazil?

THE EARLY DEVELOPMENT OF THE TELECOMMUNICATIONS SECTOR IN BRAZIL: THE IMPETUS FOR PLANNING

As is frequently the case regarding Latin American development, the early development of the telecommunications sector in Brazil was controlled largely by foreign interests (Katz 1988). As early as the 1920s, the Canadian Traction Light and Power Company established a wholly owned subsidiary, the Companhia Brasileira de Telefone (CBT), which imported equipment under government license from major multinational suppliers such as Chicago Electric, Standard Electric, and L. M. Ericsson. This resulted in little national manufacturing or technological development. It also resulted in fragmented service, largely limited to the affluent parts of urban areas and towns. Bowing to pressure in the 1950s from the nationalist oriented government of Getulio Vargas, CBT's importing of equipment was limited by import quotas and insistence on local manufacture of equipment and use of local inputs when possible (Hobday 1990). CBT soon set up local manufacturing plants to produce low technology products such as telephone handsets. Other foreign corporations such as Germany's electrical corporation Siemens and Sweden's Ericsson also established production facilities in Brazil. This resulted in limited local manufacture of telecommunications equipment (by the late 1950s, Ericsson had also begun to manufacture crossbar switching equipment) but did little to establish the development of more technologically sophisticated manufacture and resulting technology transfer.

In sharp contrast to the increasingly concentrated production of telecommunications equipment, the telecommunications infrastructure grew increasingly fragmented during the same period. By the early 1960s, CBT operated approximately 68 percent of the installed telephones but nearly 800 small private firms operated the remainder. Although the provision of service was based on federal concessions to individual firms, municipal and state governments could enact legislation affecting the federal government's ability to approve policies, investments, and operations. The lack of a planned government policy for telecommunications resulted in inefficiency and inadequacy of the network coverage (Hobday 1990; Del Fioz and Ferraz 1985).

The problems posed by an inadequate, chopped-up private infrastructure were clear to many involved in development planning in Brazil prior to the military takeover in 1964. The Brazilian government's first effort to intervene in the telecommunications planning process predates the military regime which came into power in early 1964 by two years. In 1962, the Brazilian Congress passed the Brazilian Telecommunications Code, which established an institutional framework under which telecommunications policies and operations were implemented. The major features of the code included the establishment of an agency (Contel) charged with implementing and directing national telecommunications policies, the creation of a public company (Empresa Brasileira de Telefone, Embratel) to implement and operate long-distance and international services, and the creation of a national telecommunications investment fund acquired from a surcharge on local-service and long-distance rates to supply Embratel with the financial resources necessary to establish a national telecommunications infrastructure.

After the 1964 military coup d'état, this relatively apolitical institutional framework for the telecommunications sector was absorbed under the military regime. Embratel was created in 1965 as previously planned, but in 1967 the existing telecommunications entity (Contel) was replaced by the Ministry of Communications (Mincom), an agency linked closely to the military decision-making apparatus. While telecommunications technocrats have termed this shift one which provided the sector with "a greater political authority," the Mincom was also responsible for the overall establishment of the television/radio broadcasting system and played a major role in censoring the news media during the authoritarian rule (Fadul 1989). In 1972, a state-owned enterprise, Telecommunicacoes Brasileiras S.A. (Telebras), was created to render and coordinate all the telecommunications public services in the country. As a holding company, Telebras controls twenty holding companies responsible for approximately 97 percent of total services in Brazil.

TELECOMMUNICATIONS PLANNING IN AN ERA OF SECTORAL CONSOLIDATION: 1967–1970

Planning documents during the Goulart regime, the last democratic regime before the military takeover, make little mention of telecommunications objectives (Presidencia da Republica 1962). Instead, the planning focus was on expanding services and increasing the efficiency of the postal and telegraphic services. After the military assumed power in 1964, the attention and resources awarded to the Brazilian telecommunications sector clearly increased.

The increased attention to telecommunications in strategic planning documents from the first two military regimes demonstratess the extent to which the sector was viewed as key to overall economic development policy. In 1967, a strategic planning document entitled *Diretrizes do Governo-Programa Estrategico de Desenvolvimento* (Ministerio do Planejamento 1967, 72) outlined the redirection in government goals vis-à-vis the sector. Telephone service was viewed as a key ingredient to national integration and the development of a viable industrial base in the southeastern regions of the country (Rio de Janeiro and São Paulo). This early plan was intended to be the "first step in the consolidating and quickly expanding a sector that the Government considers as a priority and whose efficiency depends substantially on the productivity of the rest of the sectors of the national economy." According to the plan, the consolidation of the sector would occur by orienting and providing incentives to each Brazilian state to establish telecommunications development planning objectives synchronized with national policies. However, a nationally centralized policy for telecommunications was clearly envisioned in this document. This document reinforces the military regime's desire to move from a disparate structure with multiple service providers within the same state toward, instead, a single large-scale state company or concessionary. While stressing the military regime's clear geopolitical objective of national integration, especially in terms of providing telephone service between state capitals and the relatively new national capital, Brasilia, early planning documents such as this also establish clear regional hierarchies for development favoring the industrially developed southern and central regions of the country, with high capacity exchanges and direct dialing capabilities among other services.

Within the telecommunications sector, this post-1964 period generally is viewed as one of consolidation and reorganization. Events such as the creation of Embratel, the incorporation of Contel into the Mincom, the creation of a self-capitalizing mechanism through which potential customers were obliged to "subscribe" to the telephone company, and the generous reinvestment of profits from the lucrative international telecommunications activities of Embratel transformed the formerly disorganized and poorly capitalized telecommunications system.

The late 1960s also signaled the takeoff of multinational telecommunications equipment producers in the Brazilian market and established an unquestioned dominance of MNCs in the equipment sector. Although the official policy dictates of the next twenty years often sought to reverse this situation, by the early 1970s firms such as L. M. Ericsson and other MNCs expanded their operations both vertically and horizontally and within ten years overwhelmingly dominated the equipment market, practicing very limited technology transfer and sending increasingly greater remittances to their parent companies (Hobday 1990).

While actively soliciting foreign investment in the equipment sector, the military regime singled out foreign firms, especially the Canadian-owned CBT, as being responsible for the problematic state of the telecommunications service sector, especially for residential users. In 1969, the Director of the Departmento Nacional de Telecomunicacoes stated in an interview in a popular newsmagazine that "the CBT, a Canadian firm, that is nominally Canadian, but in any case 'foreign' was guilty for the current state of disarray found in Rio and São Paulo." He went on to say "for various reasons, including the growth of a national consciousness, it is no longer acceptable for Brazilians to finance a foreign owned company." The end result of this was the nationalization of CBT in 1967 ("A Politica . . ." 1969). However, CBT continued to operate as a private firm under the regulatory control of the Mincom, and CBT itself began importing foreign equipment. CBT officials began criticizing the MNCs manufacturing equipment for production delays and supplying substandard equipment (Pelo Telefone 1970), triggering growing displeasure with the state of telephone service and the dominance of foreign ownership in the equipment sector and contributing to a growing national debate during the following decade.

TELECOMMUNICATIONS PLANNING AND POLICY
DURING SECTORAL EXPANSION: 1970–1980

By the early 1970s, national planning documents began to link the development of the telecommunications sector with increases in productivity and economic development in general. A 1970 strategic planning document, which established overall priorities for telecommunications and was a forerunner to the First National Development Plan which set telecommunications policy during the 1970s, stressed that through the consolidation of efforts already underway Brazil would embark upon one of the largest telecommunications investment policies in the world (Presidencia da Republica 1970). Throughout the decade, planning documents underscored the link between expansion of the national telecommunications system and increased economic growth and investment opportunities.

Telecommunications was also included in broader efforts to implement a national technology policy. For example, specific development plans for the telecommunications sector were not listed in the First National Development Plan (I Plano Nacional de Desenvolvimento), in effect from 1972 to 1974 (Presidencia da Republica 1972). Instead, telecommunications was absorbed into more general planning objectives, such as the implementation of a national technology policy. The establishment of such policies would, according to the plan, "permit the acceleration and orient technology transfer for the country, associated with a strong component of national technological elaboration."

Largely embedded in a nationalistic rhetoric of modernity, the perception that advances in telecommunications would lead to economic and social modernity was reinforced by the national media. The prominent news magazine *Veja,* published by the powerful media consortia ABRIL, routinely showcased even the most basic telecommunications technology. A series of articles in April 1970 extolling the military regime's decision to establish a Ministry of Communications noted that the government had "irreversibly opted to abandon the bitter past of inefficiency and politicking in order to adopt technology as the only possible future path" ("O Brasil se" 1970).

The geopolitical objectives of the military regime—national integration and national security—continued to be evident in planning documents. However, it is important to note that by the 1970s planning documents and the rhetoric of the telecommunications equipment sector began to resemble each other and coincide with one another. For example, an advertisement placed by the Brazilian Association of Telecommunications in *Veja* described the positive impact that the telecommunications sector could have on national development and lobbied for increased investment in the sector. Throughout the 1970s, we note a convergence of official rhetoric and the discourse of private capital with respect to the impact of telecommunications on overall economic development. However, the assumption that private capital would contribute and, in many cases, lead telecommunications policy is also evident even in early strategic planning documents. For example, the 1967 Strategic Program for Development (Programa Estrategico de Desenvolvimento) states that "the national telecommunications system should remain under the control and fiscalization of the federal government, with the possibility that its expansion, with the exception of what has been reserved by the government, may be the object of [federal] authorization or concession" (Ministerio do Planejamento 1967). The same plan outlines the government's position vis-à-vis national industry. "The expansion plan of the telecommunications system, should continue to benefit the national telecommunications equipment industry, which already finds itself equipped to supply equipment for the urban systems. . . . This will permit the utilization of any future excess capacity existing in the industrial sector, with positive benefits in the reduction of production costs, which are at the moment still relatively high in comparison to similar foreign goods" (112). Between 1968 and 1970, official planning documents continued to emphasize a major role for private national capital in the development of the telecommunications sector, especially the electronic components and equipment industry.

Throughout the 1970s and early 1980s, strategic planning documents articulated policies through which the state could include the telecommunications sector in its broader economic policy goal of import substitution, as well as promoting the development of nonforeign technology in the sector. For example, during the Figureido regime (Brazil's last military president) planning documents outlined new roles for Mincom and new developments in the telecommunications sector (Secretaria de Communicacao 1980), including a greater articulation between Mincom and other federal agencies such as the Ministries of Industry and Commerce to "consolidate the process of integration in the areas of telecommunications and informatics" (87). R&D activities were to be aimed at stimulating advanced technological research in the field, developing products which could be adapted to the specific needs and conditions of Brazil, and assuring the consolidation of a "genuinely national industry" which could benefit the state-controlled telecommunications sector. This document urged that federal purchasing power be utilized to attract Brazilian entrepreneurs to the telecommunications industry to increase the level of Brazilian-held industries in the equipment sector and to allow the country to reach a level of technological development sufficient enough to ensure that future industrial and technological policy in the telecommunications sector be made nationally.

The primary mechanisms developed by the Brazilian government to carry out such policies in the telecommunications industry were the regulation of trade, investment, and purchasing in the sector. Because the Brazilian government policy for electronics was sectoral in nature, the state became a potentially influential force (Erber 1985). For example, the Ministry of Communications was charged with ensuring the supply of telecommunications equipment to be used in the development of the national telephone network. The impact of the state-controlled telecommunications system on the telecommunications equipment sector was based largely on Telebras's centralization of purchasing power, especially the limiting of the number of suppliers of a specific item to a minimum of two and a maximum of four to allow simultaneously for competition and economies of scale while promoting standardization (ITA 1989). A second means of exerting influence on the sector was through the establishment of the Brazilian Telecommunications Research Center (CPqD) in 1976, to further the development of digital systems. Hobday (1990) provides a very comprehensive evaluation of the major role of CPqD in the technological and economic development of the telecommunications sector. Since its establishment, CPqD has focused on two goals, the formation of highly skilled manpower and the selection of R&D guidelines appropriate to Brazil's needs. Although complete technological parity with MNC levels has not been achieved yet, the creation of CPqD has enabled the Brazilian telecommunications system to accelerate autonomous technological development (Graciosa 1989).

During this period, the Brazilian state also began to more strongly advocate domestic participation in the manufacture of telecommunications equipment through its purchasing policies. For example, although the three firms considered by Telebras to develop digital switching equipment technology for the Centrais de Programacao Armazenada (CPA) program were foreign ("Uma Decisao Dificil" 1978), the contract stipulated that the winning firm must agree to transfer 51 percent of its stock to firms controlled by domestic capital. An initial decision to award the contract to Ericsson was canceled because the firm did not fully meet this stipulation ("A Novela Continua" 1978). A few months later, the three principal MNCs competing for the lucrative contract to install 50,000 CPA terminals in São Paulo—Ericsson, NEC, and Standard Electric—each announced that they would transfer majority control to Brazilian hands. (GTE followed within a year). This nationalization of foreign capital was the result of a concerted effort by then Minister of Communication Euclides Quadndt de Oliveira and was supported by Telebras ("Caminho Inverso" 1979).

Developments such as the centralization of purchasing power, the establishment of CPqD, and Telebras's commitment to "buy Brazilian" were clearly defined objectives in the planning documents during the early 1970s. They also provided an important means through which national capital began to replace MNC suppliers in the equipment sector (Hobday 1990). However, through two other factors—the carefully crafted and mutually lucrative alliances between national and multinational capital, and the emergence of new technologies such as cellular telephones for which Brazilian companies were not able to supply technology—the actual practice and degree of nationalization of the telecommunications equipment sector deviates from the planning discourse heretofore outlined. Prior to these measures, foreign capital led the expansion of the telecommunications equipment sector, which accompanied the government's increased investments in the telecommunications sector as a whole. The concerted effort by telecommunications policy makers to reduce the reliance on foreign equipment manufacturers and promote national industry led to a limited nationalization of the telecommunications equipment sector. But in association with Brazilian financial capital, the Brazilian market is currently dominated by local, wholly owned subsidiaries of mainly European and Japanese firms such as Ericsson, Siemens, NEC, Equitel, Standard Electronica (a former IT&T subsidiary), Multitel (a former GTE joint venture), Elebra Telcon, and Sul-America Teleinformatica (a former Philips joint venture) (ITA 1989). The following section describes how this current situation developed despite the state's efforts to increase national participation in the sector.

TELECOMMUNICATIONS PLANNING DURING THE TRANSITION TO DEMOCRACY: NEW SECTORAL OBJECTIVES EMERGE

Unlike many other Latin American nations, Brazil's return to democracy was a planned and orderly process, referred to as *abertura,* or opening. While it did not mean that the military freely relinquished power to civilian forces, a growing disillusionment within the military establishment led to a transition largely "directed" by the military. Even as the military came to power in 1964, various military presidents indicated that Brazil would at some point reestablish a democratic process (Bruneau and Faucher 1981). However, few of these pronouncements were taken seriously until the mid-1970s, when the business and industrial classes began to exert pressure on the military to step down from power. This action was based on the perception among these groups that authoritarian rule could not sufficiently stimulate economic growth and that democracy was the best form of government to understand and defend the interests of the business classes.

During the period of abertura and subsequent democratic transition, the rhetoric of telecommunications planning documents took on a decidedly different tone. In terms of sectoral objectives and the telecommunications sector's link to the rest of the economy, the planning documents during the very latest period of military rule and the early years of democratic regime bore little resemblance to earlier documents. The first major development plan of this period, the Third National Development Plan (1980–1985), included only three objectives for the sector (Presidencia da Republica 1980). The objectives were the following: prioritizing specific social needs, such as those of residential users in urban peripheries or rural communities, preferably through the installation of public telephone facilities; practicing a rate policy compatible with the need to expand the sector but within the constraints of the anti-inflationary economic measures adopted; and giving preference to the installation of communications infrastructure in housing units financed by the government's national housing development agency.

Within the context of development planning documents, the role envisioned for telecommunications continued to change substantially during the Sarney administration, Brazil's first nonmilitary leadership in almost thirty years. The First National Development Plan of the New Republic, a comprehensive development plan, clearly favored the social functions of the telecommunications network over the security functions promoted by previous military regimes (Republica Federativa do Brasil 1985). For example, the document implicitly criticizes previous telecommunications investment policies by stating that they focused primarily on more lucrative long-distance service and resulted in an inequitable distribution of telephone service which "privileges urban sectors with greater purchasing power in detriment of low income populations in urban peripheries and at the same time is of little assistance to rural areas." In this plan, the justification for expanding telephone service to rural regions also differs from the earlier rhetoric of the military regime. Now better service to the interior regions is called for to support a policy of "interiorization" aimed at increasing agricultural production and curtailing high levels of rural out-migration. There is no mention of "national integration," a phrase frequently used during military rule which has come to denote the incorporation and acceptance of military rule throughout the country. Instead, economic differences between urban and rural Brazil are acknowledged rather than avoided, as they were within the telecommunications policy planning discourse of the military. Another response to the transition to democracy is a sectoral objective for the "democratization" of the telecommunications system through the installation of public and semipublic telephones for use by the poor.

In addition to these broader thematic shifts in telecommunications policy discourse, the First National Development Plan restated many of the more service-oriented objectives found in the development plan it followed, the Third National Development Plan (covering the period from 1980–1985). Expanding and improving telephone service to urban and rural users, as well as continuing to focus on developing long-distance and international service, top the list of priority projects and programs for the telecommunications sector. While it is unlikely that this focus on service emerged solely in direct response to the increasingly precarious state of telephone service in Brazil, these policy statements coincide with a general deterioration in the level of telephone service during the mid-1980s. This was mainly caused by Telebras's inability to meet the demand for new lines which grew out of the economic boom of the 1970s.

This lack of expansion is related directly to the contradictions of the abertura process, begun in the mid-1970s and continuing through the early and mid-1980s. As the late military governments became more worried about public opinion and their own popularity, they began to be less willing to keep telecommunications prices high to cross-subsidize the expansion of services into new areas, which had been an element of policy since 1964. For example, in order to receive residential service, prospective customers in the 1960s and 1970s had to buy shares in Telebras. This provided investment capital, as did relatively high tariffs. Beginning in the Figuereido administration in 1979, tariffs were held below the cost of inflation in order to meet popular demands to contain inflation. While this made populist political sense, it devastated the telecommunications system's ability to generate investment for expansion of services (Siquerra 1993). The suppression of tariffs and the resultant lack of investment in expansion continued, and even accelerated, with the civilian government of Sarney in 1985.

In 1986, the estimated deficit for business and residential lines was 2.5 million (almost 50% of the total number of lines in place at the time). Growth in the parallel or speculative market for phone lines soared. The government responded by making the sale of lines by third parties illegal. Increased economic activity contributed in part to this situation, but a significant drop in government investment in the telecommunications sector certainly aggravated it. Between 1976 and 1986, investment dropped from US$1.7 billion to US$800 million.

The growing dissatisfaction with telephone service also sparked a debate concerning the privatization of certain segments of the national telecommunications sector, throughout which representatives of Telebras lobbied fiercely to maintain their monopoly over telephonic and data transmission services and to maintain Embratel's control of the long-distance market. In 1984, a Mincom sponsored seminar for the telecommunications industry focused heavily on the issue of privatization of services (Seminario Telebrasil 1984). One of the main arguments for privatization was the need to depoliticize tariff policy (or, at a minimum, to allow tariffs to match inflation) and to acquire new resources from private investors to replace the resources that government was no longer able to supply, either through tariff income or through foreign borrowing, which was no longer an option, given Brazilian foreign debt levels (some of which had resulted from telecommunications investments made during the military governments).

Representatives of Telebras and Embratel both argued against the privatization of any type of service based on Telebras's record of service and the tendency of the private sector to respond only to the most lucrative ventures at the expense of less profitable but more service-oriented activities. The discourse surrounding this issue was identical to the major themes found in strategic planning documents—national integration through service to remote areas and low income populations and so on. Despite the arguments presented by Telebras, events in the 1980s show that the direction taken by the telecommunications sector in Brazil was one of greater participation of national capital, most notably the entry of a limited number of firms which already controlled related industries such as broadcasting and computer and consumer electronics. For example, new firms were entering manufacturing, and a few new firms, along with some of the existing manufacturing alliances (like Globo–NEC), were entering liberalized competitive areas such as cellular services.

The return to democracy and the accompanying rhetorical shift found in sectoral plans did not mean that the interests of the private sector, long intertwined with the development of the telecommunications sector, would be relegated to a secondary position in favor of a continued or even strengthened role for the state. One of the direct beneficiaries of the nationalization of Brazil's largest foreign telecommunications equipment firms in late 1979 and early 1980 was Roberto Marinho, owner of the Globo media conglomerate. The Globo Organization, which dominates television production and broadcasting, publishes a prominent Rio de Janeiro newspaper, and holds countless related interests, purchased 51 percent controlling interest of NEC six years after the shares were originally purchased by a prominent Brazilian investment and holding company, BRASILINVEST, during the nationalization efforts in the telecommunications equipment sector. NEC, which two years earlier had generated US$59 million in sales and employed approximately two thousand workers in its primary manufacturing facility in São Paulo, was purchased by Marinho for less then US$1 million. In addition, NEC ranked far behind other former multinationals in terms of technological integration or technological R&D investment within Brazil (Hobday 1990). The Japanese, who still controlled 49 percent of the company's shares, were influential in approaching Roberto Marinho and in facilitating the sale of the company. Despite the financial difficulties of its former Brazilian owners, NEC remained Embratel's largest supplier of digital equipment. With the sale to Globo, controlling interest in NEC was held by Embratel's largest client, the Globo organization ("Linha Direta" 1986). Marinho's indisputably positive relationship and lucrative past dealings with both the former military and current civilian regime were key in NEC's favorable performance in the Brazilian telecommunications equipment market after its purchase by the Globo corporation.

Within a year, the influence and autonomy with which private capital could directly appropriate certain components of the telecommunications infrastructure became apparent again. In October 1987 the Globo conglomerate and one of Brazil's largest private financial and banking interests, Bradesco, were able to obtain direct control from Embratel to commercially operate a line of the Brasilsat (Brazil's communications satellite). Viewed by Embratel's unions as a privitazation of the most lucrative part of the Embratel system, the implementation of spread spectrum technology allowed Globo to transmit and receive video images throughout the country and Bradesco to further establish a nationwide electronic banking network. The formal contract, signed in September 1987 between Embratel and Victori Comunicacoes (Vicom) led to an intense debate within Embratel. Ceding to pressure from its employees' union, the organization's board of directors cancelled the contract that would have dismissed all but one of the board members by the Minister of Communications and reinstated the contract with Victori ("O Sovieteda Embratel" 1987).

Beyond the competition in manufacturing, the liberalization of new competitive telecommunications services offered firms an opportunity to expand into the previously monopolized areas of services. Like many governments, Brazil began to liberalize entry into new services well before privatizing existing state companies and services (Straubhaar 1991). Brazil allowed new entrants to compete for licenses in cellular telephony, VSAT satellite dish receiving services, packet switching, and other new services in which Telebras or state-level companies, like Telesp in São Paulo, were not yet ready.

The Globo corporation was not the only Brazilian company to establish a close and often lucrative relationship with foreign-owned telecommunications equipment suppliers. Sharp Electronics, and one of its principal subsidiaries, SID Telecom, established a partnership with AT&T in the late 1980s with the aim of becoming a major force in the cellular market. Cellular technology serves as a prime example of an area in which the Telebras system has made the decision not to become a service provider and has instead negotiated the right to run such services with private Brazilian interests closely allied with MNCs such as NEC and SID. The current scenario for cellular service is based on almost six years of bureaucratic and private-sector in-fighting over the licensing of service providers. At the center of the developments in the cellular phone sector is the manner in which Telebras divided the Brazilian market between the country's two major and most directly foreign-backed telecommunications interests (NEC and SID). The degree to which foreign technology and foreign interests were the driving force behind the proposals submitted by firms such as NEC or SID was also crucial to the debate. The end result of the proposal process was a geographic division of the Brazilian cellular market with service for Rio de Janeiro awarded to Globo–NEC; Brasilia to Ericsson do Brasil; and São Paulo to SID. The São Paulo licenses were successfully disputed and new licensing processes conducted. The São Paulo market, estimated at a potential 100,000 new subscribers per year, has been at the center of contention between NEC and SID. Throughout the proposal and contracting period, Roberto Marinho and SID president Mathias Machline aggressively lobbied the Mincom and took advantage of close personal and business relationships with Mincom officials and the Brazilian President Jose Sarney ("Uma Guerra de Titas" 1989). Part of the solution was to open São Paulo to more than one cellular licensee and two different frequency bands (Siquerra 1993).

Each of these firms benefited from Brazil's post-1974 policy aimed at encouraging and supporting wholly owned national firms. This policy, which included state-sponsored technological support through the national R&D center, import restrictions, and a Telebras purchasing policy stipulating national producers, has been considered largely successful in its effort to promote domestic industry in the telecommunications sector. To be fair we should note that NEC and SID are somewhat atypical cases because of their size and backing and the political influence of their owners. However, Hobday (1990), in an analysis of the entire telecommunications equipment sector, shows similar trends in growth among small- and medium-size telecommunications equipment producers resulting from the state policies described previously. In addition, the major Brazilian subsidiaries of telecommunications equipment manufacturers drew heavily on foreign technology provided by MNC partners such as Equitel, which used technology from its parent company Siemens, and Ericsson, which operated in Brazil in conjunction with the Monteiro Aranha group ("Triplice Alianca" 1990).

It is important to note that while SID and NEC are the most visible examples of the alliance of foreign technology and Brazilian capital in the telecommunications sector, their significance lies in their role as legitimating conduits of new and non-Brazilian (i.e., foreign) cellular technology. They also lobbied for the privatization of the cellular system and were quick to make the technological alliances necessary to implement other services locally. These operational alliances, initially formed to compete in the cellular market, also have been used in competing for non-cellular equipment. SID-Telcom announced an "operational alliance with AT&T and the Italian telecommunications company Italtel in July 1990 to compete aggressively with NEC for major Telebras equipment contracts" ("Triplice Alianca" 1990). In December 1993, SID-Telecom's three largest competitors—NEC, Ericsson, and Siemens—took judicial action in an attempt to stop a US$200 million contract from being awarded to SID to furnish AT&T manufactured equipment for the Telebras system. Despite his family company's own long-standing alliance with foreign capital, Roberto Marinho Jr., NEC's comptroller, protested Telebras' initial decision to award the contract based only on lowest bid with only secondary regard to technical consideration. "By accepting the participation of AT&T the government is sentencing factories in Brazil to extinction . . . The competition from the American company is unfair" ("Ruido na Linha" 1993). Despite its opposition to AT&T's possible entry into the market, NEC Brazil has established similar advantageous commercial alliances with its own Japanese parent company.

The parallels in telecommunications policy objectives during the late 1970s and Brazil's increasing commitment to market reserve policies protecting domestic computer manufacturers cannot be ignored. The two sectors are highly related, most obviously because of the telecommunications sector's reliance on digital technology. In both sectors, private national capital promoted and responded to the policies established to favor the development of national technology. Policies—again in both sectors—promoting import substitution or outright restriction of foreign products to spur the development of indigenous technology often were based on political determination rather than economic need. The similarity between telecommunications policy and informatics was not lost on Brazilian legislators, who in 1984 debated the establishment of the market reserve. For example, Fadul (1989) quotes a Brazilian congressman who argues that, "In the telecommunication sector where a market-reserve already effectively exists, but one in which there are industries which are pseudo-joint-ventures . . . The telecommunications model was successful with relation to use, but it was not successful in terms of the development of national technology, which is what we really want for informatics" (17). This demonstrates that events in the telecommunications sector may have had an impact on shaping an informatics policy which more radically closed the market to foreign manufacture and technology in an effort to develop its own technology.

In the case of the telecommunications sector, the extent of indigenous technological development is debatable. Hobday's (1990) analysis of the telecommunications equipment sector and its link to national policies aimed at supporting the development of wholly Brazilian-owned industries showed that through specific "buy Brazilian" policies promoted by Telebras, technological leapfrogging took place, enabling the Brazilian telecommunications system to move more rapidly than most developing countries from mechanical to digital switching systems. However, in Brazil the largest telecommunications equipment manufacturers have maintained old links with foreign subsidiaries and developed new alliances to ensure access to new technology. The "pseudo-market" reserve created a "pseudo-national" industry, which, if the latest AT&T–SID alliance is used as a gauge, has done little to promote a truly national telecommunications equipment industry in Brazil or to lessen the national telecommunications system's reliance on "operational alliances" of foreign and domestic capital. Most important, for many end users of both telecommunications and computers, the maintenance of market reserve policies forced them to pay much higher costs than did many of their competitors in other countries. By the 1980s, even though some of its main members were, benefiting from the market reserve as manufactures of telecommunications equipment and/or computers, the very influential Federacao de Industrias do Estado de São Paulo was actively lobbying for an end to the informatics reserve policy and, somewhat more hesitantly, beginning to express support for privatization, or at least liberalization of competition in telecommunications services.

By the election of Fernando Henrique Cardoso in 1994, a long debate about privatization of telecommunications and other sectors began to be resolved in favor of increased privatization. Union concerns about loss of jobs were increasingly outweighed by concerns over efficiency, need for outside capital for expansion, and the desire to limit state functions to a smaller range of critical activities, such as health and education.

Telecommunications did emerge as one of the two most controversial areas for privatization, due in part to a lingering concern about its importance to national security. Cardoso promoted privatization as a way to expand services and increase the equity of access to telecommunications, but members of his cabinet were not united on the issue and Congress was divided. Sufficient unanimity was achieved to allow modest privatization to proceed, in the form of liberalized competition in new services; however, the government was still moving slowly and cautiously on the idea of actual privatization of the Telebras holding company, the Embratel long-distance services, and the state-level operating companies who offer local wireline service (since cellular services are now expanding much faster than wired services and are increasingly competitive).

DISCUSSION

Our review of Brazilian national strategic telecommunications planning documents reveals that specific planning objectives for the sector were linked to broader political, economic, and social policies. During the first period reviewed, the military regime tied the consolidation of the telecommunications sector to so-called "national integration," allowing the regime to consolidate its own power. Similar national policies also were evident in the military's approach to consolidating the national broadcasting system. Both telecommunications and broadcasting consolidation and penetration of the countryside helped promote critical goals for national political and cultural integration and the creation of a national consumer marketplace.

During the 1970s, strategic planning documents began to emphasize the telecommunications sector's role in national economic growth and development. The development of a modern telecommunications system was viewed as a vehicle that would more closely ally Brazil with the developed world and lead to an increasing modernization of Brazilian society. As Brazil returned to democratic rule in the early 1980s, the rhetoric of strategic planning documents changed again. The role of telecommunications in Brazil was redefined from a means of uniting the country under authoritarian rule to a means through which Brazil's citizenry could more freely communicate and more equitably benefit from the telecommunications infrastructure. Now telecommunications was viewed as a means to democratize Brazilian society, with a more open and competitive broadcasting system which encouraged expansion of other national television networks to compete with TV Globo, which had been favored by the military.

In addition to tracing these major trends in sectoral planning, this chapter also demonstrates that economic planning documents are not created in a vacuum. In Brazil, the clearly articulated interests of key players, both within the state telecommunications bureaucracy and within the telecommunications equipment industry, are clearly detected in planning documents. At other times, broader issues such as economic nationalism find their way into planning documents and become apparent in the statements of those charged with directing the country's telecommunications infrastructure or by representatives of Brazilian firms competing with multinational capital in the telephone equipment sector. From the late 1970s to the present, telecommunications tariff policy fell short of larger government ambitions to visibly restrain inflation in those prices which it controlled. Finally, the inability of the telecommunications sector to establish real national control of the sector may have influenced the way that Brazilian informatics policy was crafted. Stronger controls on the importation of foreign equipment and a direct bureaucratic separation for national informatics policy, resulting in a Special Secretariat for Informatics, separated Brazil's computing policy from the Ministry of Communications, which maintained control over the telecommunications sector.

Two significant questions remain unanswered. First, is it possible to develop a methodological framework from this examination of the Brazilian case which might enable researchers to deconstruct the official rhetoric of sectoral planning documents when analyzing similar telecommunications scenarios? And second, does this analysis tell us anything new and, perhaps, more specific about the outcome or consequences of the Brazilian state's actions in the development and increasing privatization of a national telecommunications system? Within the telecommunications sector we have isolated how policy has responded to the needs and interests of the state, local capital, and multinational telecommunications equipment concerns and how local and multinational capital have established mutually beneficial strategic alliances. For example, Lesser and Osberg (1981) define the main functions of telecommunications as (1) security functions, (2) social functions, and (3) business and economic functions. Our analysis shows how the state directed its telecommunications policies to meet these varying functions at different points in the development of the country's telecommunications infrastructure.

While this limited analysis cannot trace every way that these groups interacted in setting policy for the telecommunications sector and in benefiting from the potential functions of telecommunications, certain patterns emerge. We see that throughout Brazil's economic and political trajectory from authoritarian to democratic rule, post-1964 telecommunications policies functioned at a number of distinct levels and responded to the needs of varying interests within Brazilian society. With respect to Brazilian civil society as a whole, the state used telecommunications policies in a number of distinct ways. First, it used them to consolidate power after the 1964 coup d'état under the premise of national integration, and, second, to respond to the desire of civil society as a whole to modernize and promote economic development during the so-called Brazilian economic miracle of the 1970s. Third, as the country rejected authoritarian rule in the early 1980s, the rhetoric of telecommunications policy focused on the sector's potential role in assisting in the redemocratization and equalization of Brazilian society. Finally, telecommunications policies were adjusted once more as major private interests and business users pushed for increased liberalization of competition in services and even privatization of state telecommunications companies in the 1990s.

In these instances, the Brazilian state appropriated telecommunications policy to (1) provide security functions (i.e., the maintenance of the authoritarian state through the centralization of the telecommunications system and (2) to provide social functions (i.e., the cohesion of civil society by promoting "national integration" through national telecommunications links as a means of redemocratizing Brazilian society). Within Brazil, the state-directed telecommunications policy also clearly responded to a number of economic functions. The sector was incorporated and often seen as a cornerstone of broader economic policies, such as economic development and modernization, as well as a catalyst to the policies aimed specifically at import substitution. Within this context, state policy promoted the interests of national capital which viewed the telecommunications sector as a lucrative sector under the strict control of foreign capital. The state also constructed and maintained a telecommunications infrastructure which facilitated the operation of other important sectors such as manufacturing, banking, and broadcasting.

State telecommunications policies directly responded to the interests of national capital by promoting a limited nationalization of the telecommunications equipment sector. However, the state stopped short of fully nationalizing the sector in response to the interests of local capital, which, by maintaining a slim majority stake in former MNC equipment concerns, could benefit from foreign technology (without heavy investments in R&D) through advantageous alliances with MNCs. As the interests of major manufacturers and potential service providers changed, along with the demands being placed on the telecommunications system by both business and unserved residential users, the national system began to focus on liberalization of competition to allow new national and foreign competitors, usually in very familiar alliances, and to move slowly towards privatization of state companies. The most notable beneficiaries of Brazilian telecommunications policy in the post-1964 period are the representatives of Brazilian capital who provided the local ownership and alliances to allow MNCs to enter the market despite the government's policy initiatives to the contrary.

How can this research effort be useful to those analyzing national telecommunications policies in developing country settings? We believe further research using case-study approaches should look at telecommunications policy in individual countries. Research also should ask more fundamental questions about the role and objectives of the key players from the private sector who often act in tandem with the state or national telecommunications bureaucracy. While this currently takes the form of debate over liberalization and privatization, earlier impulses that had led to more nationalistic policies have not disappeared entirely. The literature that is used as a base for examining the impact of telecommunications policies in the developing world, either in the earlier nationalist phase or in current movements toward privatization, often ignores the political factors and economic consequences which motivate the private sector.

REFERENCES

Adler, E. 1986. "Ideological guerrillas and the quest for technological autonomy: Development of a domestic computer industry in Brazil." *International Organization.*

"A Novela Continua." *Veja,* August 30, 1978, 33.

"A Politica do Bom Telefone." *Veja*, September 6, 1969, 38.

Bruneau, T., and P. Faucher. eds. 1981. *Authoritarian Capitalism: Brazil's Contemporary Economic and Political Development.* Boulder, Colo.: Westview.

"Caminho Inverso." *Veja*, February 15, 1979, 86–87.

Daland, R. 1967. *Brazilian Planning: Development Politics and Administration.* Chapel Hill: University of North Carolina Press.

Del Fioz, R.A., and J.E. Ferraz. 1985. "National Telecommunications Planning in Brazil." *Telecommunications Policy*, 229–239.

Erber, F. 1985. "The Development of the 'Electronics Complex' and Government Policies in Brazil." *World Development*, 3(13): 293–309.

Evans, P. 1986. "State, Capital, and the Transformation of Dependence: The Brazilian Computer Case." *World Development* 14 (7): 791–808.

Fadul, A. 1989. "Communicacao, cultura e informatica no Brasil: desafios atuais." *Intercom Revista Brasileira de Communicacao* 61: 13–32.

Fadul, A., and J. Straubhaar. 1995. "From PTT to Private: Liberalization and Privatization in Eastern Europe and the Third World." In *Telecommunications Politics: Ownership and Control of the Information Highway in Developing Countries,* edited by B. Moody and J. Bauer. Mahwah, N.J.: L. Erlbaum.

Gellerman, R.F. 1977. "Measuring the Benefits of Telecommunications." In *Telecommunications and Economic Development,* edited by P. Polishuk and M. O'Bryant. Dedham, Mass.: Horizon House International.

Gonzalez-Manet, E. 1987. "El mundo desconocido de la informatica." *Communicacao e Politica*, 8: 157–160.

Gonzalez-Manet, E. 1992. *Informatics and Society: The New Challenges*. Norwood, N.J.: Ablex.

Graciosa, H.M. 1989. "Telecommunications Research and Development in Brazil." *IEEE Communications 27*(9): 33–41.

Hobday, M. 1990. *Telecommunications in Developing Countries: The Challenge from Brazil*. New York: Routledge.

Hudson, H.E. 1984. *When Telephones Reach the Village: The Role of Telecommunications in Rural Development*. Norwood, N.J.: Ablex.

International Trade Adminstration (ITA) (U.S. Department of Commerce). 1989. *A Guide to Telecommunications Markets in Latin America*. Washington, D.C.: U.S. Government Printing Office.

Jequier, N. 1984. "Telecommunications for Development: Findings of the ITU-OECD Project." *Telecommunications Policy*, 83–88.

Jussawalla, M., and C. Cheah. 1987. *The Calculus of International Communications: A Study in the Political Economy of Transborder Data flow*. Littleton, Colo.: Libraries Unlimited.

Katz, R. L. 1981. "Nationalism and Computer Technology Transfer: The Brazilian Case." Unpublished Master's thesis, Massachusetts Institute of Technology.

Katz, R. L. 1988. *The International Society: An International Perspective*. New York: Praeger.

Kling, R. 1983. "Value Conflicts in Computing Developments: Developed and Developing Countries." *Telecommunications Policy* 3: 12–34.

Kottack, C. 1990. *Prime Time Society*. Belmont, Calif.: Wadsworth.

Lesser, B., and L. Osberg. 1981. *The Socio-economic Development Benefits of Telecommunications*. Geneva: International Telecommunications Union.

"Linha Direta." *Veja*, November 5, 1986, 72.

Ministerio do Planejamento e Coordenacao Geral. *Diretrizes do governo programa estrategico de desenvolvimento,* June, 1967.

Nora, S., and A. Minc. 1981. *The Computerization of Society*. Cambridge: MIT Press.

"O Brasil se Comunica." *Veja*, April 11, 1970, 26–36.

Ortiz, R. 1985. *Cultura brasileira e identidade nacional*. São Paulo: Brasiliense.

"O Soviet da Embratel." *Veja*, November 18, 1987, 114–115.

O'Sullivan-Ryan, J. 1983. "Telecommmunications Planning in Venezuela."

"Pelo Telefone." *Veja*, February 9, 1970, 34.

Presidencia da Republica. 1962. *Plano trienal de desenvolvimento economico e social 1963–1965*. Brasilia.

Presidencia da Republica. 1970. *Metas e bases para a acao de governo*. Brasilia.

Presidencia da Republica. 1972. *Primeiro plano nacional de desenvolvimento 1972–1974*. Brasilia: Departamento de Imprensa Nacional.

Presidencia da Republica (Republica Federativa do Brasil). 1980. *III Plano nacional de desenvolvimento 1980/85*. Brasilia.

Ramos, M.C. 1993. "Politicas nacionais de comunicacao e crise dos paradigmas." *Communicacao e Politica na America Latina* 6(17): 61–70.

Republica Federativa do Brasil. 1985. *IPND I Plano nacionalde desenvolvimento da nova republica 1986–1989*. Brasilia.

Rosenberg, V. 1982. "Information Policies of Developing Countries: The Case of
    Brazil." *Journal of the American Society for Information Science* 7: 203–207.
"Ruido na Linha." *Veja*, December 8, 1993, 117.
Secretaria de Communicacao Social da Presidencia da Republica. 1980. *Diretrizes
    setoriais do Presidente Joao Figueiredo*. Brasilia.
Seminario Telebrasil. *Anais: As telecommunicacoes em um ambiente de mudancas*.
    Proceedings from Telebrasil Seminar, June, 1984, sponsored by the Brazilian
    Association of Telecommunications, São Paulo.
Salles, M. 1977. Communicacao Social. Escola Superior de Guerra, Departamento de
    Estudos, CE-I-77, T 6.
Saunders, R., J. Warford, and B. Wellenius. 1983. *Telecommunications and Economic
    Development*. Baltimore: Johns Hopkins University Press.
Straubhaar, J., and E. Senger. 1990. "Breaking Technological Dependence? A History
    of Brazilian Microcomputer Policy." *International Communication Associa-
    tion Meeting, Human Communication*.
Straubhaar, J. 1991. "Communications, Culture, and Information in Brazil: The Cur-
    rent Challenges." In *Transnational Communication: Wiring the Third World*,
    edited by G. Sussman and J. Lent.
Siquerra, E., Ed. 1993. *Telecomunicacao, Privatizacao ou Caos*. São Paulo: Telepress
    Editora.
"Triplice Alianca." *Veja*, July 18, 1990, 70.
"Uma Decisao Dificil." *Veja*, May 31, 1978, 76–77.
"Uma Guerra de titas." *Veja*, September 6, 1989, 102–104.
United Nations Center on Transnational Corporations (UNCTC). 1984. *Transborder
    Data Flows and Brazil: A UNCTC Case Study*. Amsterdam: Elsevier.
Wellenius, B. 1984. "On the Role of Telecommunications in Development." *Telecom-
    munications Policy*, 59–65.
Westman, J. 1985. "Modern Dependency: A 'Crucial Case' Study of the Brazilian
    Government Policy in the Minicomputer Industry." *Studies in Comparative
    International Development* 3:25–47.

PRIVATIZATION AND LIBERALIZATION IN THE DEVELOPING WORLD

13

The Need for Innovative Policies and Strategies

Heather E. Hudson

> We believe that by the early part of the next century virtually the whole of mankind should be brought within easy reach of a telephone and, in due course, the other services telecommunications can provide.
>
> > The Maitland Commission, *The Missing Link*, 1984

> We will use this [GII] to help our respective economies and to promote health, education, environmental protection, and democracy . . . . [The ITU] adopted five principles for a GII which the nations of the world have been putting into practice: Private investment. Market-driven competition. Flexible regulatory systems. Non-discriminatory access. And universal service.
>
> > U.S. Vice President Al Gore,
> > address to the ITU Plenipotentiary Conference, September 1994

In 1984, the Maitland Commission noted that telecommunications was a "missing link" in much of the developing world. A decade later, policy makers were calling for a "Global Information Infrastructure" that will link everyone into a worldwide network, or more likely, a network of networks. Yet a majority of individuals and whole communities in the developing world still have no access to telecommunications. And where telecommunications facilities exist in developing regions and remote parts of the industrialized world, limited capacity and unreliability may leave users decades behind their better-equipped counterparts who are able to take advantage of converging technologies and new services.

This chapter examines the progress that has been made toward bringing the "whole of mankind within easy reach of a telephone," what problems remain, and the effects of changing technologies and policies. It then proposes strategies to achieve the goal of universal access to reliable and affordable telecommunications services.

ACCESS TO TELECOMMUNICATIONS: THE GAP REMAINS

Although there has been a dramatic increase in telecommunications investment in the past decade, there are still enormous gaps between the developed and developing world in accessibility to telecommunications, and within the developing world, between urban and rural areas. While there are now almost 50 lines per 100 people in high-income industrialized countries, there is still an average of less than 1 line per 100 in the poorest countries. The gaps are even greater between urban and rural areas. There are almost three times as many telephone lines per 100 in the largest city of lower–middle-income countries as there are in their rural areas, and more than seven times as many lines per 100 in the largest city of low income countries as in their rural areas. These gaps are even more significant given the fact that more than 50 percent (as much as 80 percent) of the population in the poorest countries live in rural areas (see Table 13.1).

INDICATORS OF PENT-UP DEMAND

Access to Television versus Telephones

The lack of telephones cannot necessarily be attributed to lack of demand or purchasing power. In many developing countries, television sets are much more prevalent than telephone lines. In industrialized countries, both television sets and

Table 13.1
Access to Telecommunications

	Teledensity (lines/100 pop)	Urban Density	Rest of Country
High Income Countries	48.8	51.7	48.5
Upper Middle Income Countries	12.9	21.9	10.6
Lower Middle Income Countries	8.1	19.0	6.8
Low Income Countries	0.9	5.2	0.7

Source: ITU, World Telecommunication Development Report (Geneva: ITU, 1995).

telephone lines are almost universally accessible. However, in lower–middle-income countries there are almost two-and-a-half times as many television sets as telephone lines, and in low income countries, there are more than thirteen times as many television sets as telephone lines (see Table 13.2). The problem appears to be a bottleneck in provision of telephone service rather than lack of sufficient disposable income to pay for telephone calls.

Put another way, it appears that where television is available, a significant percentage of families will find the money to buy television sets. These numbers indicate a potential pent-up demand for other communications services and the availability of disposable income if the service is deemed important.

Indicators of Entrepreneurship

Another approach to determine whether current strategies for telecommunications investment are somehow missing the mark is to examine indicators of communications entrepreneurship. While comparative data are not available, the following activities in a country would indicate that there are entrepreneurs willing to offer communications services, and customers to support them:

- Video shops: Shops that rent video cassettes and video recorders and players. These are found in even relatively poor developing countries where there would appear to be very little disposable income for most families.
- Cable television systems: Cable television systems (government-authorized or otherwise) that have been installed to provide access to television channels (e.g., from a satellite) for a fee. The most striking current example is India, where cable television systems have sprung up in urban neighborhoods to deliver programming from AsiaSat. Cable and MMDS are expanding rapidly in other developing Asian countries, such as Thailand and the Philippines.
- Kiosks and copy shops: Entrepreneurs who offer communications facilities such as telephones and facsimile services. Some countries such as Indonesia have introduced this model for pay phone service, while retaining government control over operation of the public switched network. Entrepreneurs typically retain a percentage of the toll revenues.

Table 13.2
Access to Telephones and Television Sets

	Tel Lines/100	TV Sets/100	TV Sets/ Tel Lines
High Income Countries	48.8	59.7	1.2
Upper Middle Income Countries	12.9	24.1	1.9
Lower Middle Income Countries	8.1	19.8	2.4
Low Income Countries	0.9	11.8	13.1

Source: ITU, World Telecommunication Development Report (Geneva: ITU, 1995).

THE CHANGING TELECOMMUNICATIONS ENVIRONMENT

An analysis of strategies for increasing access to telecommunications in developing countries must be placed in context. First, telecommunications technologies have changed dramatically in the past decade, and many recent innovations offer promising solutions for extending services at lower costs than were generally thought possible. Perhaps the most telling evidence of change is the cover of the Maitland Commission report itself, which showed two rotary dial telephones. This is not to say that digital switching did not exist in 1984, but it was not considered necessary or perhaps even appropriate for developing regions. A second indicator is that the commission specifically identified only telephone service, and proposed access "in due course [to] the other services telecommunications can provide." Today, many of those services would be available as soon as telecommunications service is provided.

There are many recent technological innovations that can make telecommunications services more reliable and cheaper to provide. Among the technological changes are the following:

- Wireless technologies: Advances in radio technology such as cellular radio and rural radio subscriber systems offer affordable means of reaching less isolated rural customers. Cellular networks can be used for pay phones and other "fixed" services, as well as for mobile communications. "Wireless local loop" technologies can link subscribers to the network without the need for laying cable or stringing copper wire.

- Digital compression: Digital video can be "compressed" so that video conferencing may require as few as two 64 kilobit per second circuits. Digital audio can also be compressed so that eight or more conversations can be carried on a 64 kilobit per second channel, thus reducing transmission costs.

- VSATs: Small satellite earth stations are proliferating in developing regions, usually for distribution of television signals. However, VSATs also can be used for interactive voice and data, and for data broadcasting. Multiple channels of voice communications can be provided using digital compression. Satellite terminals also can serve as hubs for wireless local networks.

- Voice messaging: Voice mail systems can do much more than replace analog answering machines. TeleBahia in northeastern Brazil is using voice messaging technology to offer "virtual telephone service" to people who are still without individual telephone service. They can rent a voice-mail box for a monthly fee. Callers can leave messages in their mail boxes, which the subscribers retrieve from a pay phone. (A similar approach has been used in some U.S. homeless shelters to enable job seekers to have a way to be contacted by prospective employers.)

- Store-and-forward data: Development organizations seeking cheap ways to communicate with field projects are using single satellite LEO systems for electronic messaging. For example, SatelLife, a nonprofit association of physicians based in Boston, operates "Health Net" using a microsatellite to provide store-and-forward data communications to small terminals in developing countries.

THE CHANGING POLICY ENVIRONMENT

In addition to technological change, the policy environment is also changing dramatically, with increasing emphasis on private-sector investment and market-driven competition, as advocated by Vice President Al Gore in his address to the ITU Plenipotentiary in 1994. We may view the various models of restructuring the telecommunications sector as experiments whose impacts will not be fully known in this decade. The major models for restructuring the telecommunications sector include the following:

Ownership

- Autonomous public sector corporations: The first strategy for creating incentives to improve efficiency and innovation in the telecommunications sector is to create an autonomous organization operated on business principles. This often is seen as an intermediate step between a PTT structure and some form of privatization. Most developing countries have taken this step, which is advocated by the World Bank and other funding agencies.

- Privatized corporations: Privatization models range from minor investments by private companies to joint ventures between private carriers and governments, to full privatization without any government stake or with a small government "golden share."

Structure

- Monopoly: Most countries began with a national monopoly model that now is being eroded. Most maintain some level of monopoly, for example in the local loop, but alternative providers using wireless and fiber are also beginning to challenge the assumption of natural monopoly in the local loop.

- Open entry for unserved areas: An intermediate step between national monopoly and competition is a policy of open entry for unserved areas. For example, the United States, Finland, Hungary, and Poland have small companies or cooperatives that were formed to provide services in areas ignored by the national monopoly carrier.

- Competition: Competition can range from terminal equipment (now commonly competitive in most countries, including developing countries) to new services such as cellular telephony, to value-added services such as packet data networks, to full competition in the network.

IMPLICATIONS FOR PLANNING

Changing Assumptions

Developing economies undergo changes that are likely to result in new and changing demands for telecommunications services, while the introduction of new technologies is changing the economic viability of rural telecommunications.

- Voice and Data: While basic voice communication is still the first priority, many users now have requirements for data communications as well, particularly facsimile and relatively low-speed data communications. Demand for Internet access is also growing enormously for universities, libraries, and schools, as well as for government and business applications and private use. Thus transmission channels must be reliable enough to handle data as well as voice traffic.

- Urban and Rural: The availability of relatively low-cost radio and satellite technologies for serving rural areas makes it possible to reach even the most remote locations and to base priorities for service on need rather than proximity to the terrestrial network. The combination of increased demand and lower-cost technologies makes rural areas more attractive for investment. As a result, other institutional structures besides public-sector monopolies also may be suitable for rural service provision.

Setting Goals and Targets

Before taking major steps to encourage investment or restructure the telecommunications sector, planners should set national telecommunications goals. Nations in general seek to improve educational standards, to provide health care for all, to create jobs, and to reduce disparities between haves and have-nots, both urban and rural. As shown in several studies, telecommunications can contribute to many of these goals (see, for example, Hudson 1984; Parker and Hudson 1995; Saunders, Warford, and Wellenius 1994).

These general development goals must be translated into specific telecommunications goals, which might include:

- Universal access to basic communications: Access may be defined using a variety of criteria such as

  population: for example, a telephone for every permanent settlement with a minimum population

  distance: for example, a telephone within a certain distance of all rural residents

  time: for example, a telephone within an hour's walk or bicycle ride of all rural residents

- Reliability: Standards for reliable operation and availability; quality sufficient for voice, facsimile, and data communications

- Emergency Services: A simple way to reach help immediately, so that anyone, including children and illiterate adults, would be able to call a hospital, the police, and so on

- Pricing: Pricing based on communities of interest; for example, to regional centers where stores and government offices are located; to other locations where most relatives are located (surrounding villages, regional towns, etc.)

In North America, we (Parker and Hudson 1995) have advocated that in order to ensure that telecommunications technologies and services can be put to optimal use for rural development, the basic goal should be to provide rural and remote areas affordable access to telecommunications and information services *comparable to those available in urban areas*. The underlying rationale is that universal access to information is critical to the development process.

While planners may want to modify this goal for lower-income countries, there is no longer a compelling technological or financial reason to limit rural services. The same technologies that are used to transmit voice can also transmit facsimile and data and, through digital compression, video as well. As noted previously, access criteria may differ in rural areas, but they actually may be comparable to access criteria in high-density urban areas, where the goal is not to provide a line for every dwelling, but access for everyone through public phones in kiosks, shops, common areas, and so on.

It is important to note that this goal is, in effect, a "moving target": it does not specify a particular technology, but assumes that as facilities and services become widely available in urban areas, they also should be extended to rural areas. Information can be accessed and shared through a range of technologies such as satellite earth stations, microwave and cellular radio links, optical fiber, and copper wire. Indeed, the technologies used to deliver the services in rural areas may differ from those installed in urban areas; for example, satellite links and radio networks may be less costly for rural communications than optical fiber or even copper wire.

It is necessary to devise a set of strategies to achieve these goals. Strategies are needed to create incentives to increase telecommunications investment and to drive the investment toward achieving these goals.

INDUSTRY STRUCTURE

The Maitland Commission paid little attention to the structure of the telecommunications sector, beyond advocating that telecommunications be set up "as a separate, self-sustaining enterprise, run along business lines" (38). At the time, many developing countries were still running telecommunications through a government department, with revenues subsidizing the postal services, and often turning foreign exchange earnings over to the national treasury. Today, a majority of developing countries are running their telecommunications administrations as autonomous government-owned enterprises, and many are in the process of privatizing these operations.

Yet, as the data show, a more entrepreneurial national monopoly may not have adequate incentives to invest in facilities to accomplish the goals outlined previously, given the unmet demands of business and upper-middle-class residential customers in the cities. The following are some strategies that can create incentives to invest in rural and less profitable areas:

- New services—franchise or competition: The introduction of a new service may be accelerated by issuing licenses for franchises. This approach has been used for cellular radio in Argentina and Mexico, for example. It allows foreign investors with the necessary capital and expertise to provide the service more quickly than could be offered through the PTT. Satellite services such as data communications also may be offered through one or more private licensed carriers. For example, private banking networks using VSATs have now been authorized in Brazil.

- Local companies: Although in most countries there is a single carrier that provides both local and long-distance services, it may make sense to delineate territories that can be served by local entities. In the United States, the model of rural coopera- tives fostered through the Rural Electrification Administration (REA) has been used to bring telephone service to areas ignored by the large carriers. Local enter- prises are likely to be more responsive to local needs, whether they be urban or rural. An example of this approach in urban areas is India's Metropolitan Telephone Corporation established to serve Bombay and Delhi. Local companies also provide telephone service in Colombia. Cooperatives have been introduced in Hungary. A disadvantage of this approach is the need for local expertise to operate the system, which is likely to be in particularly short supply in many developing countries.

- Franchises for unserved areas: Another approach to serving presently unserved ar- eas is to open them up to private franchises. Large carriers may determine that some rural areas are too unprofitable to serve in the near term. However, this conclusion may be based on assumptions about the cost of technologies and implementation that could be inappropriate.

  It should be noted that wireless technologies could change the economics of pro- viding rural services, making rural franchises much more attractive to investors. For example, while companies such as GTE and US West are selling rural franchises, other companies with a more optimistic assessment of rural profitability are buy- ing them. For example, Rochester Telephone has bought properties in the rural East and Midwest. Citizens Communications spent US$1.1 billion to buy 500,000 ac- cess lines, primarily in the rural western United States; and Pacific Telecom, the parent of Alascom, also has recently bought rural properties.

- Resale: Third parties may be permitted to lease capacity in bulk and resell it in units of bandwidth and/or time appropriate for business customers and other major users. This approach may be suitable where some excess network capacity exists (e.g., between major cities or on domestic or regional satellites). Resale is one of the simplest ways to introduce some competition and lower rates for users, but it is not legal in most devel- oping countries, even where some excess capacity exists in backbone networks.

INCENTIVES

Another strategy that may be used with a variety of institutional structures is to introduce incentives that are designed to achieve policy goals such as extension of telecommunications services into rural areas. These may include

- Incentive regulation: Some countries and U.S. states have introduced changes in regulation that allow the carriers considerable pricing flexibility in return for meet- ing certain conditions (e.g., price caps). An alternative to financial incentives would be a management-by-objectives approach where policy makers and regulators would set objectives and carriers would be rewarded for achieving them. These objectives could include service upgrades such as extension of service to rural areas or meeting quality-of-service targets. For example, the Philippines is requiring new franchisees for international gateways and cellular systems to install a specified number of lines in currently unserved rural areas.

- Investment incentives: Several countries, including Indonesia and Thailand, have encouraged investors to build new facilities through schemes known as Build–Operate–Transfer (BOT), where the investors build the system, operate it, receive a percentage of the revenues for a specified period, and then turn it over to the government. Joint ventures also may include incentives for investment in rural areas.

- Service incentives: Some countries have encouraged private entrepreneurs to offer telecommunications services. For example, in Indonesia and Rwanda, entrepreneurs may install telephones in kiosks that also sell soft drinks and newspapers. The entrepreneurs receive a percentage of the revenue; also, they typically stay open much longer than post offices and provide a secure location for the telephone.

- Limiting exclusivity: While investors may require a predictable industry environment to commit capital, countries must resist pressure to issue indefinite or long-term licenses. The technology and the industry is changing too fast for countries to assume that what seems to be adequate investment and performance today will be adequate five years —let alone ten years—from now. Thus, franchise awards should be for five years or less; and exclusivity agreements should not exceed five years.

OTHER SOURCES OF REVENUE

Internal cross-subsidies have been the primary means of sustaining rural services in the past. However, with the restructuring of the sector, if competition is introduced, or even contemplated, for some services, subsidies must be separately accounted for so that monopoly services are not used to subsidize competitive services. If subsidies are required, they should be targeted for specific services or classes of customers. Funds may be generated in several ways:

- Pooled revenues: Carriers may pool a percentage of their revenues, which would then be allocated to provide services in high-cost areas. In the United States, a "High Cost Fund" set up after the divestiture of AT&T is administered by the National Exchange Carriers Association (NECA).

- Taxes on usage: A tax on usage may be imposed, with the revenue used to provide services that would otherwise not be economical. This is one of the models used to support universal service in the United States.

- Taxes on revenues: Carriers or service providers may be taxed on revenues generated, with these taxes allocated for service upgrades or rate subsidies.

- License or franchise fees: Carriers may be charged fees for a franchise and use of spectrum, or other resources. These fees could be allocated to a fund for upgrading or extending services. The goal here should be to raise income to support upgrading and oversight of the telecommunications sector (and possibly applications such as pilot projects for education and health care), not to provide a new source of revenue for the national treasury.

- Aggregating demand: Rural areas often lack economies of scale that would make provision of new services attractive. And though government is usually a major telecommunications user, government traffic is often carried on dedicated networks. One approach to aggregating demand would be to require that all government traffic be carried on the public switched network. Government expenditures would then generate revenue that could be used to upgrade and extend the public network.

MONITORING PROGRESS

No matter what approach or combination of approaches countries choose to adopt, they must have some way of monitoring progress toward their goals. Incentives have been stressed because most countries do not have the legal history or regulation, nor sufficient available expertise to staff regulatory bodies. However, these countries can establish a small oversight group with the legal authority to require licensed carriers to provide data on the number of lines available, quality of service, sample period traffic data, and so on.

A second strategy is for this oversight group to schedule regular opportunities for users to present their needs and problems to carriers. Formal hearings may not always be appropriate, but there needs to be some mechanism for carriers and users to share information and for regulators to be made aware of user issues and perspectives.

BRINGING TELECOMMUNICATIONS WITHIN THE REACH OF ALL

The strategies discussed in this chapter are designed to reflect the changing technological, policy, and financial environments of the 1990s. In particular, they are designed to reflect three themes:

- an awareness that telecommunications goals will be moving targets because of changes in technology and user needs
- a broadening of the definition of "public interest" beyond the simple assessment of price to customers, which is the indicator most often used in industrialized countries
- an assumption that incentives are likely to be more successful than regulations in encouraging development-oriented investment, but that sanctions must be available if agreed-upon targets are not met

These themes of moving targets, public interest, and incentives with sanctions need to be incorporated in the policies that embrace privatization and liberalization if telecommunications services are to become universally accessible throughout the developing world.

BIBLIOGRAPHY

Al-Ghunaim, Abdul R. K. 1988. *The Missing Link and After.* Kuwait, Al Kuwait: Kuwait Government Printing Press.

Chowdary, T. H. 1992. "Telecommunications Restructuring in Developing Countries." *Telecommunications Policy* 16(9): 699–704.

Clements, Charles. 1991. "HealthNet." Cambridge, Mass.: SatelLife, May.

Davidson, William H., Anne C. Dibble, and Sandra H. Dom. "Telecommunications and Rural Economic Development." Redondo Beach, Calif.: MESA Inc., October.

Dillman, Don A., and Donald M. Beck. 1988."Information Technologies and Rural Development in the 1990s." *Journal of State Government* 61(1): 29–38.

Gallottini, Giovanna T. 1991. "Infrastructure: The Rural Difference." *Telecommunications Engineering and Management* 95(1): 48–50.

Gore, Albert, Jr. 1991. "Infrastructure for the Global Village: Computers, Networks and Public Policy." *Scientific American* 265(3): 150.

Hardy, Andrew P. 1980. "The Role of the Telephone in Economic Development." *Telecommunications Policy,* December.

Hudson, Heather E. 1990. *Communication Satellites: Their Development and Impact.* New York: Free Press.

Hudson, Heather E. 1992. *Applications of New Technologies in Distance Education: Telecommunications Policy Issues and Options.* Melbourne, Australia: Centre for International Research on Communication and Information Technologies (CIRCIT).

Hudson, Heather E. 1992. "Developing Countries' Communications: Overcoming the Barriers of Distance." *Froehlich/Kent Encyclopedia of Telecommunications* 4: 351–368.

Hudson, Heather E. 1993. "Maximizing Benefits from New Telecommunications Technologies: Policy Challenges for Developing Countries." In *Global Telecommunications Policies: The Challenge of Change,* edited by Meheroo Jussawalla. Westport, Conn.: Greenwood Press.

Hudson, Heather E. 1984. *When Telephones Reach the Village: The Role of Telecommunications in Rural Development.* Norwood, N.J.: Ablex.

International Development Research Centre. 1989. *Sharing Knowledge for Development: IDRC's Information Strategy for Africa.* Ottawa: IDRC.

International Telecommunication Union. 1995. *World Telecommunication Development Report.* Geneva: ITU.

Johnson, Tony. "Microsatellite that Turns Information into Medical Power." *The (Manchester) Guardian,* April 26, 1991.

Lawton, Raymond A. 1990. "Telecommunications Modernization: Issues and Approaches for Regulators." National Regulatory Research Institute, Columbus, Ohio.

Maitland Commission (International Commission for Worldwide Telecommunications Development). 1984. *The Missing Link.* Geneva: International Telecommunication Union.

Mayo, John K., G.R. Heald, S.J. Klees, and M. Cruz de Yanes. 1987. *Peru Rural Communication Services Project Final Evaluation Report.* Washington, D.C.: Academy for International Development.

National Research Council, Board on Science and Technology for International Development. 1990. *Science and Technology Information Services and Systems in Africa.* Washington, D.C.: National Academy Press.

Parker, Edwin B., and Heather E. Hudson. 1995. *Electronic Byways: State Policies for Rural Development through Telecommunications,* 2nd ed. Washington, D.C.: The Aspen Institute.

Saunders, Robert, J. Warford, and B. Wellenius. 1994. *Telecommunications and Economic Development,* 2nd ed. Baltimore: Johns Hopkins University Press.

INDEX

ABOUT THE EDITOR
AND CONTRIBUTORS

MARCUS BROOKS
British Telecom Regulatory Affairs Department

ANNA CANNING
Centre for Economic Reform and Transformation
Heriot-Watt University, Edinburgh

ROGER CARLSON
Business Development Strategy
NYNEX Network Systems Company

LILIA PÉREZ CHAVOLLA
Department of Communication
Ohio State University, Columbus

CHRISTINE HORAK
Center for Survey Research
University of Nevada, Las Vegas

HEATHER E. HUDSON
Telecommunications Management and Policy Program
McLaren School of Business
University of San Francisco

PIOTR JASIŃSKI
Regulatory Policy Research Centre
Hertford College, Oxford University

MEHEROO JUSSAWALLA
Program on International Economics and Politics
East West Center
Honolulu, Hawaii

JEONG-JA LEE
Dongbang Peregrine Securities Co. Ltd.
Seoul, South Korea

MARIA MICHALIS
International Institute for Regulators in Telecommunications
School of Social Sciences
City University, London

BEN PARK
International Business Development Strategy
NYNEX Network Systems Company

MAUREEN D. PICHÉ
Business Development Strategy
NYNEX Network Systems Company

BRUCE ROWE
Comstream
San Diego, California

DANIEL J. RYAN
Department of Economics
Temple University, Philadelphia

ROHAN SAMARAJIVA
Department of Communications
Ohio State University, Columbus

JOSEPH STRAUBHAAR
Department of Communications
Brigham Young University
Provo, Utah

LINA TAKLA
CIS-Middle Europe Centre
London Business School

JOHN URE
Telecommunications Research Project
Centre of Asian Studies
University of Hong Kong

ARAYA VIVORAKIJ
Hong Kong Consumer Council